ATLAS
of the
WORLD

GW00374152

HEMA
Maps

Published by Hema Maps Pty Ltd.
PO Box 4365 Eight Mile Plains QLD 4113 Australia
Ph: +61 7 3340 0000 Fax: +61 7 3340 0099
Web: www.hemamaps.com
E-mail: manager@hemamaps.com.au

Hema Maps NZ Limited
PO Box 58924 Greenmount,
East Tamaki, Auckland, New Zealand
Ph: +64 9 273 6459 Fax: +64 9 273 6479
E-mail: sales.hema@clear.net.nz

Second edition 2003

World Pocket Atlas   ISBN 1 86500 225 9
Atlas of the World Mini Edition   ISBN 1 86500 248 8

Printed by PMP Print, Brisbane, Australia

*Wherever possible the latest comparable
data has been used in the compilation
of the 'World flags and statistics' section.*

*The Map section uses local spellings.
The 'World flags and statistics' section
uses the conventional English translation
where it is different from the local
form of the name.*

Contents

Legend and key map

The physical world
Time zones
Flight distances and
     journey times   1
Major airports of
     the world   1
Country flags and
     statistics   1

World   3

Europe   4
Scandinavia   4
Central Europe   4
Germany   4
Benelux   4
British Isles   5
France   5
Spain and Portugal   5
The Alpine States   5
Italy   5
The Balkans   6
Greece and
     Western Turkey   6

European Russia	64	**North America**	**106**
		Canada	108
Asia	**66**	United States	110
Northwest Asia	68	Northwest	
Northeast Asia	70	United States	112
Eastern China	72	Northeast	
Japan and Korea	74	United States	114
Southeast Asia	76	Southeast	
Malaysia and		United States	116
Indonesia	78	Southwest	
Southern Asia	80	United States	118
Middle East	82	Central America and	
Turkey	84	the Caribbean	120
Israel	86		
Gulf States	87	**South America**	**122**
		Northern	
Africa	**88**	South America	124
Northeast Africa	90	Southern	
Northwest Africa	92	South America	126
West Africa	94		
Central Africa	96	**Polar Regions**	**128**
Southern Africa	98		
		Index to	
Oceania	**100**	country maps	129
Australia	102	Index	130
New Zealand	104		

Legend and key map

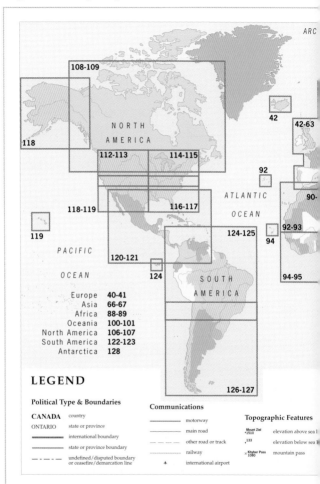

ARC

108-109

NORTH AMERICA

118

42

42-63

112-113   114-115

92

ATLANTIC

OCEAN

90-

118-119   116-117

119

PACIFIC

120-121

124

94

92-93

OCEAN

124-125

94-95

Europe   **40-41**
Asia   **66-67**
Africa   **88-89**
Oceania   **100-101**
North America **106-107**
South America **122-123**
Antarctica   **128**

SOUTH AMERICA

126-127

LEGEND

Political Type & Boundaries

CANADA   country

ONTARIO   state or province

━━━━━━   international boundary

────────   state or province boundary

─ · ─ · ─   undefined/disputed boundary or ceasefire/demarcation line

Communications

─────   motorway

─────   main road

─ ─ ─   other road or track

············   railway

✈   international airport

Topographic Features

Mount Ziel
+1510   elevation above sea l

,133   elevation below sea l

✕ **Khyber Pass**
1080   mountain pass

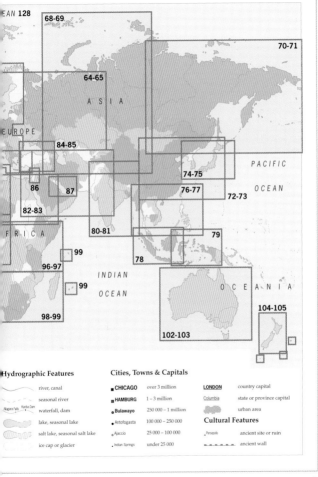

68-69

70-71

64-65

A S I A

EUROPE

84-85

PACIFIC

OCEAN

86   87

74-75

76-77

72-73

82-83

F R I C A

80-81

99

79

96-97

78

99

INDIAN

OCEAN

O C E A N I A

104-105

98-99

102-103

Hydrographic Features

~~~~~ river, canal

········ seasonal river

Niagara Falls Kariba Dam waterfall, dam

lake, seasonal lake

salt lake, seasonal salt lake

ice cap or glacier

Cities, Towns & Capitals

■ **CHICAGO**   over 3 million

■ **HAMBURG**   1 – 3 million

● **Bulawayo**   250 000 – 1 million

● Antofogasta   100 000 – 250 000

○ Ajaccio   25 000 – 100 000

· Indian Springs   under 25 000

<u>**LONDON**</u>   country capital

<u>Columbia</u>   state or province capital

urban area

Cultural Features

. Persepolis   ancient site or ruin

▪ ▪ ▪ ▪ ▪   ancient wall

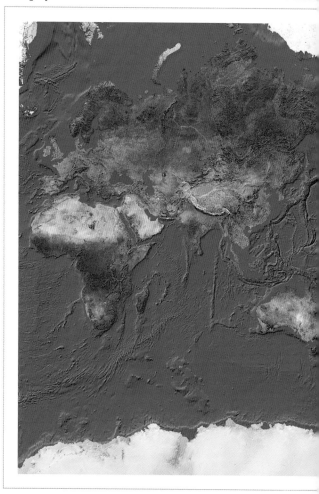

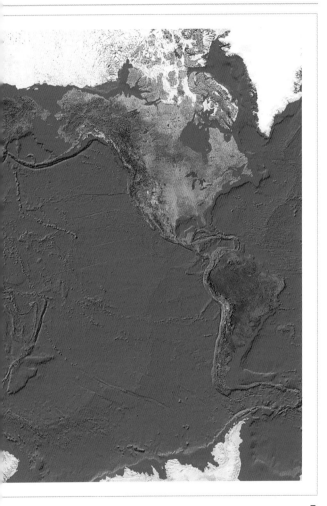

Time zones

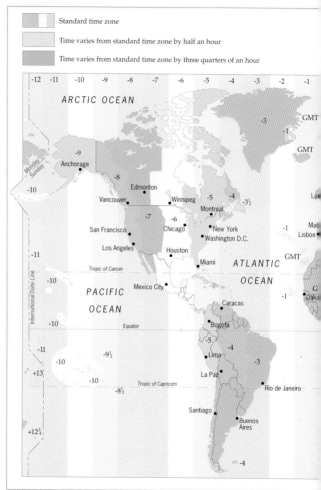

Standard time zone

Time varies from standard time zone by half an hour

Time varies from standard time zone by three quarters of an hour

MT	Greenwich Mean Time
1 to +12	hours ahead of GMT
to -12	hours behind GMT

The world is divided into 24 standard time zones, each covering 15' longitude. All places to the west of Greenwich are one hour behind GMT for every 15' longitude and all places to the east one hour ahead for every 15'. Most countries establish a single time zone based on their location west or east of Greenwich; some however, particularly those with a large west-east extent, establish more than one, usually separated by political or physical boundaries.

9

Flying times

Approximate flying times between some major cities. Times quoted (in hours and minutes) are 'flying time' only. In many cases, in order to travel between two points, it is necessary to change aircraft one or more times. Time between flights has not been included.

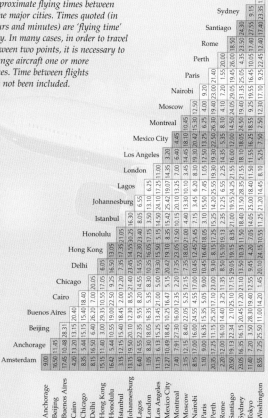

Air distances

Great circle distances between some major cities, given in kilometres. To convert to miles, multiply number given by 0.6214.

The great circle distance is the shortest distance between any two points on the earth's surface.

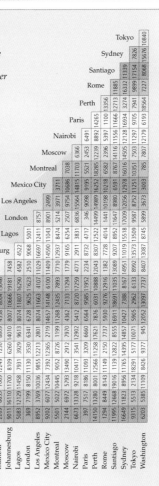

From \ To	Anchorage	Beijing	Buenos Aires	Cairo	Chicago	Delhi	Hong Kong	Honolulu	Istanbul	Johannesburg	Lagos	London	Los Angeles	Mexico City	Montreal	Moscow	Nairobi	Paris	Perth	Rome	Santiago	Sydney	Tokyo	Washington
Amsterdam	7198	7826	11454	3286	6608	6392	9270	11652	2209	9011	5083	369	8952	9202	5501	2144	6673	397	14150	1294	11995	16649	9315	6203
Anchorage		6358	13412	9861	456	9171	8164	4470	8653	16110	12129	7199	3769	6077	5022	6972	13216	7536	13280	8449	13328	11823	5513	5385
Beijing			19279	7530	10560	3806	1990	8129	7069	11700	11458	8150	10036	12434	10445	5793	9218	8218	8001	8143	19016	8956	2134	11109
Buenos Aires				11846	9043	15786	18431	12162	12249	8109	7931	11130	9855	7392	9052	13490	10417	11051	12566	11149	1199	11765	18291	8426
Cairo					9869	4402	8096	14202	1230	6260	3929	3530	12213	12365	8726	2912	3541	3210	11258	2150	13600	14395	9577	9377
Chicago						12017	12519	6817	8809	14010	9613	6341	2801	2719	1199	7970	12902	6650	17621	7737	8555	14857	10071	945
Delhi							3742	11910	4558	8807	8074	6728	12817	14657	11268	4362	5412	6600	7836	5930	16911	10427	5905	12052
Hong Kong								8945	8004	10666	11807	9625	11663	14148	12435	7133	8720	9630	6031	9276	18691	7388	2962	13097
Honolulu									13046	19181	16290	11623	4107	6100	7893	11342	17259	11910	10888	12916	10888	8167	6133	7737
Istanbul										7458	4582	2510	11029	11409	8074	1779	4771	2234	10035	1382	13089	14951	8992	8406
Johannesburg											4522	9068	16697	14590	12952	9165	2911	8732	8307	7728	9074	11019	13573	13087
Lagos												5001	12411	11043	8891	6254	3831	4717	13089	4014	9585	15518	13509	8745
London													8757	8901	5214	2507	6836	346	14499	1441	11258	16994	9587	5899
Los Angeles														2499	3929	9754	15564	9085	14989	10198	8981	12056	8752	3673
Mexico City															3711	10686	14815	9213	16252	10218	6564	12978	11251	3003
Montreal																7038	11703	5522	17977	6591	8621	16016	10351	785
Moscow																	6366	2486	12239	2396	14116	14505	7503	7807
Nairobi																		6491	8767	5397	13100	12128	11297	12179
Paris																			14265	1100	11642	16934	9705	6193
Perth																				13356	12713	3274	7941	18564
Rome																					11885	16332	9899	7227
Santiago																						11339	17754	8068
Sydney																							7826	15676
Tokyo																								10840

Major airports of the world

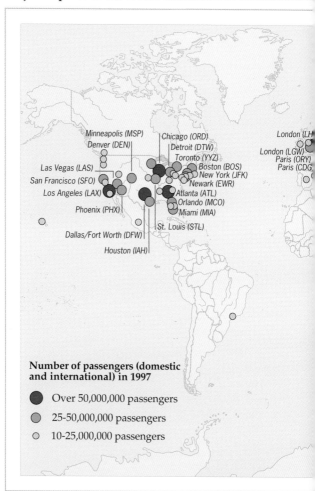

Minneapolis (MSP)
Denver (DEN)
Chicago (ORD)
Detroit (DTW)
Toronto (YYZ)
Boston (BOS)
New York (JFK)
Newark (EWR)
Las Vegas (LAS)
San Francisco (SFO)
Los Angeles (LAX)
Atlanta (ATL)
Orlando (MCO)
Miami (MIA)
Phoenix (PHX)
St. Louis (STL)
Dallas/Fort Worth (DFW)
Houston (IAH)
London (LH
London (LGW)
Paris (ORY)
Paris (CDG

Number of passengers (domestic and international) in 1997

Over 50,000,000 passengers

25-50,000,000 passengers

10-25,000,000 passengers

erdam (AMS)
kfurt/Main (FRA)

ne (FCO)

Seoul (SEL)   Tokyo (NRT)
                              Tokyo (HND)
Hong Kong (HKG)

              Bangkok (BKK)

Singapore (SIN)

nly those airports handling over 25 million passengers are named on the map

Country flags & statistics

Afghanistan

Area: 647,500 km²
Capital: Kabul
Population: 26.8m

Languages: Dari, Pushtu
Religion: Sunni Muslim
Currency: Afghani

Albania

Area: 28,748 km²
Capital: Tirana
Population: 3.5m

Main language: Albanian
Religion: Muslim
Currency: Lek

Algeria

Area: 2,381,741 km²
Capital: Algiers
Population: 31.7m

Languages: Arabic, Berber, French
Religion: Muslim
Currency: Algerian dinar

Andorra

Area: 468 km²
Capital: Andorra la Vella
Population: 68,000

Languages: Spanish, Catalan, French
Religion: Roman Catholic
Currency: Euro

Angola

Area: 1,246,700 km²
Capital: Luanda
Population: 10.4m

Main language: Portuguese
Religions: Roman Catholic, Protestant
Currency: Readjusted kwanza

Antigua & Barbuda

Area: 442 km²
Capital: St John's
Population: 67,000

Main language: English
Religion: Protestant
Currency: East Caribbean dollar

Argentina

Area: 2,766,890 km²
Capital: Buenos Aires
Population: 37.4m

Main language: Spanish
Religion: Roman Catholic
Currency: Peso

Armenia

Area: 29,800 km²
Capital: Yerevan
Population: 3.3m

Languages: Armenian, Russian
Religion: Armenian Apostolic
Currency: Dram

ustralia

Area: 7,686,850 km²
Capital: Canberra
Population: 19.4m

Main language: English
Religion: Protestant
Currency: Australian dollar

ustria

Area: 83,858 km²
Capital: Vienna
Population: 8.2m

Main Language: German
Religion: Roman Catholic
Currency: Euro

zerbaijan

Area: 86,600 km²
Capital: Baku
Population: 7.8m

Main language: Azerbaijani
Religion: Muslim
Currency: Manat

ahamas, The

Area: 13,940 km²
Capital: Nassau
Population: 297,900

Main language: English
Religions: Protestant, Roman Catholic
Currency: Bahamian dollar

Bahrain

Area: 620 km²
Capital: Manama
Population: 645,400

Languages: Arabic, English
Religion: Shi'a Muslim
Currency: Bahraini dinar

Bangladesh

Area: 143,998 km²
Capital: Dhaka
Population: 131.3m

Languages: Bengali, English
Religion: Muslim
Currency: Taka

Barbados

Area: 430 km²
Capital: Bridgetown
Population: 275,300

Main language: English
Religion: Protestant
Currency: Barbados dollar

Belarus

Area: 207,600 km²
Capital: Minsk
Population: 10.4m

Languages: Belarussian, Russian
Religion: Russian Orthodox
Currency: Rouble

Belgium

Area: 30,510 km²
Capital: Brussels
Population: 10.3m
Languages: French, Flemish
Religion: Roman Catholic
Currency: Euro

Belize

Area: 22,966 km²
Capital: Belmopan
Population: 256,000
Languages: English, Spanish
Religion: Christian
Currency: Belize dollar

Benin

Area: 112,622 km²
Capital: Porto Novo
Population: 6.6m
Main language: French
Religion: Traditional beliefs
Currency: Franc CFA

Bhutan

Area: 47,000 km²
Capital: Thimphu
Population: 2.0m
Languages: Dzongkha, English
Religion: Mahayana Buddhist
Currency: Ngultrum

Bolivia

Area: 1,098,581 km²
Capital: Sucre
Population: 8.3m
Languages: Spanish, Quechua, Ayma
Religion: Roman Catholic
Currency: Boliviano

Bosnia-Herzegovina

Area: 51,129 km
Capital: Sarajev
Population: 3.9r
Languages: Serbo-Croat, Croato-Ser
Religion: Muslim
Currency: Convertable marka

Botswana

Area: 581,730 km²
Capital: Gaborone
Population: 1.5m
Languages: Setswana, English
Religion: Traditional beliefs
Currency: Pula

Brazil

Area: 8,511,965 km²
Capital: Brasilia
Population: 174.5m
Main language: Portuguese
Religion: Roman Catholic
Currency: Real

Brunei

Area: 5,765 km²
Cap: Bandar Seri Begawan
Population: 343,700

Languages: Malay, English
Religion: Muslim
Currency: Brunei dollar

Bulgaria

Area: 110,910 km²
Capital: Sofia
Population: 7.7m

Main language: Bulgarian
Religion: Christian
Currency: Lev

Burkina

Area: 274,200 km²
Capital: Ouagadougou
Population: 12.2m

Main language: French
Religion: Traditional beliefs
Currency: Franc CFA

Burundi

Area: 27,834 km²
Capital: Bujumbura
Population: 6.2m

Languages: Kirundi, French, Kishwahili
Religion: Roman Catholic
Currency: Burundi franc

Cambodia

Area: 181,035 km²
Capital: Phnom Penh
Population: 12.5m

Languages: Khmer, Chinese, Vietnamese
Religion: Buddhist
Currency: Riel

Cameroon

Area: 475,442 km²
Capital: Yaoundé
Population: 15.8m

Languages: English, French
Religion: Traditional beliefs
Currency: Franc CFA

Canada

Area: 9,976,140 km²
Capital: Ottawa
Population: 31.6m

Languages: English, French
Religions: Roman Catholic, Protestant
Currency: Canadian dollar

Cape Verde

Area: 4,033 km²
Capital: Praia
Population: 405,200

Languages: Portuguese, Creole
Religion: Roman Catholic
Currency: Cape Verde escudo

Central African Republic

Area: 622,984 km²
Capital: Bangui
Population: 3.6m

Languages: French, Sango
Religions: Christian, Muslim
Currency: Franc CFA

Chad

Area: 1,284,000 km²
Capital: Ndjamena
Population: 8.7m

Languages: Arabic, French, Sara
Religion: Muslim
Currency: Franc CFA

Chile

Area: 756,950 km²
Capital: Santiago
Population: 15.3m

Main language: Spanish
Religion: Roman Catholic
Currency: Chilean peso

China

Area: 9,596,961 km²
Capital: Beijing
Population: 1,273.1m

Languages: Mandarin, Cantonese
Religion: Confucianist
Currency: Renminbi yuan

Colombia

Area: 1,138,914 km²
Capital: Bogotá
Population: 40.3m

Main language: Spanish
Religion: Roman Catholic
Currency: Colombian peso

Comoros

Area: 2,170 km²
Capital: Moroni
Population: 596,200

Languages: French, Arabic, Comoran
Religion: Muslim
Currency: Comoran franc

Congo

Area: 342,000 km²
Capital: Brazzaville
Population: 2.9m

Languages: French, Lingala, Kikongo
Religion: Roman Catholic
Currency: Franc

Congo, Democratic Republic of

Area: 2,345,410 km²
Capital: Kinshasa
Population: 53.6m

Languages: Swahili, Lingala, French
Religions: Christian, local beliefs
Currency: Congolese franc

Costa Rica

Area: 51,100 km²
Capital: San José
Population: 3.8m

Main language: Spanish
Religion: Roman Catholic
Currency: Costa Rican colón

Cyprus

Area: 9,251 km²
Capital: Nicosia
Population: 762,900

Languages: Greek, Turkish
Religions: Greek Orthodox, Muslim
Currency: Cyprus pound

Cote d'Ivoire

Area: 322,463 km²
Capital: Yamoussoukro
Population: 16.4m

Main language: French
Religion: Traditional beliefs
Currency: Franc CFA

Czech Republic

Area: 78,866 km²
Capital: Prague
Population: 10.3m

Main Language: Czech
Religion: Roman Catholic
Currency: Koruna

Croatia

Area: 56,542 km²
Capital: Zagreb
Population: 4.3m

Languages: Croato-Serb, Serbo-Croat
Religion: Roman Catholic
Currency: Kuna

Denmark

Area: 43,094 km²
Capital: Copenhagen
Population: 5.3m

Main language: Danish
Religion: Evangelical Lutheran
Currency: Kroner

Cuba

Area: 110,861 km²
Capital: Havana
Population: 11.1m

Main language: Spanish
Religion: Roman Catholic
Currency: Cuban peso

Djibouti

Area: 22,000 km²
Capital: Djibouti
Population: 460,700

Languages: Arabic, French
Religion: Christian
Currency: Djibouti franc

Dominica

Area: 754 km²
Capital: Roseau
Population: 71,000

Languages: English, Creole
Religion: Roman Catholic
Currency: East Caribbean dollar

Dominican Republic

Area: 48,734 km²
Capital: Santo Domingo
Population: 8.6m

Main language: Spanish
Religion: Roman Catholic
Currency: Dominican Republic peso

East Timor

Area: 19,000 km²
Capital: Dili
Population: 800,000

Languages: Tetum, Portugese
Religion: Roman Catholic, Muslim
Currency: US dollar

Ecuador

Area: 283,561 km²
Capital: Quito
Population: 13.2m

Languages: Spanish, Quechua
Religion: Roman Catholic
Currency: Sucre

Egypt

Area: 1,001,449 km²
Capital: Cairo
Population: 69.5m

Main language: Arabic
Religion: Muslim
Currency: Egyptian pound

El Salvador

Area: 21,041 km²
Capital: San Salvador
Population: 6.2m

Main language: Spanish
Religion: Roman Catholic
Currency: El Salvador colón

Equatorial Guinea

Area: 28,051 km²
Capital: Malabo
Population: 486,000

Languages: French, Spanish
Religion: Christian
Currency: Franc CFA

Eritrea

Area: 121,320 km²
Capital: Asmara
Population: 4.3m

Languages: English, Arabic
Religions: Coptic Christian, Muslim
Currency: Nakfa

Estonia

Area: 45,226 km²
Capital: Tallinn
Population: 1.4m

Languages: Estonian, Russian
Religion: Evangelical Lutheran
Currency: Kroon

Ethiopia

Area: 1,127,127 km²
Capital: Addis Ababa
Population: 65.9m

Main language: Amharic
Religions: Muslim, Christian
Currency: Ethiopian birr

Fiji

Area: 18,274 km²
Capital: Suva
Population: 844,300

Languages: Fijian, Hindi
Religion: Christian
Currency: Fiji dollar

Finland

Area: 337,030 km²
Capital: Helsinki
Population: 5.2m

Languages: Finnish, Swedish
Religion: Evangelical Lutheran
Currency: Euro

France

Area: 547,030 km²
Capital: Paris
Population: 59.6m

Main language: French
Religion: Roman Catholic
Currency: Euro

Gabon

Area: 267,668 km²
Capital: Libreville
Population: 1.2m

Languages: French, Fang, Eshira
Religion: Roman Catholic
Currency: Franc CFA

Gambia, The

Area: 11,295 km²
Capital: Banjul
Population: 1.4m

Languages: English, local dialects
Religion: Muslim
Currency: Dalasi

Georgia

Area: 69,700 km²
Capital: Tbilisi
Population: 5.0m

Languages: Georgian, Russian
Religion: Georgian Orthodox
Currency: Lari

Germany

Area: 357,021 km²
Capital: Berlin
Population: 83.0m

Main Language: German
Religion: Protestant
Currency: Euro

Guatemala

Area: 108,889 km²
Capital: Guatemala Ci
Population: 13m

Main language: Spanish
Religion: Christian
Currency: Quetzal

Ghana

Area: 238,533 km²
Capital: Accra
Population: 19.9m

Languages: English, Twi, Fanti
Religions: Traditional beliefs, Muslim
Currency: Cedi

Guinea

Area: 245,857 km²
Capital: Conakry
Population: 7.6m

Languages: French, Susu, Malinké
Religion: Muslim
Currency: Guinea franc

Greece

Area: 131,940 km²
Capital: Athens
Population: 10.6m

Main language: Greek
Religion: Greek Orthodox
Currency: Euro

Guinea-Bissau

Area: 36,126 km²
Capital: Bissau
Population: 1.3m

Languages: Portuguese, Creole
Religion: Traditional beliefs
Currency: Franc CFA

Grenada

Area: 340 km²
Capital: St George's
Population: 89,200

Main language: English
Religion: Roman Catholic
Currency: East Caribbean dollar

Guyana

Area: 214,967 km²
Capital: Georgetow
Population: 697,200

Languages: English, Creole
Religions: Christian, Hindu
Currency: Guyana dollar

Haiti

Area: 27,750 km²
Capital: Port-au-Prince
Population: 7.0m

Languages: French, Creole
Religion: Roman Catholic
Currency: Gourde

Honduras

Area: 112,088 km²
Capital: Tegucigalpa
Population: 6.4m

Languages: Spanish, English
Religion: Roman Catholic
Currency: Lempira

Hungary

Area: 93,030 km²
Capital: Budapest
Population: 10.1m

Languages: Magyar, German
Religion: Roman Catholic
Currency: Forint

Iceland

Area: 103,000 km²
Capital: Reykjavik
Population: 277,800

Languages: Icelandic, Danish
Religion: Evangelical Lutheran
Currency: Icelandic króna

India

Area: 3,287,590 km²
Capital: New Delhi
Population: 1,030m

Languages: Hindi, English
Religion: Hindu
Currency: Indian rupee

Indonesia

Area: 1,919,440 km²
Capital: Jakarta
Population: 228.4m

Languages: Bahasa Indonesian, Dutch
Religion: Muslim
Currency: Rupiah

Iran

Area: 1,648,000 km²
Capital: Tehran
Population: 66.1m

Languages: Persian, Kurdish, Arabic
Religion: Shi'a Muslim
Currency: Rial

Iraq

Area: 437,072 km²
Capital: Baghdad
Population: 23.3m

Languages: Arabic, Turkic, Aramaic
Religion: Shi'a Muslim
Currency: Iraqi dinar

Ireland, Republic of

Area: 70,280 km²
Capital: Dublin
Population: 3.8m

Languages: English, Irish
Religion: Roman Catholic
Currency: Euro

Israel

Area: 20,770 km²
Capital: Jerusalem
Population: 5.9m

Languages: Hebrew, Arabic
Religion: Jewish
Currency: Shekel

Italy

Area: 301,230 km²
Capital: Rome
Population: 57.7m

Main language: Italian
Religion: Roman Catholic
Currency: Euro

Jamaica

Area: 10,990 km²
Capital: Kingston
Population: 2.7m

Languages: English, Spanish
Religion: Christian
Currency: Jamaican dollar

Japan

Area: 377,835 km²
Capital: Tokyo
Population: 126.8m

Main language: Japanese
Religions: Shinto, Buddhist
Currency: Yen

Jordan

Area: 92,300 km²
Capital: Amman
Population: 5.2m

Languages: Arabic, English, French
Religion: Muslim
Currency: Jordanian dinar

Kazakhstan

Area: 2,717,300 km²
Capital: Astana
Population: 16.7m

Languages: Kazakh, Russian
Religion: Muslim
Currency: Tenge

Kenya

Area: 582,650 km²
Capital: Nairobi
Population: 30.8m

Languages: English, Swahili
Religions: Roman Catholic, Protestant
Currency: Kenyan shilling

Kiribati

Area: 717 km²
Capital: Bairiki
Population: 94,100

Languages: I-Kiribati, English
Religion: Roman Catholic
Currency: Australian dollar

Latvia

Area: 64,589 km²
Capital: Riga
Population: 2.4m

Languages: Latvian, Russian
Religion: Evangelical Lutheran
Currency: Lats

Kuwait

Area: 17,820 km²
Capital: Kuwait
Population: 2.0m

Languages: Arabic, English
Religion: Muslim
Currency: Kuwaiti dinar

Lebanon

Area: 10,400 km²
Capital: Beirut
Population: 3.6m

Languages: Arabic, French, English
Religion: Muslim
Currency: Lebanese pound

Kyrgyzstan

Area: 198,500 km²
Capital: Bishkek
Population: 4.7m

Languages: Kirghiz, Russian
Religion: Muslim
Currency: Som

Lesotho

Area: 30,355 km²
Capital: Maseru
Population: 2.2m

Languages: Sesotho, English
Religion: Roman Catholic
Currency: Loti

Laos

Area: 236,800 km²
Capital: Vientiane
Population: 5.6m

Languages: Lao, French, Vietnamese
Religion: Buddhist
Currency: Kip

Liberia

Area: 111,369 km²
Capital: Monrovia
Population: 3.2m

Languages: English & local languages
Religion: Traditional beliefs
Currency: Liberian dollar

Libya

Area: 1,759,540 km²
Capital: Tripoli
Population: 5.2m
Main language: Arabic
Religion: Muslim
Currency: Libyan dinar

Macedonia

Area: 25,333 km²
Capital: Skopje
Population: 2.0m
Main language: Macedonian
Religion: Christian
Currency: Dinar

Liechtenstein

Area: 160 km²
Capital: Vaduz
Population: 32,500
Main Language: German
Religion: Roman Catholic
Currency: Swiss franc

Madagascar

Area: 587,041 km²
Capital: Antananariv
Population: 16m
Languages: Malagasy, French
Religion: Traditional beliefs
Currency: Malagasy franc

Lithuania

Area: 65,200 km²
Capital: Vilnius
Population: 3.6m
Languages: Lithuanian, Russian
Religion: Roman Catholic
Currency: Litas

Malawi

Area: 118,484 km²
Capital: Lilongwe
Population: 10.5m
Languages: Chichewa, English
Religions: Protestant, Catholic
Currency: Kwacha

Luxembourg

Area: 2,586 km²
Capital: Luxembourg
Population: 443,000
Languages: Luxembourgish, French, German
Religion: Roman Catholic
Currency: Euro

Malaysia

Area: 329,750 km²
Cap: Kuala Lumpu
Putrajaya
Population: 22.2m
Languages: Malay, English
Religion: Muslim
Currency: Malaysian dollar

Maldives

Area: 298 km²
Capital: Male
Population: 310,760
Main Language: Maldivian
Religion: Sunni Muslim
Currency: Rufiyaa

Mali

Area: 1,240,192 km²
Capital: Bamako
Population: 11m
Languages: French, local dialects
Religion: Muslim
Currency: Franc CFA

Malta

Area: 316 km²
Capital: Valletta
Population: 394,600
Languages: Maltese, English
Religion: Roman Catholic
Currency: Maltese lira

Marshall Islands

Area: 181 km²
Cap: Dalap-Uliga-Darrit
Population: 70,800
Languages: Marshallese, English
Religion: Protestant
Currency: US dollar

Mauritania

Area: 1,030,700 km²
Capital: Nouakchott
Population: 2.7m
Languages: Arabic, Pulaar, French
Religion: Muslim
Currency: Ouguiya

Mauritius

Area: 1,860 km²
Capital: Port Louis
Population: 1.2m
Languages: Creole, French, English
Religion: Hindu
Currency: Mauritius rupee

Mexico

Area: 1,972,550 km²
Capital: Mexico
Population: 101.9m
Main language: Spanish
Religion: Roman Catholic
Currency: Peso

Micronesia, Federated States of

Area: 702 km²
Capital: Palikir
Population: 134,600
Languages: English, Yapese, Ulithian
Religion: Roman Catholic
Currency: US dollar

Moldova

Area: 33,843 km²
Capital: Chisinau
Population: 4.4m

Languages: Moldavian, Russian
Religion: Romanian Orthodox
Currency: Leu

Monaco

Area: 2 km²
Capital: Monaco
Population: 32,000

Main language: French
Religion: Roman Catholic
Currency: Euro

Mongolia

Area: 1,566,500 km²
Capital: Ulan Bator
Population: 2.7m

Languages: Mongolian, Kazakh
Religion: Tibetan Buddhist
Currency: Tugrik

Morocco

Area: 446,550 km²
Capital: Rabat
Population: 30.6m

Languages: Arabic, Berber
Religion: Muslim
Currency: Dirham

Mozambique

Area: 801,590 km²
Capital: Maputo
Population: 19.4m

Main language: Portuguese
Religion: Traditional beliefs
Currency: Metical

Myanmar (Burma)

Area: 678,500 km²
Capital: Rangoon
Population: 42.0m

Languages: Burmese, English, Shan
Religion: Buddhist
Currency: Kyat

Namibia

Area: 825,418 km²
Capital: Windhoek
Population: 1.8m

Languages: English, Afrikaans, German
Religion: Christian
Currency: Namibian dollar

Nauru

Area: 21 km²
Capital: Yaren
Population: 12,100

Languages: Nauruan, French
Religion: Christian
Currency: Australian dollar

Nepal

Area: 147,181 km²
Capital: Kathmandu
Population: 21.9m
Main language: Nepali
Religion: Hindu
Currency: Nepalese rupee

Netherlands

Area: 41,526 km²
Capital: Amsterdam
Population: 16.0m
Main language: Dutch
Religion: Roman Catholic
Currency: Euro

New Zealand

Area: 268,680 km²
Capital: Wellington
Population: 3.9m
Main language: English
Religion: Protestant
Currency: New Zealand dollar

Nicaragua

Area: 129,494 km²
Capital: Managua
Population: 4.9m
Languages: Spanish, English
Religion: Roman Catholic
Currency: Córdoba

Niger

Area: 1,267,000 km²
Capital: Niamey
Population: 10.4m
Languages: French, Hausa
Religion: Muslim
Currency: Franc CFA

Nigeria

Area: 923,768 km²
Capital: Abuja
Population: 126.6m
Languages: English, Hausa
Religions: Christian, Muslim
Currency: Naira

North Korea

Area: 120,538 km²
Capital: Pyongyang
Population: 22m
Main language: Korean
Religion: Traditional beliefs
Currency: Won

Norway

Area: 324,220 km²
Capital: Oslo
Population: 4.5m
Main language: Norwegian
Religion: Evangelical Lutheran
Currency: Krone

Oman

Area: 212,460 km²
Capital: Muscat
Population: 2.6m
Languages: Arabic & local dialects
Religion: Ibadi Muslim
Currency: Omani rial

Pakistan

Area: 803,940 km²
Capital: Islamabad
Population: 144.6m
Languages: Punjabi, Urdu, Sindi
Religion: Sunni Muslim
Currency: Pakistan rupee

Palau

Area: 459 km²
Capital: Koror
Population: 19,100
Languages: Palauan, English
Religion: Christian
Currency: US dollar

Panama

Area: 78,200 km²
Capital: Panama City
Population: 2.8m
Languages: Spanish, English
Religion: Roman Catholic
Currency: Balboa

Papua New Guinea

Area: 462,840 km²
Capital: Port Moresby
Population: 5m
Languages: English, Pidgin English
Religion: Christian
Currency: Kina

Paraguay

Area: 406,752 km²
Capital: Asuncion
Population: 5.7m
Languages: Spanish, Guaraní
Religion: Roman Catholic
Currency: Guaraní

Peru

Area: 1,285,216 km²
Capital: Lima
Population: 27.5m
Languages: Spanish, Quechua, Ayma
Religion: Roman Catholic
Currency: New Sol

Philippines

Area: 300,000 km²
Capital: Manila
Population: 82.8m
Languages: Filipino, English
Religion: Roman Catholic
Currency: Philippine peso

oland

Area: 312,685 km²
Capital: Warsaw
Population: 38.6m

Main language: Polish
Religion: Roman Catholic
Currency: Zloty

ortugal

Area: 92,391km²
Capital: Lisbon
Population: 10.1m

Main language: Portuguese
Religion: Roman Catholic
Currency: Euro

atar

Area: 11,437 km²
Capital: Doha
Pop: 769,150

Languages: Arabic, English
Religion: Sunni Muslim
Currency: Qatar riyal

omania

Area: 237,500 km²
Capital: Bucharest
Population: 22.4m

Main Language: Romanian
Religion: Romanian Orthodox
Currency: Leu

Russia

Area: 17,075,200 km²
Capital: Moscow
Population: 145m

Main language: Russian
Religion: Russian Orthodox
Currency: Rouble

Rwanda

Area: 26,338 km²
Capital: Kigali
Population: 7.3m

Languages: Kinyarwanda, French, English
Religion: Roman Catholic
Currency: Rwanda franc

Samoa

Area: 2,860 km²
Capital: Apia
Population: 179,000

Languages: Samoan, English
Religion: Protestant
Currency: Tala

San Marino

Area: 61 km²
Capital: San Marino
Population: 27,300

Main language: Italian
Religion: Roman Catholic
Currency: Euro

São Tomé & Príncipe

Area: 1001 km²
Capital: São Tomé
Population: 165,000

Main language: Portuguese
Religion: Roman Catholic
Currency: Dobra

Saudi Arabia

Area: 1,960,582 km²
Capital: Riyadh
Population: 22.8m

Languages: Arabic, English
Religion: Sunni Muslim
Currency: Saudi riyal

Senegal

Area: 196,190 km²
Capital: Dakar
Population: 10.34m

Languages: French, local dialects
Religion: Muslim
Currency: Franc CFA

Serbia and Montenegro

Area: 102,350 km²
Capital: Belgrade
Population: 10.7m

Languages: Serbo-Croat, Albanian
Religion: Orthodox
Currency: New dinar

Seychelles

Area: 455 km²
Capital: Victoria
Population: 80,000

Languages: French, English, Creole
Religion: Roman Catholic
Currency: Seychelles rupee

Sierra Leone

Area: 71,740 km²
Capital: Freetown
Population: 4.5m

Languages: English, French, Creole
Religion: Traditional beliefs
Currency: Leone

Singapore

Area: 647 km²
Capital: Singapore
Population: 4.3m

Languages: Malay, Mandarin, Tamil
Religion: Buddhist
Currency: Singapore dollar

Slovakia

Area: 48,845 km²
Capital: Bratislava
Population: 5.4m

Languages: Slovak, Magyar, Czech
Religion: Roman Catholic
Currency: Koruna

Slovenia

Area: 20,253 km²
Capital: Ljubljana
Population: 2m

Languages: Slovene, Magyar, Italian
Religion: Roman Catholic
Currency: Tolar

Solomon Islands

Area: 28,450 km²
Capital: Honiara
Population: 480,400

Main language: English
Religion: Christian
Currency: Solomon Island dollar

Somalia

Area: 637,657 km²
Capital: Mogadishu
Population: 7.5m

Languages: Somali, Arabic, English
Religion: Sunni Muslim
Currency: Somali shilling

South Africa

Area: 1,219,912 km²
Capital: Pretoria
Population: 43.6m

Languages: English, Afrikaans, Zulu
Religion: Protestant
Currency: Rand

South Korea

Area: 98,480 km²
Capital: Seoul
Population: 47.9m

Main language: Korean
Religion: Mahayana Buddhist
Currency: Won

Spain

Area: 504,782 km²
Capital: Madrid
Population: 40.0m

Main language: Castilian Spanish
Religion: Roman Catholic
Currency: Euro

Sri Lanka

Area: 65,610 km²
Cap: Sri
Jayewardenepura Kotte

Population: 19.4m
Languages: Sinhala, Tamil, English
Religion: Buddhist *Currency:* Sri Lankan rupee

St Kitts-Nevis

Area: 261 km²
Capital: Basseterre
Population: 38,700

Main language: English
Religion: Protestant
Currency: East Caribbean dollar

St Lucia

Area: 622 km²
Capital: Castries
Population: 158,200
Main language: English
Religion: Roman Catholic
Currency: East Caribbean dollar

St Vincent & the Grenadines

Area: 388 km²
Capital: Kingstown
Population: 115,900
Main language: English
Religion: Protestant
Currency: East Caribbean dollar

Sudan

Area: 2,505,813 km²
Capital: Khartoum
Population: 36.1m
Languages: Arabic, English
Religion: Muslim
Currency: Sudanese dinar

Suriname

Area: 163,265 km²
Capital: Paramaribo
Population: 434,000
Languages: Dutch, Sranang Togo
Religions: Christian, Hindu
Currency: Surinam guilder

Swaziland

Area: 17,364 km²
Capital: Mbabane
Population: 1.1m
Main language: SiSwati, English
Religion: Protestant
Currency: Rand

Sweden

Area: 449,964 km²
Capital: Stockholm
Population: 8.9m
Main language: Swedish
Religion: Evangelical Lutheran
Currency: Swedish krona

Switzerland

Area: 41,290 km²
Capital: Bern
Population: 7.3m
Languages: French, German, Italian
Religion: Roman Catholic
Currency: Swiss franc

Syria

Area: 185,180 km²
Capital: Damascus
Population: 16.7m
Languages: Arabic, Kurdish, Turkish
Religion: Sunni Muslim
Currency: Syrian pound

Taiwan

Area: 35,980 km²
Capital: Taipei
Population: 22.4m

Languages: Mandarin, Chinese
Religions: Buddhist, Confucianist
Currency: New Taiwan dollar

Togo

Area: 56,785 km²
Capital: Lomé
Population: 5.2m

Languages: French, Ewe
Religion: Traditional beliefs
Currency: Franc CFA

Tajikistan

Area: 143,100 km²
Capital: Dushanbe
Population: 6.6m

Languages: Tajik, Uzbek, Russian
Religion: Sunni Muslim
Currency: Tajik rouble

Tonga

Area: 747 km²
Capital: Nuku'alofa
Population: 104,200

Languages: Tongan, English
Religion: Protestant
Currency: Pa'anga

Tanzania

Area: 945,087 km²
Capital: Dodoma
Population: 36.2m

Languages: Swahili, English
Religion: Traditional beliefs
Currency: Shilling

Trinidad & Tobago

Area: 5,130 km²
Capital: Port of Spain
Population: 1.2m

Main language: English
Religion: Christian
Currency: Trinidad & Tobago dollar

Thailand

Area: 513,115 km²
Capital: Bangkok
Population: 61.8m

Languages: Thai, Chinese, Khmer
Religion: Buddhist
Currency: Baht

Tunisia

Area: 163,610 km²
Capital: Tunis
Population: 9.7m

Languages: Arabic, French, English
Religion: Muslim
Currency: Tunisian dinar

Turkey

Area: 780,580 km²
Capital: Ankara
Population: 66.5m

Main language: Turkish
Religion: Muslim
Currency: Turkish lira

Turkmenistan

Area: 488,100 km²
Capital: Ashkhabad
Population: 4.6m

Languages: Turkmenian, Russian
Religion: Muslim
Currency: Manat

Tuvalu

Area: 26 km²
Capital: Fongafale
Population: 11,000

Languages: Tuvaluan, English
Religion: Protestant
Currency: Australian dollar

Uganda

Area: 236,040 km²
Capital: Kampala
Population: 24m

Languages: English, Swahili
Religions: Roman Catholic, Protestant
Currency: Uganda shilling

Ukraine

Area: 603,700 km²
Capital: Kiev
Population: 48.8m

Main language: Ukrainian, Russian
Religion: Ukrainian Orthodox
Currency: Hryvna

United Arab Emirates

Area: 82,880 km²
Capital: Abu Dha
Population: 2.4m

Languages: English, Arabic
Religion: Sunni Muslim
Currency: UAE dirham

United Kingdom

Area: 244,820 km
Capital: London
Population: 59.6m

Main language: English
Religion: Protestant
Currency: Pound

United States

Area: 9,629,091 km
Capital: Washington
Population: 278m

Languages: English, Spanish
Religions: Protestant, Roman Catho
Currency: US dollar

Uruguay

Area: 176,220 km²
Capital: Montevideo
Population: 3.4m

Main language: Spanish
Religion: Roman Catholic
Currency: New Uruguayan peso

Uzbekistan

Area: 447,400 km²
Capital: Tashkent
Population: 25.2m

Languages: Uzbek, Russian
Religion: Muslim
Currency: Sum

Vanuatu

Area: 12,189 km²
Capital: Port-Vila
Population: 192,900

Languages: Bislama, English, French
Religion: Protestant
Currency: Vatu

Vatican City

Area: 0.44 km²
Capital: Vatican City
Population: 1,000

Main language: Italian
Religion: Roman Catholic
Currency: Euro

Venezuela

Area: 912,050 km²
Capital: Caracas
Population: 23.9m

Main language: Spanish
Religion: Roman Catholic
Currency: Bolívar

Vietnam

Area: 329,560 km²
Capital: Hanoi
Population: 80.0m

Languages: Vietnamese, French, English
Religion: Buddhist
Currency: Dông

Yemen

Area: 527,970 km²
Capital: San'a
Population: 18.1m

Main language: Arabic
Religion: Sunni Muslim
Currency: Riyal

Zambia

Area: 752,618 km²
Capital: Lusaka
Population: 9.8m

Languages: English, Nyanja, Tonga
Religion: Christian
Currency: Kwacha

Zimbabwe

Area: 390,580 km²
Capital: Harare
Population: 11.4m

Languages: English, Shona, Ndebele
Religion: Syncretic
Currency: Zimbabwe dollar

© Hema Maps Pty Ltd. Based on original data © Research Machines plc

0   200   400   600 km

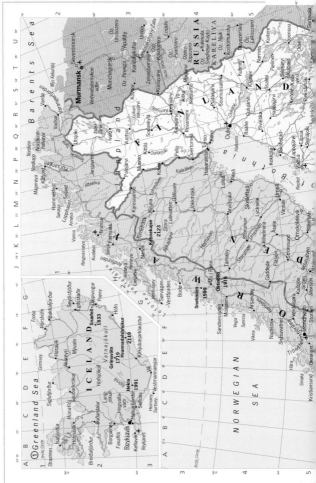

© Hema Maps Pty Ltd. Based on original data © Research Machines plc

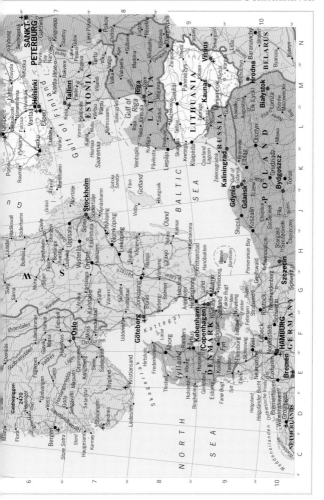

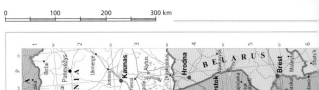

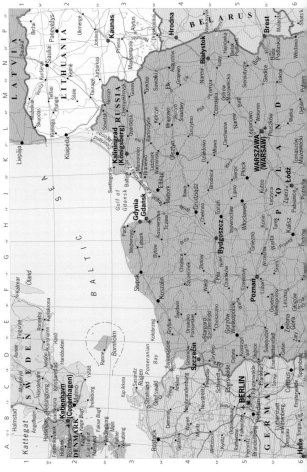

44

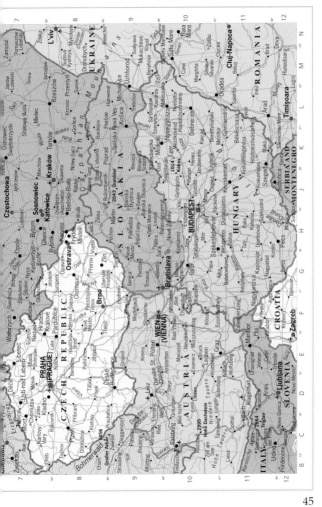

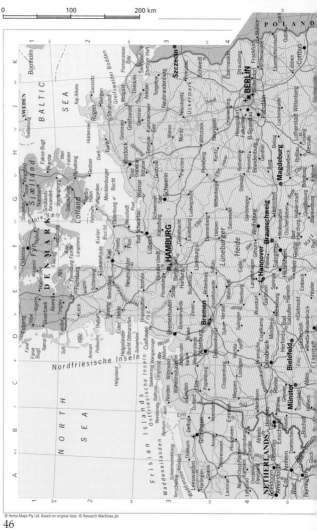

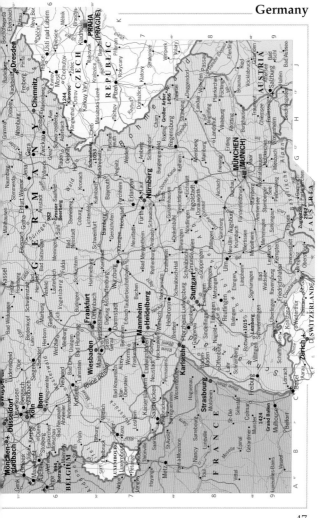

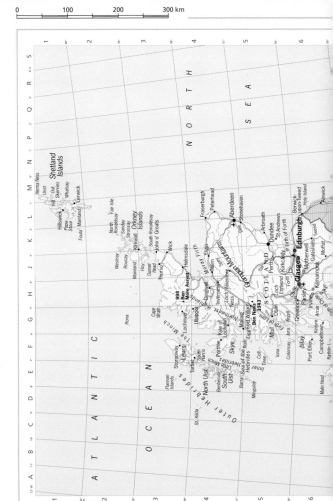

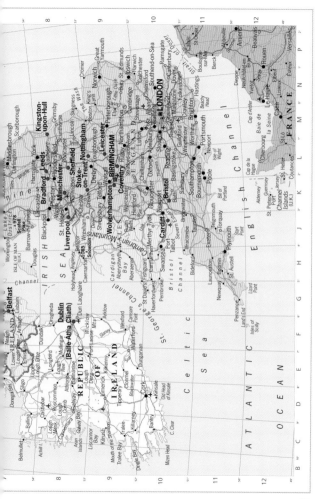

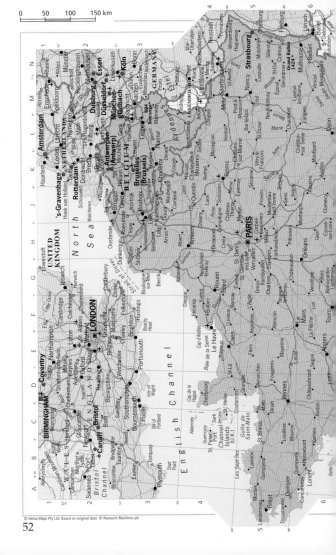

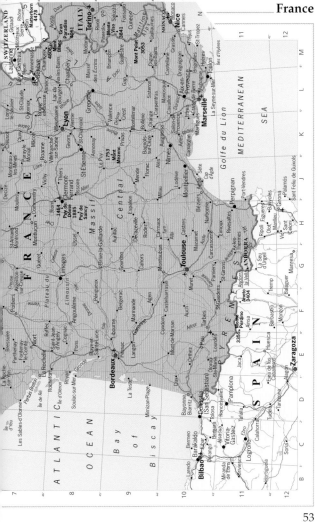

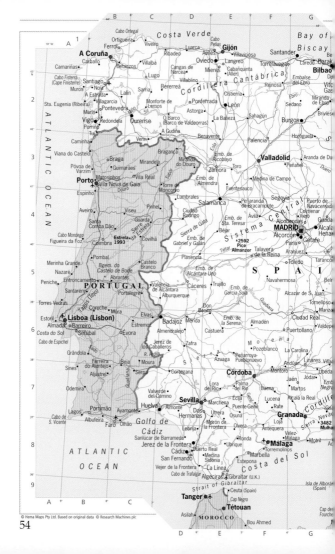

0   100   200 km

J   K   L   M   N   P   Q

Biarritz
Bayonne   Orthez   Muret   Béziers   Cap d'Agde
Donostia   Oloron   Pau   Tarbes   Aude   Carcassonne   Narbonne
(San Sebastián)   Ste-Marie   **FRANCE**   Pamiers   Limoux   Golfe du Lion
para Tolosa   Lourdes   St-Gaudens   St-Girons   Ax-les-Thermes   Rivesaltes   Perpignan
Alsasua   Roncesvalles   P   Y   R   E   N   E   E   S   **ANDORRA**   Port-Vendres
Pamplona   Jaca   Monte   Aneto   Andorra   Tet   Figueres
ogroño   Tafalla   3355 Perdido   3404   la Vella   La Seu   Ripoll   Banyoles   Costa
alahorra   Ejea de los   Huesca   Ainsa   d'Urgell   Manlleu   Girona   Palamós   Brava
•Tudela   Caballeros   Barbastro   Tremp   Vic   Sant Celoni   Sant Feliu
oria   •Tarazona   Alagón   Monzón   Balaguer   Manresa   Terrassa   de Guixols
inazán   Calatayud   **Zaragoza**   Lleida   Igualada   Sabadell   Mataró
Medinaceli   Daroca   Azaila   Fraga   Montblanc   Vilanova   **BARCELONA**
    Alcañiz   Caspe   Reus   la Geltrú   El Prat de Llobregat
Calamocha   Montalbán   Tortosa   Tarragona   Sitges
    Teruel   Amposta   Costa   Dorada
•Cuenca   Sierra   Morella   Islas Baleares
    de Gúdar   Vinaròs   (Balearic Islands)   Menorca
    Castelló de la Plana   Ciutadella   Mahón
Emb. de   Utiel   Borriana   Islas Columbretes   Cap de Formentor
Contreras   Sagunt   La Vall d'Uixó   Pollença   Arta
robledo   Cofrents   Paterna   Golfo de   Sóller   Inca   Manacor
Roda   Júcar   Torrent   **Valencia**   Valencia   **Palma**   Mallorca
    Almansa   Algemesí   Llucmajor
•Albacete   Alzira   Cabrera   Cap de ses
Chinchilla   Cullera   Salines
de Monte-Aragón   Gandía   Eivissa
Icaraz   Jumilla   Alcoi   Dénia   (Ibiza)
    Benidorm   San Antonia   Eivissa (Ibiza)
Hellín   Novelda   **Alicante**   Abad   Formentera
    Cieza   Elda   Santa Pola
Alcantarilla   Elch
Murcia   Orihuela
Zarzadilla   Costa   Blanca
enibética   de Totana   La Unión
Lorca   Cartagena
Albox   Aguilas   Golfo de   M   e   d   i   t   e   r   r   a   n   e   a   n   S   e   a
    Mazarrón
Vera   Dellys   Tizi
Nijar   **ALGER**   Ain   Ouzou
•Almería   **(ALGIERS)**   Taya   Thenia
o de   Cabo   Bou   Cherchell   Larbaa   Lakhdaria   Bouira
ería de Gata   Ismail   Blida
    Ténès   Bouzghaia   Miliana   Medéa   Beni   Sour el
    Khemis   Slimane   Ghozlane
Ain-Tédeles   Chélif   Miliana   Berrouaghia   **A L G E R I A**
Mostaganem   Ech Chélif   Mountains
    Bou   Thenet   Ksar el   Ain el
    Kadir   el Had   Boukhari   Hadjel
Mers el   Relizane   A   t   l   a   s
Kébir   Godyel
Oran   El Amria   Mohammadia
Beni Saf   Mascara

J   K   L   M   N

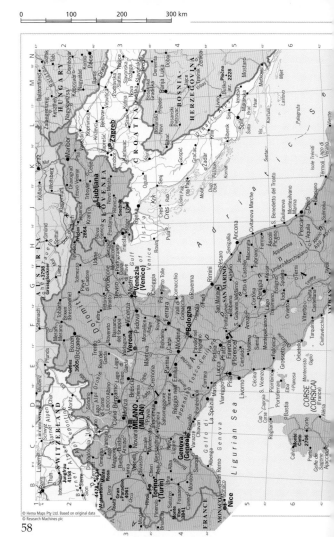

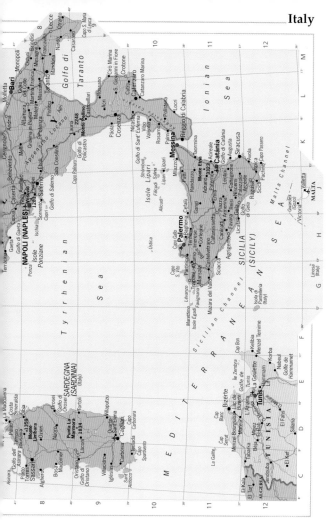

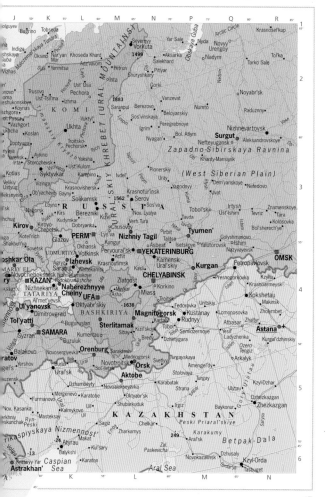

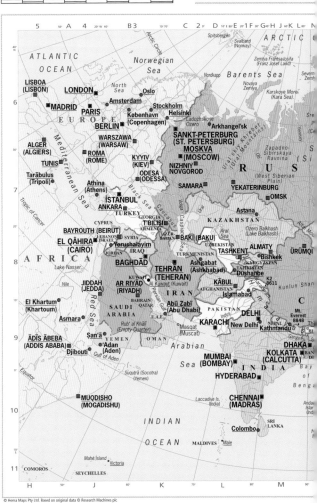

© Hema Maps Pty Ltd. Based on original data © Research Machines plc

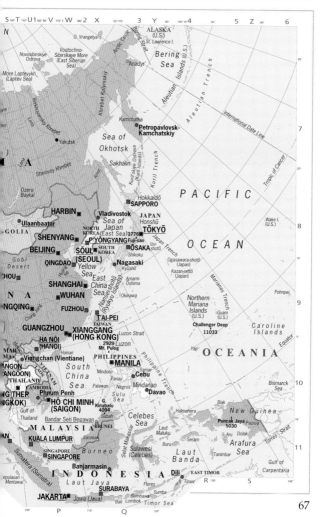

S 140° T 150° U 160° V 170° W 2 X 70°/170° Y 60° 180° 4 50° 5 Z 40° 6

N

ALASKA (U.S.)

Novosibirskiye Ostrova

Vostochno-Sibirskoye More (East Siberian Sea)

More Laptevykh (Laptev Sea)

Khrebet Kolymskiy

Ostrov Vrangelya

Arctic Circle

Bering Strait

St. Lawrence I.

Bering Sea

Anadyr'

Aleutian Islands (U.S.)

Aleutian Trench

International Date Line

Verkhoyanskiy Khrebet

Lena

Yakutsk

Kamchatka

Petropavlovsk-Kamchatskiy

A

Stanovoy Khrebet

Sea of Okhotsk

Sakhalin

Kuril Trench

Kuril'skiye Ostrova (Kuril Islands)

Tropic of Cancer

Ozero Baykal

Kuril'skiye Ostrova (Kuril Islands)

PACIFIC

Wake I. (U.S.)

HARBIN

Hokkaidō

SAPPORO

Vladivostok

JAPAN

Honshū

3776▲ Fuji-san

Ulaanbaatar

NORTH KOREA

Sea of Japan (East Sea)

TŌKYŌ

OCEAN

GOLIA

SHENYANG

P'YŎNGYANG

BEIJING

SŎUL (SEOUL)

SOUTH KOREA

ŌSAKA

Shikoku

Ryūkyū shotō

Japan Trench

QINGDAO

Yellow Sea

Nagasaki

Kyūshū

Amami Ōshima

Ogasawara-shotō (Japan)

Kazan-rettō (Japan)

'HOU

SHANGHAI

East China Sea

Nansei-shotō (Ryūkyū Islands)

Mariana Trench

Pohnpei

N A

WUHAN

Chang Jiang

Okinawa

Northern Mariana Islands (U.S.)

Guam (U.S.)

Caroline

NGQING

FUZHOU

Equator

GUANGZHOU

XIANGGANG (HONG KONG)

TAIWAN

T'AI-PEI

Challenger Deep 11033

Islands

Yap

HA NỘI (HANOI)

Hainan

2929 Luzon ▲ Mt. Pulog

Luzon Strait

MARS

Viangchan (Vientiane)

PHILIPPINES

OCEANIA

ANGON

South China Sea

MANILA

Philippine Trench

Mindoro

Cebu

Bismarck Sea

ANGON)

THAILAND

Panay

Palawan

Negros

Mindanao

New Guinea

G THEP

GKOK)

CAMBODIA

HỒ CHÍ MINH (SAIGON)

Phnom Penh

Sulu Sea

Davao

Biak

Puncak Jaya 5030

Papua

Gulf of Thailand

Bandar Seri Begawan

Kinabalu 4094 ▲

Sabah

Celebes Sea

Halmahera

Laut Maluku

AN

MALAYSIA

BRUNEI

Sarawak

KUALA LUMPUR

SINGAPORE

SINGAPORE

Borneo

Buru

Seram

Laut Banda

Aru

Dolak

Arafura Sea

Torres Strait

Gulf of Carpentaria

Sumatera (Sumatra)

epulauan

Mentawa

Banjarmasin

Sulawesi (Celebes)

Selat Makasar

I N D O N E S I A

JAKARTA

SURABAYA

Jawa (Java)

Laut Jawa

Bali Lombok

Flores

Sumba

Dili

Timor

EAST TIMOR

Timor Sea

R

S

180°

P

150°

Q

120°

67

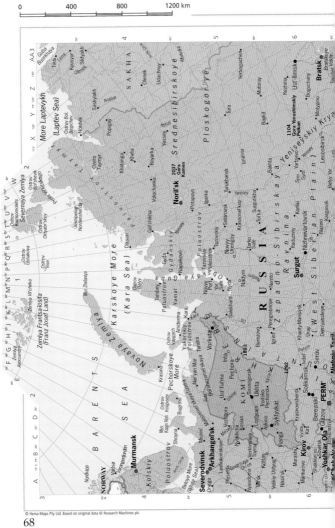

0   400   800   1200 km

AA 3

Guba Buorkhaya
Tiksi
Olenek
Kyusyur
Siklyakh

More Laptevykh
(Laptev Sea)

SAKHA

Olenek
Udachnyy
Yerbogachen
Saskylakh
Anabar
Nordvik
Popigay
Ust'-Ilimsk
Bratsk
Bratskoye Vdkhr.
Tura
Baykit
Kazhim
Mutoray
Severnaya Zemlya
Ostrov Komsomolets
Ostrov Oktyabr'skoy
Ostrov Bol'shevik
Mys Chelyuskin

Ostrov Ushakova

Ostrov Vize

Zemlya Frantsa-Iosifa
(Franz Josef Land)
Zemlya
Aleksandry
Zemlya Vil'cheka

Ostrovnoy
Nordenshel'da

Ostrova
Sergeya Kirova

Ploskogor'ye

1104
Gora Enashimskiy Polkan

Yeniseyskiy Kryazh

Moloyma
Boguchany
Taseyevo Vdkhr.

Ozero Taymyr
Khatanga
Boyarka
Kheta

Sredne-sibirskoye

Yessey
Noril'sk 2037
Gora Kamen'

Baykit
Taravaka
Tutonchany
Teya
Tura

Kras-noyarskoye Vdkhr.

Norilka
Korlki
Lesosibirsk
Belyy Yar
Karasuk
Achinsk

P O L O U S T R O V

Ostrov Vrangelya

Karskoye More
(Kara Sea)

Mys Zhelaniya

Kras-nino

Dudinka
Igarka
Potapovo
Turukhansk
Sidorovsk
Krasnosel'kup
Surgutikha
Yeniseysk

G y d a n s k i y
Gyda
Napalkovo
Tazovskiy
Novyy Port
Yar-Sale
Nyda
Nadym
Nurmato
Sym
Yart-sevo

Surgut

Z a p a d n o - S i b i r s k a y a
R a v n i n a
(W e s t   S i b e r i a n   P l a i n)

B A R E N T S
S E A

P o l u o s t r o v
Yamal

Ostrov Belyy

Kharasavey
Tambey
Yar-Sale
Salekhard
Labytnangi
Aksarka

Nizhnevartovsk

R U S S I A

Novaya Zemlya

Ostrov Kolguyev
Bugrino

Pechorskoye More

Yugorskiy Poluostrov
Amderma
Varnek
Ust'-Kara
Kara

Khanty-Mansiysk
Igrim
Berezovo
Pelym
Serov
Nizhniy Tagil

Poluostrov
Kanin

Mys Kanin Nos

Shoyna

Indiga
Nar'yan-Mar
Khal'mer-Yu
Vorkuta
1883
Inta
Ust'-Tsil'ma
Pechora
Troitsko-Pechorsk
Il'ych
1292
Krasnovishersk
Solikamsk
Berezniki
PERM'
Glazov
Kirs

NORWAY
Nordkapp
Vadsø
Kirkenes

K o l ' s k i y
P o l u o s t r o v

Murmansk

Beloye More
(White Sea)

Onega

Severodvinsk Arkhangel'sk

Leshukonskoye
Mezen'
Nes'
Pinega
Karpogory
Plesetsk
Onega

K O M I

Syktyvkar
Ukhta
Vuktyl
Sosnogorsk

Kotlas
Velikiy Ustyug
Nikol'sk
Murashi
Kirov
Yoshkar-Ola

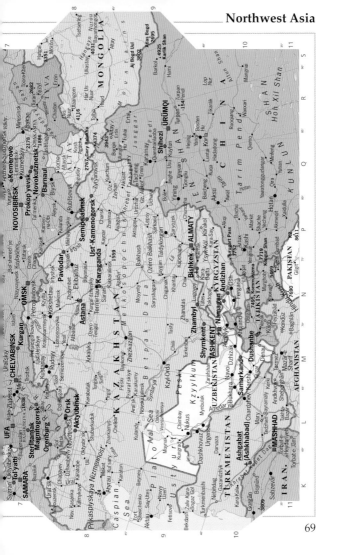

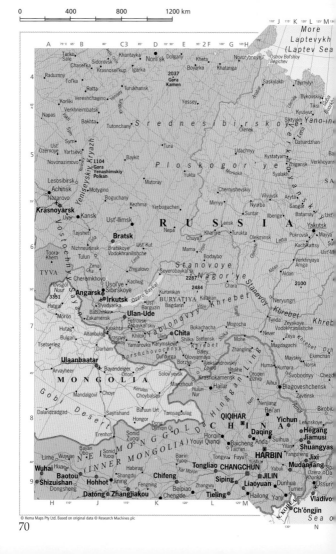

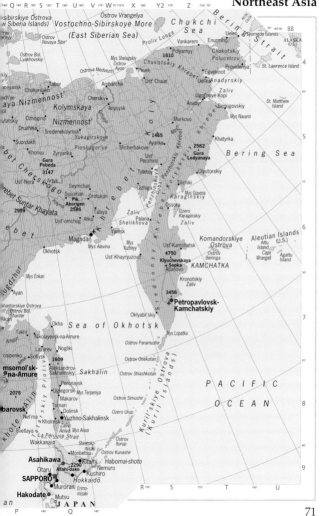

140° Q 145° R 150° S 155° T 160° U 165° V 170° W 75°/175°E X 180° Y2 175° Z 170° 70° **BB**

sibirskiye Ostrova
oy Siberia Islands)   Ostrov Vrangelya   Arctic Circle   65° 165°W   **BB**
rov   Ostrov Novaya Sibir'   **Vostochno-Sibirskoye More**   C h u k c h i   B e r i n g
alayy   **(East Siberia Sea)**   S e a   Uelen   Enurmino   Diomede Islands
         Ostrov Bol.   Proliv Longa   Strait   ALASKA
         Lyakhovskiy   Mys Shelagskiy   Chukotskiy   Egvekinot   (U.S.)
neyansk   Tabor   Ostrova Medvezhi   Ostrov   Polyarnyy   Poluostrov   Providenya St. Lawrence Island
         Chokurdakh   Ayon   1810   Ue'kal Anadyrskiy
aya **Nizmennost'**   Ambarchik   Pevek   Chukotskiy Khrebet Uelkal Anadyrskiy
va   Ust' Chaun   Anadyr'   Ugol'nyye Kopi   Beringovskiy   St. Matthew
utatskiy   Ozhogino   **Kolymskaya**   Cherskiy   Mys Navarin   Island
            Druzhina   **Nizmennost'**   Anyuysk   Markovo   Khatyrka
               Sredenekolymsk   Ayanka   1485
         Suordakh   Yukagirskoye   Shicherbakovo   2562   **Bering Sea**
bet Chetskogo Ploskogor'ye   Zyryanka   Ust'   Gora
Gora   Penzhino   Ledyanaya
Pobeda   Tylkhoy   Olyutorskiy
3147   Ust'-Nera   Seymchan   Gizhiga   Tilichiki
bet Suntar Khayata Susuman   Orotukan **Pik** Mys Govena
2959   **Aborigen** Zaliv   Karaginskiy
         Ust'-omchug   Atka **2586** Shelikhova   Ossora   Ozero
                        Yamsk   Palana   Karaginskiy   Zaliv
              Magadan   Mys Alevina   Mys   Komandorskiye   Aleutian Islands
dzhur Okhotsk   Yuzhnyy   Ustʼ-Kamchatsk   **Ostrova**   (U.S.)
                     Ust'-Khayryuzovo   **Kamchatka**   Attu   Cape
Mys Enkan   **Klyuchevskaya** Ostrov Beringa Island Wrangell
                                            Sopka   Atlasovo   Agattu
Ayan   **S e a o f O k h o t s k** Kronotskiy   Island
hantarskiye Ostrova   **4750**   Zaliv
Ostrov Bol.   Oktyabr'skiy   **3456**
Shantar Takht   **Petropavlovsk-**
rikan   **Kamchatskiy**
osipenko   Nikolayevsk-na-Amure   Mys Lopatka
          Sofiysk   Noglikki   Ostrov Paramushir
msomol'sk- **1609** Aleksandrovsk-
na-Amure   Sakhalinskiy   **Sakhalin**   Ostrov Onekotan
2078   Poronaysk   Ostrov Shiashkotan   **P A C I F I C**
barovsk   Uglegorsk   Mys Terpeniya
         Makarov   Ostrov Simushir   **O C E A N**
         Tomari   Dolinsk
   Nel'ma   Kholmsk **Yuzhno-Sakhalinsk** Ozero Urup
   Svetlaya   Zaliv Mys Aniva
              La Pérouse Strait   Shiretoko-
khoe   Wakkanai   misaki   Ostrov Iturup
Asahikawa   Monbetsu   Ostrov Kunashir **Habomai-shoto**
   Ōtaru Asahi-dake   Kitami Nemuro
SAPPORO **2290**   Kushiro   Ermo-
         Muroran   **Hokkaidō**   misaki
Hakodate Mutsu
an   **J A P A N**   71

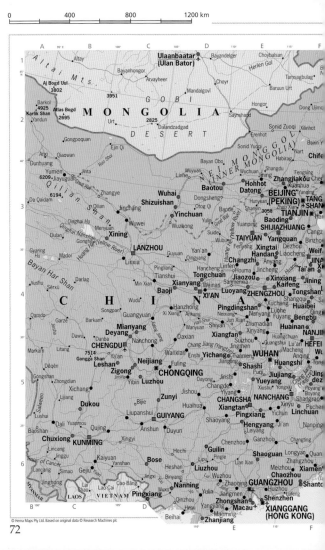

0   400   800   1200 km

72

Yichun
QIQIHAR Jiamusi Hegang
Horqin Hailin Bikin
Youyi Qianqi Daqing Anda Suihua
Baicheng Tao'an Fuyu Yushu Songhua Jiang Svetlaya La Pérouse Strait
Tongyu HARBIN Pangzheng Jixi Muling
CHANGCHUN JILIN Mudanjiang Spassk Ussuriysk
Ozéro Khanka Dal'niy
Liaoyuan Dunhua Vladivostok Tumen Nakhodka
Siping Hailong Yanji Najin
Tieling Hunjiang Hyesan
FUSHUN Benxi
ANSHAN Manp'o NORTH Kimch'aek
Jinxi Yingkou Sinŭiju Hamhŭng SEA OF
Dandong KOREA Wŏnsan
P'YŎNGYANG Namp'o JAPAN
DALIAN SŎUL Sokch'o (EAST SEA)
Yantai Kaesŏng (SEOUL) Kangnŭng
INCH'ŎN SOUTH Ullŭng do
QINGDAO Ch'ŏngju TAEJŎN P'ohang
KWANGJU Ch'ŏnju KOREA Tottori
YELLOW PUSAN
SEA Mokp'o Sunch'ŏn
Yancheng Cheju Kwangju
Nantong Cheju do Gotō-rettō
Wuxi (South Korea) Nagasaki Akune
SHANGHAI Kagoshima Miyakonojō
Suzhou Ōsumi-shotō Tanega-shima
NINGBO EAST Nirahai Yaku-shima
CHINA SEA
Wenzhou Nansei-shotō
(Ryukyu Islands) Amami-Ōshima
Naze
Okinawa
Naha
Chi-lung PACIFIC
T'AI-PEI
Chang-hua 3950 OCEAN
Yu Shan
TAIWAN
T'ai-tung Tropic of Cancer
P'ing-tung
Sakishima-shotō

Asahikawa 2290 Kitami
Nayoro Shiretoko-misaki Ostrov Iturup
Wakkanai Monbetsu Abashiri
Asahi-dake Ostrov Kunashir
Otaru SAPPORO HOKKAIDŌ Nemuro
Oshamambe Tomakomai Kushiro
Okushiri-tō Muroran Erimo-misaki
Matsumae Hakodate
Tsugaru-kaikyō Mutsu
Aomori Hachinohe
Hirosaki Odate
Morioka
Akita Kamaishi
Ichinoseki
Sakata Ishinomaki
Shinjō Sendai
Yamagata Iwaki
Niigata Fukushima
Jōetsu Utsunomiya HONSHŪ
Nagano Maebashi TŌKYŌ
Toyama Kanazawa YOKOHAMA
Fukui Gifu 3776 Shizuoka
Fuji-san Izu-shotō
KYŌTO NAGOYA Hamamatsu
Chūgoku-sanchi ŌSAKA Matsusaka
Tottori KŌBE Wakayama
Higashi-suidō Okayama Myōjin
HIROSHIMA Mats- uyama Sumisu-jima
Shimonoseki Tokushima
KITA-KYŪSHŪ Kōchi JAPAN Tori-shima
FUKUOKA Ōita SHIKOKU Sōfu-gan
Kumamoto Miyazaki
KYŪSHŪ

Stanovoy

Zhangguangcai Ling
Sikhote Alin

Song hua Jiang

Horgin

Korea Bay

handong Bandao

Eastern China

73

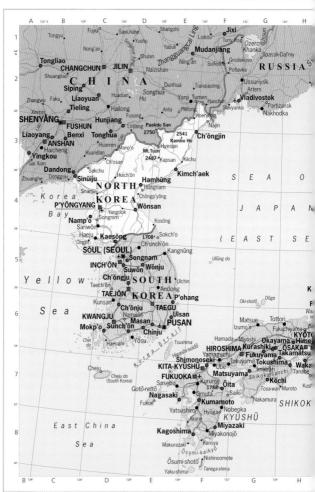

74

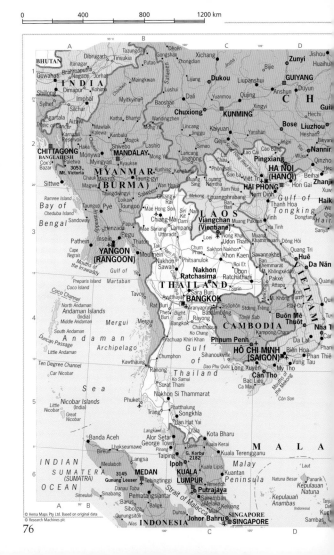

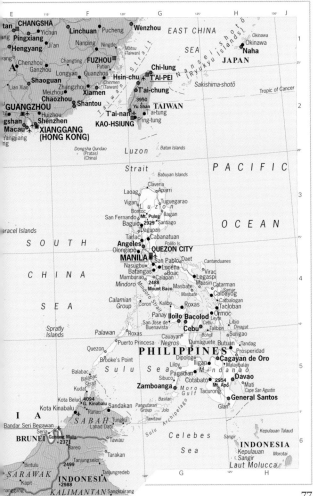

tan **CHANGSHA** Yichun
●Pingxiang ●Linchuan Pucheng ●Wenzhou EAST CHINA Okinawa
●Hengyang Ji'an ●Nanping Ningde Matsu SEA ●Naha
A ●Chenzhou Changting **FUZHOU** (Taiwan) *Nansei-shotō* **JAPAN**
Ganzhou Longyan ●Putian *(Ryukyu Islands)*
Shaoguan Zhangzhou ●Quanzhou **Chi-lung** Sakishima-shotō Tropic of Cancer
Lian Xian Meizhou ●Xiamen **Hsin-chu** **T'AI-PEI**
●**Chaozhou** ●**Shantou** Chinmen **T'ai-chung**
GUANGZHOU Huizhou (Taiwan) 3950
gshan Yu Shan **TAIWAN**
Shenzhen **T'ai-nan** ●T'ai-tung
●Macau **XIANGGANG** **KAO-HSIUNG** P'ing-tung
Yangjiang **(HONG KONG)**
ng

Luzon Batan Islands

Strait

P A C I F I C

Batan Islands

Babuyan Islands

aracel Islands

S O U T H Claveria
Laoag ●Aparri
Vigan ●Tuguegarao
Bontoc *L u z o n* ●Ilagan
C H I N A San Fernando ●Mt. Pulog Santiago
Baguio 2929 ●Cabanatuan
Dagupan
Tarlac Cabanatuan
S E A **Angeles** Polillo Is. Cantanduanes
Olongapo **QUEZON CITY**
MANILA Daet
Nasugbu San Pablo ●Virac
Spratly **Lucena**
Islands Batangas ●Boac Legaspi
Mamburao Calapan ●Maasin Catarman
2488 Masbate Samar
Mindoro **Mount Baco** ●Calbayog
Calamian Catbalogan
Group Coron *Mindoro Strait* ●Ormoc **Tacloban**
Kalibo Roxas Leyte
Palawan San Jose de **Panay** **Iloilo** **Bacolod** Ormoc
Buenavista ●Libio
●Roxas **Cebu** Talibon Dinagat
Quezon Cauayan Bohol Surigao
●Puerto Princesa *Negros* Dumaguete Butuan ●Tandag
Brooke's Point **PHILIPPINES** ●Prosperidad
Dipolog
Balabac S u l u S e a Loay Iligan ●Cagayan de Oro
Balabac Kudat 4094 *Strait* Sibuco Pagadian *M i n d a n a o* ●Malaybalay
Kota Belud **Zamboanga** Cotabato 2954 **Davao**
G. Kinabalu Sandakan Moro Mt. Apo ●Mati
I A Kota Kinabalu Ranau Pangutaran Tacurong Gulf Cape San Agustin
S A B A H Tungku Group ●Jolo ●**General Santos**
Bandar Seri Begawan Lahad Datu Tawi-Tawi ●Glan
Seria **BRUNEI** Gunung Mulu ●Tawau Kepulauan Talaud
●2371 *Sulu Archipelago* Sangir
Bareo Celebes **INDONESIA**
Bintulu **INDONESIA** Tanjungselor S e a Kepulauan Morotai
2499 Tarakan Sangir
SARAWAK Tanjungredeb *Laut Molucca*
Kapit Sangkuilrang
nangkawang **INDONESIA** *K A L I M A N T A N* ●2988

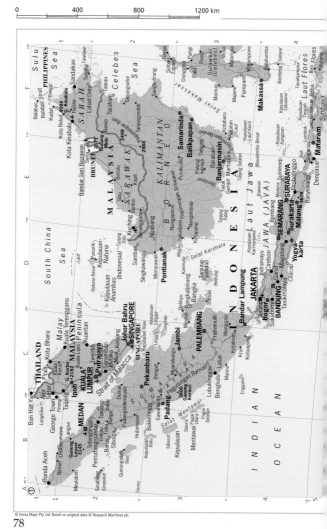

© Hema Maps Pty Ltd. Based on original data © Research Machines plc

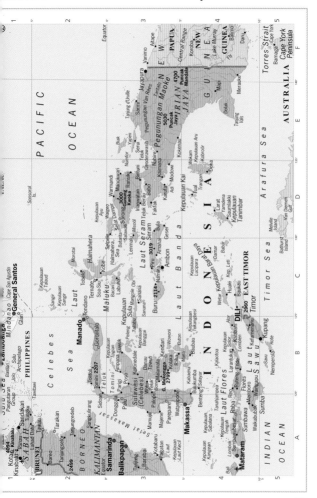

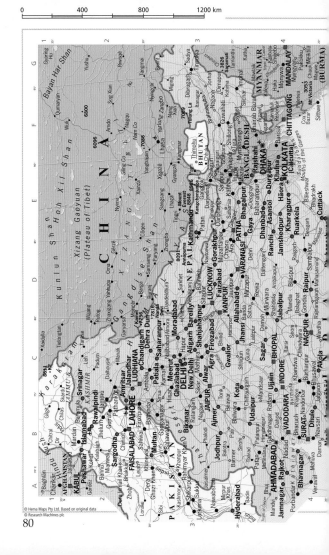

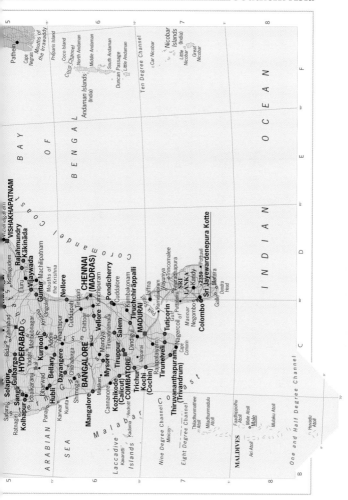

Southern Asia

BAY OF BENGAL

INDIAN OCEAN

ARABIAN SEA

Mouths of the Irrawaddy
Pathein
Cape Negrais
Préparis Island
Coco Island
Coco Channel
North Andaman
Middle Andaman
South Andaman
Duncan Passage
Little Andaman
Andaman Islands (India)
Ten Degree Channel
Car Nicobar
Nicobar Islands (India)
Little Nicobar
Great Nicobar

VISHAKHAPATNAM
Rajahmundry
Kakinada
Kottagudem
Vijayawada
Eluru
Guntur
Machilipatnam
Mouths of the Krishna
Nellore

Sataras
Solapur
Ratnagiri
Bidar
Zahirabad
Sangli
Gulbarga
Kolhapur
Ichalkaranji
Yadgir
Mahbubnagar
Dharwad
Gadag
Panaji
Karwar
Kumta
Hubli
Bellary
Davangere
Chitradurga
Shimoga
Makkere
Cannanore
Kavaratti
Kadama
Androth
Minicoy

HYDERABAD
Kurnool
Addni
Anantapur
Cuddapah
Chittor
Tirupati
Kanchipuram
Cuddalore

BANGALORE
Mandya
Mysore
Tiruvannamalai
Salem
Dindigul
Tiruppur
COIMBATORE
Valparai
Trichur
Kochi (Cochin)
Thiruvananthapuram (Trivandrum)
Tirunelveli
Rajapalayam
Cape Comorin

CHENNAI (MADRAS)
Vellore
Pondicherry
Kumbakonam
Truchchirappalli
MADURAI
Tuticorin

Jaffna
Vavuniya
Trincomalee
Anuradhapura
Puttalam
Negombo
Colombo
SRI LANKA
Kandy
2359
Sri Jayewardenepura Kotte
Pottuvil
Galle
Matara
Dondra Head

Coromandel Coast
Palk Strait
Gulf of Mannar
Mannar

Malabar Coast
Laccadive Islands

Nine Degree Channel
Eight Degree Channel

MALDIVES
Faadhippolhu Atoll
Male Atoll
Male
Ari Atoll
Miladhunmadulu Atoll
Dhuvaafaru Atoll
Maalhosmadulu Atoll
Maalaku Atoll

One and Half Degree Channel

Huvadu Atoll

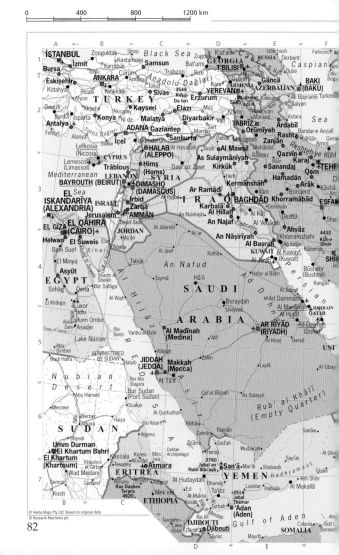

82

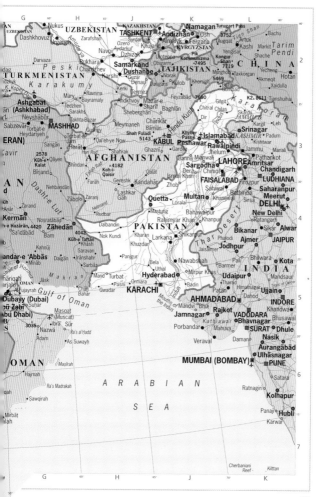

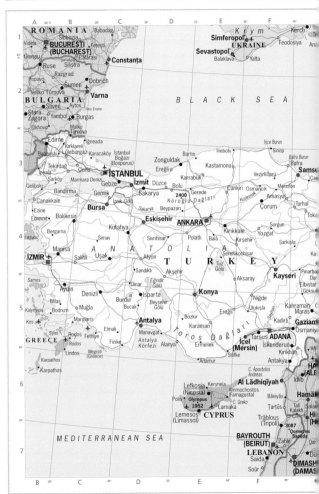

0   200   400   600 km

0   50   100   150 km

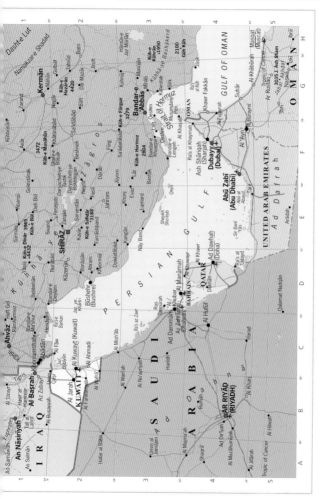

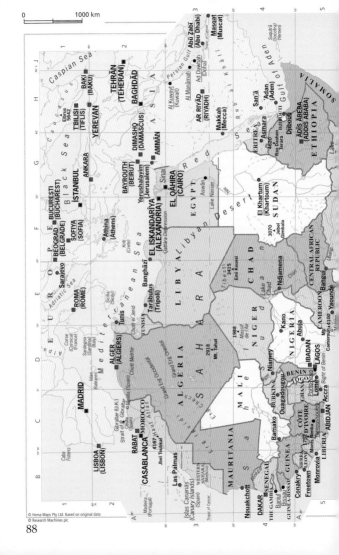

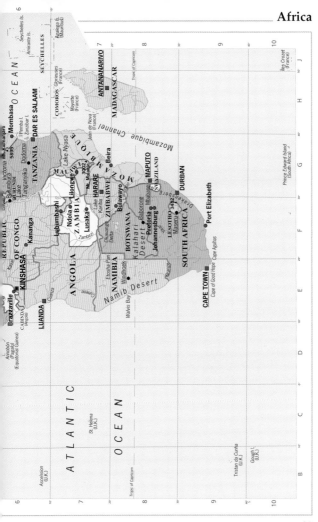

Map scale: 0 — 400 — 800 — 1200 km

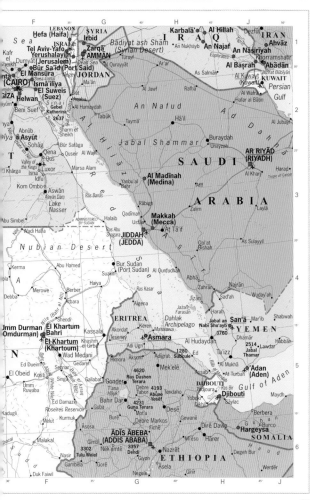

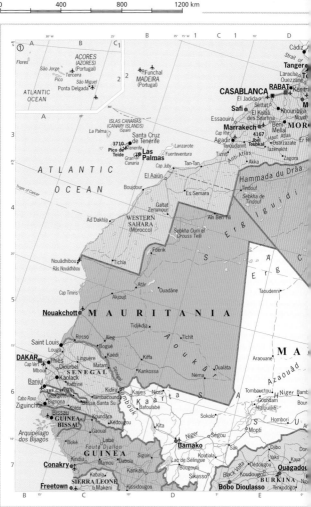

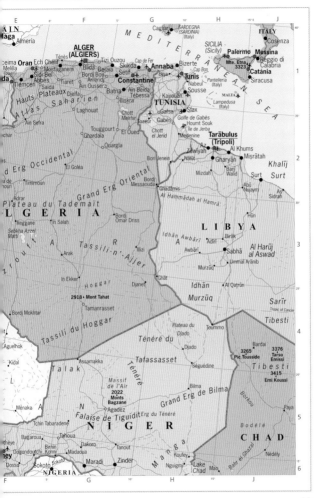

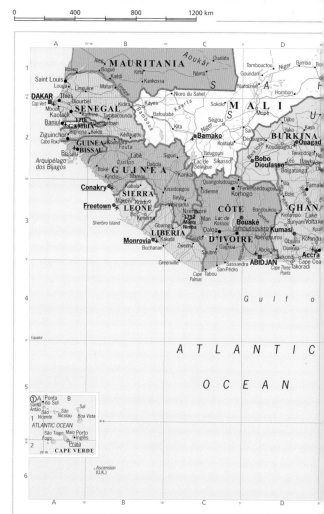

0   400   800   1200 km

| A | 15° W | B | 10° | C | 5° | D |

MAURITANIA

Aoukâr

Oualata

Rosso • Aleg • Boghé • Kaédi • Kiffa • Kankossa • Néma
Saint Louis • Louga • Biourbel • Linguère • Matam • Nioro du Sahel
Tombouctou • Niger • Bamba • Bo
Goundam • Hombori

DAKAR • Thiès • Kidira • Kayes • Sokolo
Cap Vert • Mbour • Kaffrine • Tambacounda • Bafoulabé • Kita
M A L I • Mopti • Djibo • Kaya

SENEGAL • Kaolack • Bamako • Koutiala • Ségou
Banjul • Kédougou • Fouta • **BURKINA**
THE GAMBIA • Bignona • Kolda • Bougouni • Sikasso • **Bobo** • Koudougou • Tenkodogo • Ni
Ziguinchor • Labé • Siguiri • Lac de • **Dioulasso** • Léo • Bawku
Cabo Roxo • Diallon • Dabola • Séinguè
Bissau • **GUINEA** • Kankan • Bolgatanga

Arquipélago • Boké • Mamou • Kissidougou • Ouangolodougou
dos Bijagós • Kindia • Odienné • Ferkessédougou • Bole • Tamal

Conakry • **SIERRA** • Beyla • Korhogo • **GHANA**
• Makeni • Woimama • Nzérékoré • **CÔTE** • Bondoukou • **Ouaga**
Freetown • **LEONE** • Koidu • Man • Lac de • Kintampo • Lake
• Kabala • Kossou • Sunyani • Volta
Sherbro Island • Kenema • Gbarnga • Monts • Daloa • **Bouaké** • **Kumasi**
LIBERIA • Nimba • **Yamoussoukro** • Obuasi • **Accra**
Monrovia • Zwedru • **D'IVOIRE** • Gagnoa • Dunkwa • Kofori
• Buchanan • Soubré • Aboisso • Sekondi • Cape Coa
Greenville • Sassandra • Abengourou • **ABIDJAN** • Takoradi
Cape • San-Pédro • Cape Three
Tabou • Points

Cape
Palmas

G u l f   o

Equator

A T L A N T I C

O C E A N

① A Ponta B
Santo do Sol • Sal
Antão • São • Boa Vista
• Vicente • Nicolau
ATLANTIC OCEAN
São Tiago • Maio Porto
Fogo • Inglês
Praia
CAPE VERDE

• Ascension
(U.K.)

| A | 15° | B | 10° | C | 5° | D |

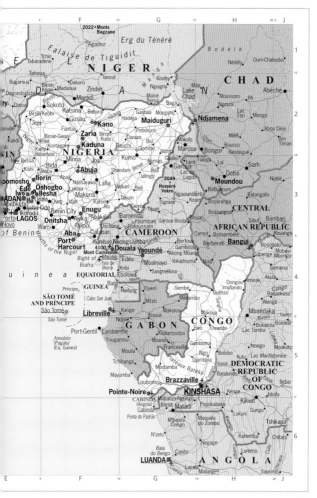

0　　　　400　　　　800　　　　1200 km

A 15° E **B** 20° **C** 25° **D**

1

DEMOCRATIC REPUBLIC
OF CONGO

Porto Amboim
Sumbe
Lobito
Benguela
Lucira
Cuanza
Quibala
•Malanje
Bailundo
Camacupa
Kuito
Cacola
Saurimo
Luau
Dilolo
Lubudi
Kasenga•
Kwilu
Mpor
•Kolwezi
•Likasi
Lake
Bang

2

Cubal
Huambo•
Chitembo
Sachanga
Lucusse
Luena
Lumbala
Kaquengue
Lóvua
Calandula
Zambezi
Mwinilunga
Solwezi•
Kasempa
•Lubumbashi
Chingola•
Kitwe•
•Mufulira
•Ndola

ANGOLA
Lubango
Caconda
Kuvango
Menongue
Cangamba
Chiume
Manyinga
Kaoma
Mumbwa
ZAMBIA
•Kabwe

3

Namibe
Tombua
Foz do
Cunene
Cape Fria
Cahama
Humbe•
Ondjiva
Caiundo
Mavinga
Cuito
Cuanavale
Cuango
Bagani
Mohembo
Okavango
Delta
Kongola
Morigu
Senanga
Mulobezi
Seshehe
Choma
Livingstone
Victoria
Hwange
Falls
Lake
Kariba
Kariba Dam
•Lusaka
Luar
Kafue•
Namwala
Kwekwe
Kadoma

Kuila Plateau
Opuwo
Sesfontein
Etosha
Pan
Tsumeb
Tsumkwe
Maun
Nata
Makgadikgadi
Lake
Xau
Francistown
Selebi-
Phikwe
Bulawayo•
Gweru
ZIMB

4

2574
Brandberg
Outjo
Grootfontein
Ghanzi
Serowe
Mochudi
Zuisha
Plumtree
Gwanda
Beitbridge

Swakopmund
Walvis Bay
Tropic of Capricorn
Omaruru
Karibib
Windhoek•
Gobabis
Mamuno
BOTSWANA
Kalahari
Tshane
Molepolole
•Gaborone
Lobatse
Mmabatho
Ellisras
Thabazimbi
Nylstroom
Trichar
LIMP

Namib
NAMIBIA
Rehoboth
Desert

5

Lüderitz
Maltahöhe
Mariental
Keetmanshoop
Seeheim
Tshabong
Vorstershoop
Tshabong
Sun City
Vryburg
Klerksdorp
NORTH WEST
Kuruman
Postmasburg
Warrenton•
•Pretoria
Johannesburg•
Soweto
Springs•
Vereenig
Kroonstad
Dur

ATLANTIC

Alexander
Bay
Port Nolloth
Springbok
Karasburg
Opington
Douglas
Prieska
Kimberley•
•Bloemfontein
Welkom
FREE STATE
Bethlehem
Mont aux Sou
3282
Bettlehem
•Maseru
LESOTHO
Ladysm

Fish
Orange
Kenhardt
NORTHERN
CAPE
Carnarvon
De Aar
Aliwal North
Elliot
Kokstad
Umtata

OCEAN

6

Vanrhynsdorp
Calvinia
SOUTH AFRICA
Victoria
West
Middelburg
Queenstown
EASTERN CAPE
King William's

St. Helena
Bay
Vredenburg
Piketberg
Sutherland
Great Karoo
Laingsburg
Beaufort
West
Graaff
Reinet
Fort
Beaufort
East London

CAPE TOWN•
Khayelitsha
Paarl•
Worcester•
WESTERN
CAPE
Little
Karoo
Oudtshoorn
Knysna
Uitenhage•
•Port Elizabeth

Cape of
Good Hope
Bredasdorp
Cape Agulhas
Mosselbaai

SEYCHELLES

Aldabra
Group

TANZANIA
Liwale
Mtwara
Lindi

Masasi
Nyamtumbo
Songea
Tunduru
Ruvuma
Cabo Delgado
Mocímboa da Praia

COMOROS
Îles Glorieuses
(France)

Moroni Njazidja
Nzwani
Antsiranana
Tanjona
Bobaomby

Mwali
Mamoudzou
Mayotte
(France)

Ambilobe
Nosy Be
Ambanja
Iharaña

Metangula
Marrupa
Montepuez
Pemba

MALAWI
Lichinga
Luchenga
Namapa
Nacala

Lilongwe
Cuamba

Massif du
2876
Analalava
Tsaratanana
Sambava
Maroantsetra

Blantyre
Zomba
2419
Monte
Namuli
Nampula
Moçambique

Mananara
Avaratra

Mount
Mulanje
3002
Angoche
Mahajanga

Changara
Tete
Chiromo
Mocuba
Moma

Maevatanana
Soanierana-Ivongo

MOZAMBIQUE
Caia
Quelimane

Tanjona
Vilanandro
Besalampy

Maintirano
Ambatondrazaka
Toamasina

RARE
tungwiza
Chinde

Nosy Barren

MADAGASCAR
ANTANANARIVO
2643
Tsiafajavona

Mutare

Antsalova
Miandrivazo
Moramanga

Beira
Belo Tsiribihina

Antsirabe
Marolambo

Ambositra

Espungabera

Morondava

Mania
Ambohipeno
Mananjary
Fianarantsoa

Save
Nova Mambone

Bassas da
India
(France)

Morombe
Mangoky

Chigubo

Île Europa
(France)

Ihosy
Vohipeno
Farafangana

Mapinhane

Mabalane

Massinga

Toliara
Ihosy
Betroka

Tropic of Capricorn

Chókwè
Chibuto

Inhambane

Betioky
Bekily
Tôlanaro

Xai-Xai

Ampanihy

MAPUTO
Bela Vista

Ambovombe

bane
LAND
hief

Tanjona
Vohimena

Mkuze

INDIAN

Empangeni
aritzburg
:BAN

OCEAN

Amirante Is.

SEYCHELLES

Praslin I.
Victoria

Mahé Island

Coëtivy I.

INDIAN OCEAN

Port Louis

MAURITIUS
INDIAN
OCEAN

Aldabra
Group

SEYCHELLES

St-Denis

Réunion
(France)

Assumption
Island

Cosmoledo Group

Astove
Island

Farquhar Group

Agalega Islands
(Mauritius)

99

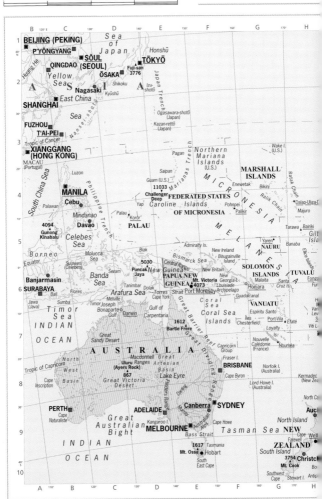

0   1000   2000   3000   4000 km

B 120° E **C** 130° **D** **E** 140° **F** 150° **G** 160° **H** 170°

1 BEIJING (PEKING) ■
Sea
of
P'YŎNGYANG ■   Japan
SŌUL   Honshū
QINGDAO (SEOUL) ■   TŌKYŌ
ŌSAKA   Fuji-san
Yellow   3776

2 Sea   Shikoku
A   S   Nagasaki   Izu-
I   A   shotō
SHANGHAI   East China   Kyūshū   Ogasawara-shotō
(Japan)
FUZHOU   Sea   Kazan-rettō
T'AI-PEI   (Japan)   Wake I.
3 Tropic of Cancer   (U.S.)
XIANGGANG   Pagan
(HONG KONG)   Northern
MACAU   Mariana
(Portugal)   Saipan (U.S.)   Islands   Eniwetok
Luzon   Guam (U.S.)   (U.S.)   MARSHALL
4 11033   ISLANDS
Challenger   FEDERATED STATES   Ralik Chain
MANILA ■   Deep   Yap   OF MICRONESIA   Bikini
Cebu ●   Palau   MICRONESIA   Dalap-Uliga-
Mindanao   Korōr   Caroline   Islands   Pohnpei   Majuro
PALAU   Palikir
4094   Tarawa   Bairiki
Gunong   Admiralty Is.   MELANESIA   Banaba
5 Kinabalu   New Ireland   NAURU
Borneo   Celebes   Biak   Bismarck Sea   Bougainville   Yaren ●
Equator   Sea   5030   New   Island   SOLOMON   TUVALU
Sulawesi   Puncak   Guinea   New Britain   ISLANDS
(Celebes)   Jaya   PAPUA NEW   Georgia I.   Malaita   Santa   Fonga
Banjarmasin ■   Moluccas   GUINEA   Mt. Victoria   Honiara ●   Cruz Is.   Fu
6 SURABAYA ■   Banda   Seram   4073   Louisiade
Jawa   Sea   Tanimbar   Port Moresby ●   Archipelago   Guadalcanal
(Java)   Flores   Dolak   Torres   Cape York   VANUATU
Bali   Sumba   Arafura Sea   Strait   Coral   Espiritu Santo   Port-Vila ●   Efaté
Timor   Melville I.   Gulf of   Sea   Iles   Levu
Timor   Sea   Timor Joseph   Carpentaria   Chesterfield   Loyalty   Viti Le
7 INDIAN   Bonaparte   Darwin ●   Coral Sea   Islands   Nouvelle
Gulf   Islands   Calédonie
OCEAN   Capricorn   (France)
Great   Group   Nouméa ●
Sandy Desert   Fraser I.
20° S   Macdonnell   Great   BRISBANE ■
AUSTRALIA   Ranges   Artesian   Norfolk I.
Uluru   Basin   (Australia)   Kermadec
Tropic of Capricorn   North   Ranges   1612   Lake Eyre   Cape Byron   (New Zea
8 West   (Ayers Rock)   Bartle Frere ●   Lord Howe I.
Basin   867   (Australia)
Cape   Great Victoria   North Cal
Inscription   Desert
PERTH ■   Canberra ●   SYDNEY ●   Auc
9 Cape   ADELAIDE ■   Cape Howe   North Island
Naturaliste   Kangaroo I.   NEW
Great   MELBOURNE ■   Farewell
Australian   Bass Strait   Tasman Sea   ZEALAND
Bight   1617   Cape   Well
INDIAN   Tasmania   Mt. Ossa ●   Hobart   South Island   3754 Christc
OCEAN   South   Mt. Cook   Bo
10 East Cape   Southwest   Stewart I.
Cape

A 110° **B** **C** 120° **D** 130° **E** 140° **F** 150° **G** 160° **H**

© Hema Maps Pty Ltd. Based on original data © Research Machines plc

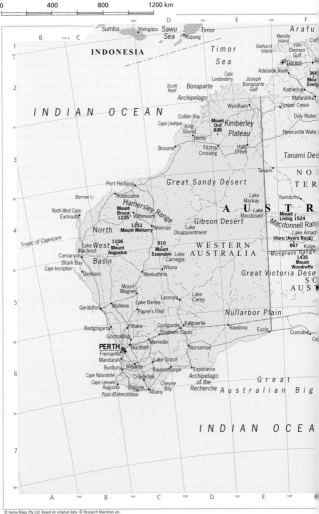

Scale: 0 400 800 1200 km

INDONESIA

Sumba Waingapu Sawu Sea Timor Arafu

Melville Island Van Diemen Gulf Col

Timor Sea Bathurst Island Darwin

Cape Londonderry Joseph Bonaparte Gulf Adelaide River 366 Mou Eveh

INDIAN OCEAN Bonaparte Archipelago Katherine Mataranka

Scott Reef Collier Bay Mount Ord 936 Kimberley Plateau Timber Creek

Cape Lévêque King Sound Daly Water

Derby Fitzroy Crossing Halls Creek Newcastle Wate

Broome Tanami Des

Port Hedland Great Sandy Desert Tanami NO TER

Barrow I. Roebourne Lake Mackay Yuendumu AUSTR

North West Cape Exmouth Mount Bruce 1235 Wittenoom Hamersley Range Gibson Desert Lake Macdonald Mount Liebig 1524 Macdonnell Ran

1253 Mount Meharry Newman Lake Disappointment Uluru (Ayers Rock) 867 Kulge

North West Basin 1106 Mount Augustus 910 Mount Essendon WESTERN AUSTRALIA Lake Carnegie Musgrave Range 1435 Mount Woodroffe

Lake MacLeod Carnarvon Wiluna Great Victoria Dese SC

Shark Bay Denham Meekatharra AUS

Cape Inscription Mount Magnet Leonora Lake Carey Nullarbor Plain

Geraldton Mullewa Lake Barlee Payne's Find

Badgingarra Pithara Coolgardie Kalgoorlie Rawlinna Eucla Coorabie Ce

Goomalling Southern Cross Norseman

PERTH Northam Merredin

Fremantle Williams Lake Grace

Mandurah Ravensthorpe Esperance Great

Bunbury Cranbrook Cheyne Bay Archipelago of the Recherche Australian Big

Cape Naturaliste Walpole Albany

Cape Leeuwin Augusta

Point d'Entrecasteaux

Tropic of Capricorn

INDIAN OCEA

© Hema Maps Pty Ltd. Based on original data © Research Machines plc.

102

A.C.T. = Australian Capital Territory

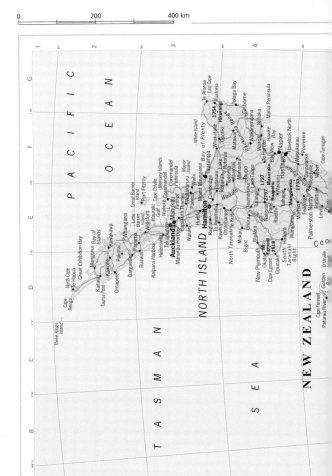

0   200   400 km

PACIFIC

OCEAN

TASMAN

SEA

NORTH ISLAND

NEW ZEALAND

Three Kings Islands

Cape Reinga
North Cape
Te Hapua
Great Exhibition Bay
Kaitaia
Taroa Point
Mangonui
Bay of Islands
Kaikohe
Kawakawa
Omapere
Paihia
Dargaville
Ruawai
Whangarei
Helensville
Little Barrier Island
Great Barrier Island
Port Fitzroy
Cape Colville
Kaipara Harbour
Pakotai
Wellsford
Coville
Mercury Islands
Mayor Island
Waiheke Island
Coromandel
Coromandel Peninsula
Manukau Harbour
Auckland
Manukau
Takanini
Papakura
Thames
Firth of Thames
Paeroa
Waihi
White Island
Huntly
Raglan
Ngaruawahia
Te Kuiti
Cambridge
Tauranga
Bay of Plenty
Hamilton
Whakatane
Opotiki
Te Araroa
East Cape
Ruatoria
Tokaga Bay
Gisborne
Te Puke
Rotorua
Mount Maunganui
Lake Rotorua
Kawhia
Otorohanga
Taumarunui
Waikato
Murupara
Matawai
Ruakumara
Wairoa
Mahia Peninsula
Mahia
North Taranaki Bight
Mokau
Ohura
Lake Taupo
National Park
1727
Makorako 2797
Ruapehu 2518
Lake Waikaremoana
Wairoa
Hawke Bay
Napier
Waipukurau
Havelock North
Hastings
1733
New Plymouth
Okato
Cape Egmont
Egmont 2518
Opunake
Raetihi
Ohakune
Taihape
Waipawa
Waiouru
South Taranaki Bight
Wanganui
Mangaweka
Marton
Feilding
Palmerston North
Dannevirke
Woodville
Pahiatua
Levin
Coo
D'Urville Island
Golden Bay
Cape Farewell
Paturau River
1754
Hikurangi

© Hema Maps Pty Ltd. Based on original data © Research Machines plc.

104

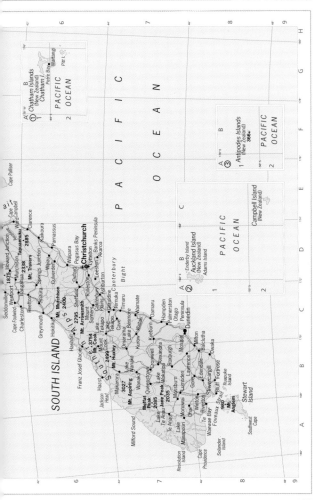

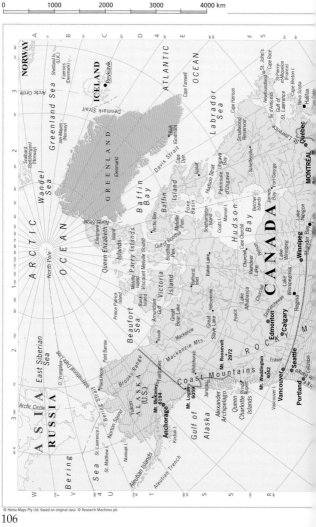

0   1000   2000   3000   4000 km

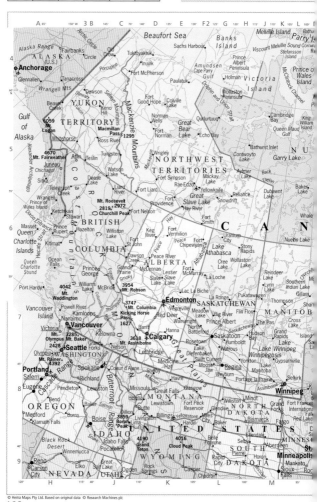

Map scale: 0 — 400 — 800 — 1200 km

A 145° B 150° W 3 B 145° C 70° 140° D 135° E 130° F 2 G 125° H 120° J 115° K 110° L

Beaufort Sea

Melville Island

Parry Isl

Banks Island

Sachs Harbour

Viscount Melville Sound

Arctic Circle

Tuktoyaktuk

Inuvik

Old Crow

Prince Albert Peninsula

Amundsen Gulf

Holman

Victoria Island

Prince of Wales Island

Fort McPherson

Paulatuk

Dolphin and Union Strait

Alaska Range

Fairbanks

Circle

Porcupine

Fort Good Hope

Colville Lake

Coppermine

Anchorage

Glennallen

Tanacross

Wrangell Mts

Dawson

Keno Hill

Norman Wells

Great Bear Lake

Qurluqtuuq

Echo Bay

Cambridge Bay

Queen Maud Gulf

Gulf of Alaska

6059 Mt. Logan

YUKON

Beaver Creek

Stewart

Ross River

Fort Norman

Wrigley

Bathurst Inlet

Contwoyto Lake

Garry Lake

NU

Whitehorse

Macmillan Pass 1295

Selwyn Mountains

Mackenzie Mountains

Fort Simpson

Rae-Edzo

Yellowknife

Aylmer Lake

Back

Dubawnt Lake

Bake Lake

4670 Mt. Fairweather

Atlin

Teslin

Tungsten

TERRITORY

Watson Lake

NORTHWEST TERRITORIES

Mackay Lake

Reliance

Dubawnt Lake

Juneau

Chichagof I.

Sitka

Telegraph Creek

Dease Lake

Liard River

Fort Liard

Fort Providence

Great Slave Lake

Snowdrift

Bake Lake

Whale

Wrangell

Prince of Wales Island

Ketchikan

Stewart

Mt. Roosevelt 2819 2972 Churchill Peak

Fort Nelson

Hay River

Fort Smith

C

A

N

Masset

Queen Charlotte Islands

Prince Rupert

Hazelton

Williston Lake

Keg River

Fort Vermilion

Peace River

Fort Chipewyan

Uranium City

Lake Athabasca

Stony Rapids

Wollaston Lake

Reindeer Lake

Nueltin Lake

Lynn Lake

Southern Indian Lake

Gillam

Kitimat

Dawson Creek

Fort St. John

McLennan

Cree Lake

La Loche

Ocean Falls

BRITISH COLUMBIA

Prince George

Grande Prairie

Peace River

Slave Lake

Fort McMurray

La Ronge

Pukatawagan

Thompson

MANITOB

Queen Charlotte Sound

4042 Mt. Waddington

Williams Lake

McBride

3954 Mt. Robson

Lac La Biche

Meadow Lake

Big River

Flin Flon

The Pas

Cross Lake

Island

Port Hardy

Powell River

Quesnel

3285 Mt. Olympus

Kamloops

3747 Mt. Columbia

Kicking Horse Pass 1627

Vegreville

EDMONTON

Wainwright

North Battleford

Prince Albert

Saskatoon

Hudson Bay

Grand Rapids

Vancouver Island

Nanaimo

Kelowna

Calgary 3618 Mt. Assiniboine

Red Deer

Hanna

Rosetown

Humboldt

Watrous

Lake Winnipegosis

Gypsumville

Vancouver

Victoria

Seattle

Mt. Baker 2428

Nelson

Grand Forks

Banff

Lethbridge

Medicine Hat

Diefenbaker

Regina

Moose Jaw

Lake Manitoba

Portage la Prairie

Selkirk

WASHINGTON

Olympia

Mt. Rainier 4392

Spokane

Coeur d'Alene

Shelby

Havre

Glasgow

Weyburn

Lake Winnipeg

Winnipeg

Portland

Salem

Eugene

Richland

Lewiston

Missoula

Great Falls

Williston

Minot

Grand Forks

International F

OREGON

Bend

Pendleton

Baker

Helena

MONTANA

Lewistown

Fort Peck Reservoir

Glendive

NORTH DAKOTA

Bismarck

Fargo

Red Lake

Medford

Burns

3859 Borah Peak

Butte

Miles City

Baker

MINNES

Klamath Falls

Boise

Lima

Billings

Hardin

Belle Fourche

Sheridan

Aberdeen

St.

Black Rock Desert

IDAHO

Idaho Falls

Pocatello

4190 Grand Teton

4016 Cloud Peak

SOUTH DAKOTA

Pierre

Minneapolis

Reno

Carson City

Elko

UTAH

Great Salt Lake

Ogden

WYOMING

Rock Springs

Rapid City

Casper

Chadron

Mankato

Sioux Falls

NEVADA

Winnemucca

Salt Lake City

120° H 115° J 110° 105° K 100° L 95° M

© Hema Maps Pty Ltd. Based on original data © Research Machines plc

0   400   800   1200   1600 km

© Hema Maps Pty Ltd. Based on original data © Research Machines plc

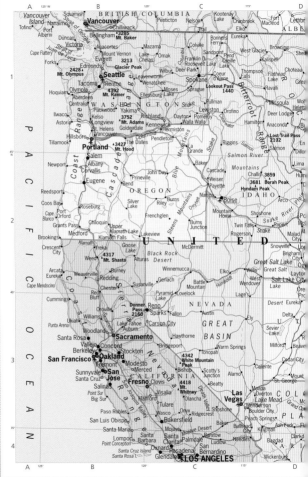

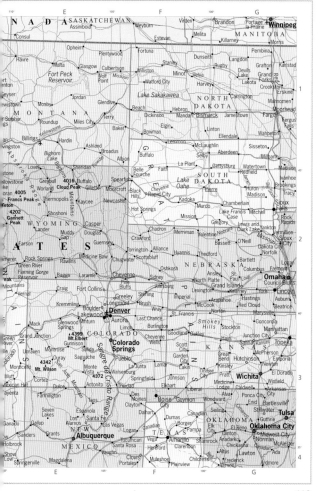

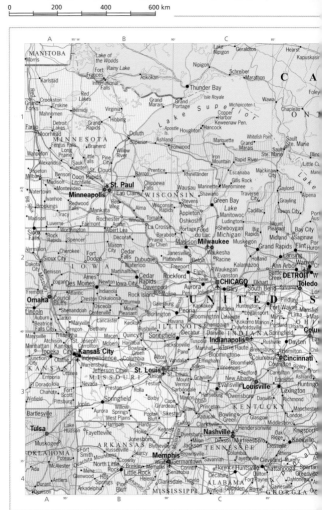

© Hema Maps Pty Ltd. Based on original data © Research Machines plc

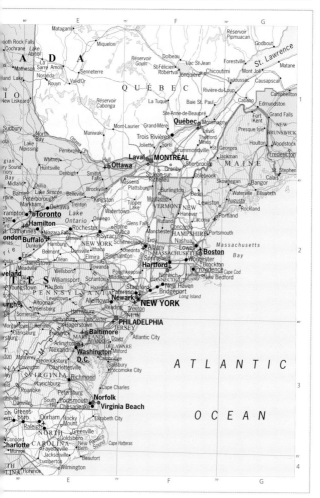

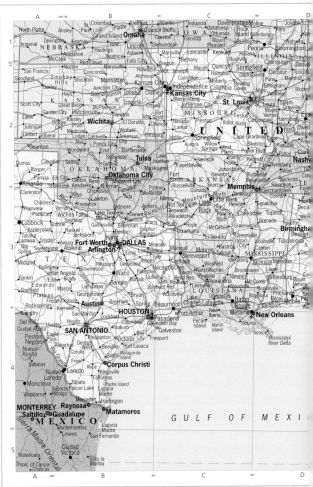

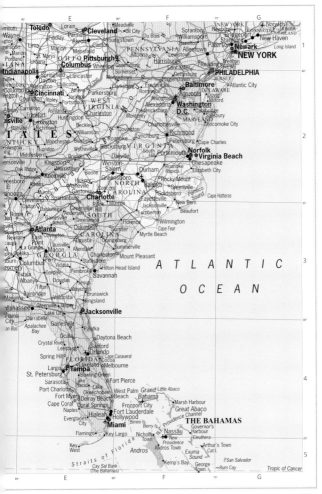

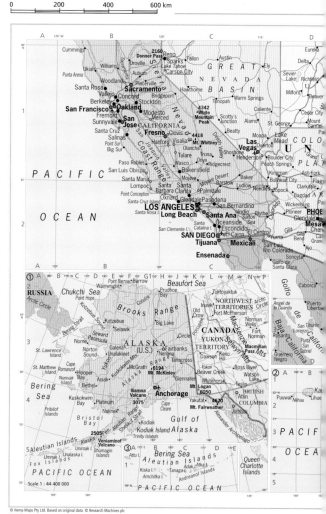

0   200   400   600 km

A 125° W   **B**   120°   **C**   115°   **D**

40°N

Cummings   Eureka

                    2160   G R E A T
Ukiah   Williams ●Donner Pass Reno
                    ●Sparks   Delta
        Oroville   Fallon   Austin   Ely
                    Lake Tahoe
Punta Arena Woodland Auburn Carson City   Sevier Richfield
        Placerville   N E V A D A   Lake
Santa Rosa Sacramento Bridgeport   Warm Springs Milford
Vallejo Concord Stockton   Beaver
Berkeley Oakland Modesto Hawthorne   Tonopah   Cedar City
San Francisco Fremont Merced   Caliente   Mount
        San   C A L I F O R N I A   ●4342   Carmel
Sunnyvale Jose Fresno●Clovis   ●White Scotty's   St. George
Santa Cruz   Hanford Visalia Mountain Junction Alamo Moapa COLO
Salinas   ●4418 Peak   Beatty   Lake U N I PLA
    Point Sur Big Sur ●Mt.Whitney Olancha   Las   Mead   Grand
                    Tulare   Death Valley Vegas   Kingman Ash Fork
P A C I F I C Coast Range Wasco Trona Shoshone Henderson● Boulder City Peach Springs
        San Luis Obispo Bakersfield Onyx Ridgecrest   Boulder City   Clarkdale A
                    ●Ridgecrest   Bullhead City   Bagdad N
        Santa Maria   Mojave Desert Baker Ludlow Needles Topock Wickenburg A
    Lompoc Santa Santa Palmdale Barstow   Kingman   PHOE
O C E A N   Barbara Clarita   Glendale●Pasadena   San Bernardino Pioneer Glendale
    Point Conception Oxnard LOS ANGELES● ●Indio Salton Blythe   Mesa
    Santa Cruz Island ●Long Beach Santa Ana Sea   Gila Cham
        Santa Rosa I. Oceanside Escondido El Cajon El Centro   San Luis Grand
    San Clemente I. SAN DIEGO● ●Mexicali Rio Colorado Sonoyta Golfo de
    San Catalina I. Tijuana●   Santa Clara
                    Ensenada●

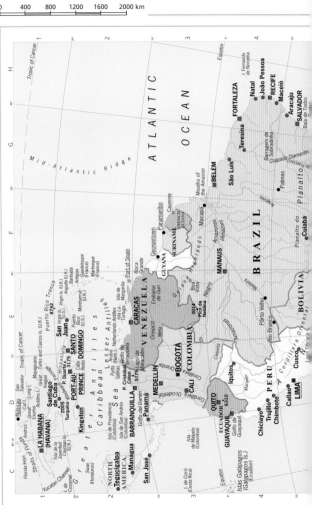

0 400 800 1200 1600 2000 km

122

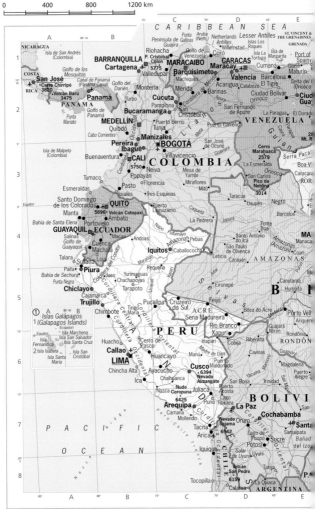

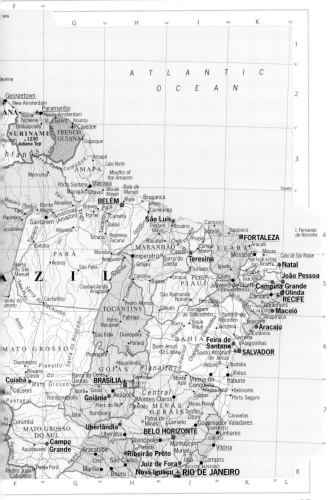

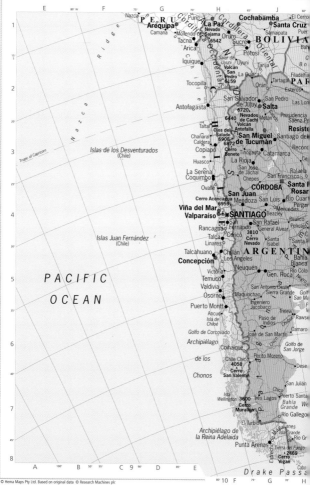

0   400   800   1200 km

PACIFIC

OCEAN

Islas de los Desventurados
(Chile)

Islas Juan Fernández
(Chile)

Archipiélago de
la Reina Adelaida

PERU
Nazca
Arequipa
Camana
Mollendo
Tacna
Arica
Iquique
Tocopilla
Antofagasta
Taltal
Chañaral
Caldera
Copiapó
Huasco
La Serena
Coquimbo
Ovalle

La Paz
Puno
Nevado
Sajama
6542
Oruro
Potosí

Cordillera Occidental
Cordillera Oriental

Salar de Uyuni
Uyuni
La Quiaca

Volcán
San
Pedro
6159
Calama

Volcán
San Pedro
6720.
6440
Nevados
de Cachi
Volcán
Antofalla
6908
Ojos del
Salado
6872
Cerro
Bonete

San Salvador
de Jujuy
Salta
San Miguel
de Tucumán
Catamarca
La Rioja
San José
de Jáchal
Chepes
San Francisco
Rafaela

Cochabamba
Sucre

Santa Cruz
Samaipata
Tarija

BOLIVIA

PAR

Filadelfia
Esteros
Orán

Presidencia
Roque
Saénz
Peña
Resiste

Reconq

Santa F
Rosar

Cerro Aconcagua
6959
Viña del Mar
Valparaíso
SANTIAGO
Rancagua
Talca
Curicó
Linares
San
Fernando
Cerro
Nevado
3810
San Rafael
Santa
Isabel

CÓRDOBA
San Juan
Mendoza
San Luis
Beazley
Río Cuar
Melincué
Pergam
Pehuajó

Talcahuano
Concepción
Chillán
Los Ángeles
Victoria
Temuco
Valdivia
Osorno

ARGENTIN

Neuquén
Gen. Roca
Río Colo

Bahía
Blanca

Puerto Montt
Ancud
Isla de
Chiloé

Golfo de Corcovado
Archipiélago
de los
Chonos

Coihaique
Chile Chico
Perito Moreno
4058
Cerro
San Valentín

Maquinchao
Sierra Grande
Ingeniero
Jacobacci
Paso de
Indios
José de San Martín

San Antonio Oeste
San Ma

Trelew
Rawso

Golfo de
San Jorge
Dese

Chico
Tres Lagos
3600
Cerro
Murallón

Isla
Wellington

El Turbio

San Julián
Puerto Deseado
Bahía
Grande
Río Gallego

Isla Grande
de Tierra del Fuego
Punta Arenas
Estrecho de Magallanes
2469
Cerro
Yogan

Tropic of Capricorn

© Hema Maps Pty Ltd. Based on original data © Research Machines plc

126

Drake Passa

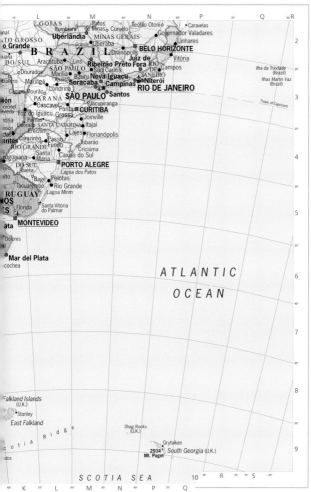

Polar Regions

0   1000   2000   3000

① (Arctic)

RUSSIA
Arctic Circle

Sakhalin
Sea of Okhotsk

Klyuchevskaya Sopka ▲ 4750

Lena

More Laptevykh (Laptev Sea)

Karskoye More (Kara Sea)

Novaya Zemlya

Severnaya Zemlya

Nordkapp

Barents Sea

MOSKVA (MOSCOW)
Arkhangel'sk

UKRAIN
BELARUS
Helsinki
FINLAND
Stockholm
SWEDEN   GERMAN
Oslo   DENMAR
NORWAY

Bering Sea
International Dateline

Novosibirskiye Ostrova (New Siberia Islands)

Vostochno-Sibirskoye More (East Siberian Sea)

Zemlya Frantsa-Iosifa (Franz Josef Land) (Russia)

Bjørnøya (Norway)

Svalbard (Norway)

Jan Mayen (Norway)

Norwegian Sea
North Sea

St. Lawrence I.   Bering Strait

O. Vrangelya

Chukchi Sea

Arctic Ocean

North Pole

Greenland Sea

ICELAND

REP. O
IRELAN

Nunivak I.

Aleutian Islands

ALASKA
(U.S.)
Mt. McKinley ▲ 6194
Anchorage

Ellesmere I.

Queen
Elizabeth
Islands

Melville I.

Banks I.

GREENLAND
(Denmark)

3700
Gunnbjørns Fjeld

Reykjavík

UNITEI
KINGDO

Kodiak I.
Gulf of
Alaska

Mt. Logan ▲ 6059

Beaufort Sea

Victoria I.

Baffin Bay

Baffin Island

Davis Strait

Nuuk
(Godthåb)

ATLANTIC

PACIFIC
OCEAN

Alexander Archipelago

Mackenzie Mountains

CANADA

Great Bear Lake

Great Slave Lake

Hudson Strait

Labrador Sea

OCEAN

② (Antarctic)

ATLANTIC
OCEAN

South Georgia (U.K.)

South Sandwich Is. (U.K.)

INDIAN
OCEAN

Scotia Sea

Falkland Islands (U.K.)

South Orkney Is. (U.K.)

Antarctic Circle

South Shetland Is. (U.K.)

ARGENTINA
CHILE

Cabo de Hornos (Cape Horn)
Isla Grande de Tierra del Fuego

Drake Passage

Antarctic Peninsula

Weddell Sea

Dronning Maud Land

Bellingshausen
Sea

Mt. Jackson ▲ 4191

Ronne Ice Shelf

Berkner I.

Mt. Menzies ▲ 3355

Amery Ice Shelf

Mackenzie Bay

East
Antarctica

Peter I Øy (Norway)

Vinson Massif ▲ 4897

South Pole

Transantarctic Mountains

**West
Antarctica**

Mt. Kirkpatrick ▲ 4528

Davis
Sea

Pine Island Bay

Marie Byrd
Land

Ross
Ice Shelf

Victoria Land

Wilkes Land

Amundsen
Sea

Sulzberger Bay

Mt. Minto ▲ 4163

Dumont
d'Urville Sea

PACIFIC
OCEAN

Limit of Pack Ice

Ross
Sea

International Dateline

Limit of Drift Ice

SOUTHERN OCEAN

INDIAN
OCEAN

Index to Country Maps

A

Afghanistan **83**
Albania **62**
Algeria **92**
Andorra **54**
Angola **96**
Antigua & Barbuda **121**
Argentina **126**
Armenia **85**
Australia **102**
Austria **57**
Azerbaijan **85**

B

Bahamas, The **121**
Bahrain **87**
Bangladesh **80**
Barbados **121**
Belarus **64**
Belgium **49**
Belize **120**
Benin **95**
Bhutan **80**
Bolivia **124**
Bosnia-Herzegovina **60**
Botswana **98**
Brazil **124**
Brunei **77**
Bulgaria **61**
Burkina **94**
Burma (Myanmar) **76**
Burundi **96**

C

Cambodia **76**
Cameroon **95**
Canada **108**
Cape Verde **94**
Central African Republic . . **96**
Chad **90**
Chile **126**
China **72**
Colombia **124**
Comoros **99**
Congo **95**
Congo, Democratic
    Republic of **96**
Costa Rica **121**
Cote d'Ivoire **94**
Croatia **60**
Cuba **121**
Cyprus **84**
Czech Republic **45**

D

Denmark **43**
Djibouti **97**
Dominica **121**
Dominican Republic . . . **121**

E

East Timor **79**
Ecuador **124**

Egypt **91**
El Salvador **120**
Equatorial Guinea **95**
Eritrea **91**
Estonia **43**
Ethiopia **97**

F

Fiji **100**
Finland **42**
France **52**

G

Gabon **95**
Gambia, The **94**
Georgia **85**
Germany **46**
Ghana **94**
Greece **62**
Grenada **121**
Guatemala **120**
Guinea **94**
Guinea-Bissau **94**
Guyana **125**

H

Haiti **121**
Honduras **121**
Hungary **45**

I

Iceland **42**
India **80**
Indonesia **78**
Iran **82**
Iraq **82**
Ireland, Republic of **51**
Israel **86**
Italy **58**

J

Jamaica **121**
Japan **75**
Jordan **86**

K

Kazakhstan **69**
Kenya **97**
Kiribati **101**
Korea, North **74**
Korea, South **74**
Kuwait **87**
Kyrgyzstan **69**

L

Laos **76**
Latvia **43**
Lebanon **86**

Lesotho **98**
Liberia **94**
Libya **90**
Liechtenstein **56**
Lithuania **43**
Luxembourg **49**

M

Macedonia **62**
Madagascar **99**
Malawi **99**
Malaysia **78**
Maldives **81**
Mali **92**
Malta **59**
Marshall Islands **100**
Mauritania **92**
Mauritius **99**
Mexico **120**
Micronesia,
    Federated States of . . **100**
Moldova **61**
Monaco **56**
Mongolia **70**
Morocco **92**
Mozambique **99**
Myanmar (Burma) **76**

N

Namibia **98**
Nauru **100**
Nepal **80**
Netherlands **49**
New Zealand **104**
Nicaragua **121**
Niger **93**
Nigeria **95**
Norway **42**

O

Oman **83**

P

Pakistan **83**
Palau **100**
Panama **121**
Papua New Guinea **100**
Paraguay **126**
Peru **124**
Philippines **77**
Poland **44**
Portugal **54**

Q

Qatar **87**

R

Romania **61**
Russia **64**
Rwanda **96**

S

Samoa **101**
San Marino **58**
São Tomé and Príncipe . . **95**
Saudi Arabia **82**
Senegal **94**
Serbia and Montenegro . . **60**
Seychelles **99**
Sierra Leone **94**
Singapore **78**
Slovakia **45**
Slovenia **57**
Solomon Islands **100**
Somalia **97**
South Africa **98**
Spain **54**
Sri Lanka **81**
St. Kitts-Nevis **121**
St. Lucia **121**
St. Vincent & the
    Grenadines **121**
Sudan **91**
Suriname **125**
Swaziland **99**
Sweden **42**
Switzerland **56**
Syria **85**

T

Taiwan **77**
Tajikistan **69**
Tanzania **97**
Thailand **76**
Togo **94**
Tonga **101**
Trinidad & Tobago **124**
Tunisia **93**
Turkey **84**
Turkmenistan **69**
Tuvalu **100**

U

Uganda **97**
Ukraine **64**
United Arab Emirates . . . **87**
United Kingdom **51**
United States **110**
Uruguay **127**
Uzbekistan **69**

V

Vanuatu **100**
Vatican City **58**
Venezuela **124**
Vietnam **76**

Y, Z

Yemen **82**
Zambia **98**
Zimbabwe **98**

Index

How to use the index

This is an alphabetically arranged index of the places and features that can be found on the maps in this atlas. Each name is generally indexed to the largest scale map on which it appears. If that map covers a double page, the name will always be indexed by the left-hand page number.

Names composed of two or more words are alphabetised as if they were one word.

All names appear in full in the index, except for 'St.' and 'Ste.', which although abbreviated, are indexed as though spelled in full.

Cross-references are indicated by the '=' sign.

Abbreviations used in this index are explained in the list on page 131.

The grid reference (see below) locates a place or feature on the map. A name can be found by referring to the red letters and numbers placed around the maps. First find the letter, which appears along the top and bottom of the map, and then the number, down the sides. The name will be found within the rectangle uniquely defined by that letter and number. A number in brackets preceding the grid reference indicates that the name is to be found within an inset map.

Name ──────	Owensboro		●	C3	114
	Owen Sound		D2	114
	Owo		●	F3	94
Symbol ──────	Owyhee		⟋	C2	112
	Oxford, New Zealand			D6	104
	Oxford, U.K.		●	A3	48
Grid reference ──────	Oxnard		──G4	94
	Oyama		●	K5	74
Page reference ──────	Oyapock		⟋	G3	124
	Oyem		●	C2	118

Symbols

✕	Continent name	▲	Mountain, volcano, peak	▭	Sea, ocean
▲	Country name	▲	Mountain range	⊠	Cape, point
▣	State or province name	◉	Physical region or feature	⊠	Island or island group,
▢	Country capital	⟋	River, canal		rocky or coral reef
▢	State or province capital	▭	Lake, salt lake	✳	Place of interest
●	Settlement	▭	Gulf, strait, bay	▨	Historical or cultural region

Abbreviations

Al. ... Alabama	Kans. ... Kansas	N.D. ... North Dakota	S.D. ... South Dakota
Ariz. ... Arizona	Ky. ... Kentucky	Nebr. ... Nebraska	Shetland Is. ... Shetland Islands
Ark. ... Arkansas	La. ... Louisiana	Nev. ... Nevada	Tenn. ... Tennessee
Calif. ... California	Mass. ... Massachusetts	Nfld. ... Newfoundland	Tex. ... Texas
Colo. ... Colorado	Md. ... Maryland	N.H. ... New Hampshire	U.K. ... United Kingdom
Conn. ... Connecticut	Me. ... Maine	N. Ire. ... Northern Ireland	U.S. ... United States
Del. ... Delaware	M.G. ... Mato Grosso	N. Mex. ... New Mexico	Ut. ... Utah
Eng. ... England	Mich. ... Michigan	N.Y. ... New York	Va. ... Virginia
Fla. ... Florida	Minn. ... Minnesota	Oh. ... Ohio	Vt. ... Vermont
Ga. ... Georgia	Miss. ... Mississippi	Okla. ... Oklahoma	Wash. ... Washington
Ia. ... Iowa	Mo. ... Missouri	Oreg. ... Oregon	Wis. ... Wisconsin
Id. ... Idaho	Mont. ... Montana	Orkney Is. ... Orkney Islands	W. Va. ... West Virginia
Ill. ... Illinois	N.B. ... New Brunswick	Pa. ... Pennsylvania	Wyo. ... Wyoming
Ind. ... Indiana	N.C. ... North Carolina	S.C. ... South Carolina	

A

Name	Ref	Page
...achen	J4	48
...alen	F8	46
...alst	G4	48
...arau	D3	56
...are	C3	56
...bā	F3	94
...bādān	C1	87
...badla	E2	92
...baji	F3	94
...bakaliki	F3	94
...bakan	S7	68
...bano Terme	G5	56
...barqū	E1	87
...bashiri	N1	74
...baya Häyk'		
...baya Wenz	G5	90
...bbeville	D4	48
...bd al Kūrī	F7	82
...béché	D3	94
...bengourou	E1	46
...benrā	E1	46
...bensberg	G8	46
...beokuta	E3	94
...beraeron	H9	50
...berdeen, U.K.	K4	50
...berdeen, S.D., U.S.	G1	112
...berdeen, Wash., U.S.	B1	112
...berystwyth	H9	50
...bhā	H4	90
...bidjan	D3	94
...bilene	G2	118
...biline	M6	106
...bnūb	F2	90
...boisso	D3	94
...bomey	E3	94
...bong Mbang	G4	94
...bou Déia	C5	90
...brantes	B5	54
...bsaroka Range	E1	112
...bū al Abyaḍ	F4	87
...bu Aweigîla	B6	86
...bu Dhabi = Abū Ẓabī	F4	87
...bu Hamed	F4	90
...buja		
...bune Yosēf	G5	90
...bū Nujaym	C1	90
...buro	E3	96
...bu Simbel	F3	90
...būẓabī	F4	87
...bu Nujaym	J2	92
...baponeta	E7	110
...capulco	E5	120
...cariguá	D3	94
...cra	D3	94
...chen See	G3	56
...hill Island	B8	50

Name	Ref	Page
Achinsk	S6	68
Achit	L3	64
Aci Gól	M7	62
A Cihanbeyli	Q6	62
Acireale	K11	58
Acklins Island	K4	120
Aconcagua	D7	124
Açores	(1)B2	92
A Coruña	B1	54
Acqui Terme	D6	56
Acre	C5	124
Acri	L9	58
Ada	K12	44
Ada	B3	116
Adak Island	(3)C1	118
Adam	G5	82
Adams Island	(2)B1	104
Adana	E7	82
Adana	E5	84
Adda	E5	56
Ad Dafrah	E5	87
Ad Dahnā	B3	87
Ad Dakhla	B4	92
Ad Dammām	D3	87
Ad Dawhah	D4	87
Ad Dir'īyah	B4	87
Addis Ababa = Ādīs Ābeba	F2	96
Adelaide	G6	102
Adelaide River	F2	102
Aden = Adan	D3	79
Adi	E7	82
Adige	C5	56
Adigrat	G5	90
Adirī	B2	90
Ādīs Ābeba	F2	96
Adi Ugri	G5	90
Admiralty Islands	E6	100
Adoni	C5	80
Adour	F11	52
Adra	H8	54
Adrano	J11	58
Adrar	E3	92
Adria	H5	56
Adriatic Sea	H4	58
Adygeya	J1	84
Adz'vavom	L1	64
Aegean Sea	H5	62
A Estrada	B2	54
Afghanistan	H3	79
Afīf	H3	90
Afikpo	F3	94
Africa	E5	88
Afrīn	G5	84
Afula	C4	86
Afyon	N6	62
Agadez	G5	92
Agadir	D2	92
Agadyr'	N8	68

Name	Ref	Page
Agalega Islands	J7	88
Agartala	F4	80
Agattu Island	W6	70
Agde	J10	52
Agen	F9	52
Agios Efstratios	H5	62
Agra	C3	80
Agrakhanskiy Poluostrov	M2	84
Agri	K4	84
Agri	L8	58
Agrigento	H11	58
Agrinio	D6	62
Agryz	K3	64
Agua Prieta	E2	118
Aguascalientes	D4	120
A Gudiña	C2	54
Aguelhok	F5	92
Águilas	J7	54
Ahar	M4	84
Ahaura	C6	104
Ahaus	K2	48
Ahlen	K3	48
Ahmadabad	B4	80
Ahmadnagar	B5	80
Ahväz	E3	82
Aichach	G8	46
Aigina	F7	62
Aihui	M6	70
Ain	N5	70
Ain Beïda	G1	92
Ain Ben Tili	D3	92
Ain el Hadjel	P9	54
Ain Oussera	F1	92
Ainsa	L2	54
Ain Sefra	E2	92
Ain Taya	P8	54
Aïn-Tédélès	L8	54
Aisne	F5	48
Aitape	F3	79
Aiud	L3	60
Aix-en-Provence	L10	52
Aix-les-Bains	L8	52
Aizawl	F4	80
Aizu-wakamatsu	K5	74
Ajaccio	C7	58
Aj Bogd Uul	B2	72
Ajdābiyā	D1	90
Ajigasawa	L3	74
Ajka	G10	44
Ajlun	C4	86
Ajmer	B4	80
Akanthou	D2	118
Akaroa	D6	104
Akcakale	H5	84
Aketi	C3	96
Akhisar	K6	62
Akhty	M3	84

Place	Ref	Page
Al Wafrā'.	B2	87
Al Wajh.	G2	90
Alwar.	C3	80
Al Wari'ah	B3	87
Alytus	P3	44
Alzey	D7	46
Alzira.	K5	54
Amādīyah	K5	84
Amadjuak Lake	S4	108
Amahai.	C3	79
Amapá	G3	124
Amapá	G3	124
Amarillo	F1	118
Amasya	F3	84
Amazon = Amazonas	F4	122
Amazonas.	D4	124
Amazonas.	E4	124
Ambala.	C2	80
Ambanjä.	H2	98
Ambarchik	U3	70
Ambato	B4	124
Ambatondrazaka	H3	98
Amberg	G7	46
Ambikapur	D4	80
Ambilobe	H2	98
Ambon	C3	79
Ambositra	H4	98
Ambovombe	H5	98
Amchitka Island	(3)El	118
Amderma	L4	68
Amdo.	F2	80
Ameland.	H1	48
American Samoa	J7	100
Americus	E3	116
Amersfoort	H2	48
Amery Ice Shelf	(2)M2	128
Ames	B2	114
Amfilochia	D6	62
Amfissa	E6	62
Amg'un'	P6	70
Amiens	E5	48
Amirante Islands	(2)B2	98
Ammān	C5	86
Ammerland	K1	48
Ammersee	F2	56
Ammochostos	E6	84
Ammochostos Bay	A1	86
Amol	F2	82
Amorgos	H8	62
Amos	E1	114
Ampana	B3	79
Ampanihy	G4	98
Amposta.	L4	54
Amritsar	B2	80
Amrum.	D2	46
Amsterdam.	G2	48
Amstetten	K2	56
Am Timan	D5	90
Amudar'ya.	L9	68
Amundsen Gulf	G2	108
Amundsen Sea.	(2)GG3	128
Amur	P6	70
Amursk	P6	70
Anabar	J2	70
Anaconda	D1	112
Anacortes	B1	112
Anadarko	G3	112
Anadolu Dağları	H3	84
Anadyr'.	X4	70
Anadyrskiy Zaliv	Y3	70
Anafi	H8	62
Ānah	J6	84
Analalava	H2	98
Anamur	E5	84
Anantapur	C6	80
Anapa	G1	84
Anápolis	H7	124
Anār	F1	87
Anatolia	M6	62
Anchorage	(1)H3	118
Ancona	H5	58
Ancud	G7	126
Anda	H1	72
Åndalsnes.	D5	42
Andaman Islands	A4	76
Andaman Sea	A4	76
Andernach	K4	48
Anderson	E3	116
Anderson	D5	122
Andfjorden	J2	42
Andizhan.	N9	68
Andkhvoy	J2	82
Andoas.	B4	124
Andong	E5	74
Andorra	L2	54
Andorra la Vella	M2	54
Andøya.	H2	42
Andreanof Islands.	(3)C1	118
Andrews	F2	118
Andria	L7	58
Andros	G7	62
Andros, Greece.	G7	62
Andros, The Bahamas.	F5	116
Andros Town.	F5	116
Androth.	C5	80
Andújar	F6	54
Aneto.	L2	54
Angarsk	G6	70
Änge	H5	42
Angel de la Guarda.	D3	118
Angeles	G3	76
Ängelholm.	G8	42
Angeln	E2	46
Angermünde	E6	52
Angers	E6	52
Anglesey	H8	50
Angmagssalik = Tasiilaq	Z3	108
Ango	D3	96
Angoche	F3	98
Angol	E7	88
Angola	E7	88
Angoulême	F8	52
Anguilla	M5	120
Aniak	(1)F3	118
Anina	J4	60
Anyaman	H5	84
Ankang.	D4	72
Ankara	E4	84
Anklam.	J3	46
Anna	H4	64
Annaba.	G1	92
Annapolis	E3	114
Annapurna	D3	80
An Nāsiriyah	J1	90
Annecy.	B5	56
Annemasse	B4	56
Anniston	F5	94
Annobón	F5	94
Annonay	K8	52
An Nukhayb	D3	82
Anqing	F4	72
Ansbach	F7	46
Anshan	B3	74
Anshun.	D5	72
Ansley	G2	112
Anson	B3	116
Ansongo	F5	92
Antakya	G5	84
Antalya	N8	62
Antalya Körfezi	N8	62
Antananarivo	H3	98
Antarctica	(2)A1	128
Antarctic Peninsula	(2)LL3	128
Antequera	F7	54
Anti-Atlas	D3	92
Antibes.	C7	56
Antigua	M5	120
Antigua and Barbuda	M5	120
Antikythira.	F9	62
Antipodes Islands.	(3)A1	104
Antlers	B3	116
Antofagasta	G3	126
Antonito	E3	112
Antrim	F7	50
Antropovo	H3	64
Antsalova	G3	98
Antsirabe	H3	98
Antsirañana	H2	98
Antu.	E2	74
Antwerp = Antwerpen	G3	48
Antwerpen	G3	48
Anuradhapura	D7	80
Anxi.	B2	72
Anyuysk	U3	70
Anzhero-Sudzhensk	R6	68
Anzio.	G7	58
Aoga-shima	K7	74
Aomori.	L3	74
Aosta.	C5	56
Aoukâr	C5	92
Aoukoukar	C1	94
Apalachee Bay.	E4	116
Aparri	G3	76
Apatin	F4	60
Apatity	F1	64
Ape	P8	42
Apeldoorn.	H2	48
Api	D2	80
Apia.	J7	100
Apostle Islands	B1	114
Apoteri.	F3	124
Appalachian Mountains	E3	116
Appennino	G5	58
Appennino Abruzzese	H6	58
Appennino Calabro	K10	58
Appennino Lucano	K8	58
Appennino Tosco-Emiliano	D6	56
Appennino Umbro-Marchigiano	H6	58
Appleton	C2	114
Apure	D2	124
Aqaba	C7	86
Aquidauana	F8	124
Ara	D3	80
Arabian Sea	H6	82
Aracaju.	K6	124
Aracati	K4	124
Aracatuba	G8	124
Arad	J3	60
Arafura Sea.	D5	79
Araguaia.	F4	122
Araguatins	H5	124
Arāk	E3	82
Arak	F3	92
Aral Sea	K8	68
Aral'sk	M5	64
Aranda de Duero	G3	54
Aran Island	D6	50
Aran Islands	B8	50
Aranjuez	G4	54
Aranyaprathet	C4	76
Araouane	E5	92
Arapahoe	G2	112
Arapiraca	K5	124
Ar'ar.	D3	82
Araras	G5	124
Ararat	L4	84

133

Entry		Ref	Page
Arbīl	•	K5	84
Arbroath	•	K5	50
Arcata	•	B2	112
Archipelago of the Recherche	⬚	D6	102
Archipel de la Société	⬚	L7	100
Archipel des Tuamotu	⬚	M7	100
Archipiélago de la Reina Adelaida	⬚	F9	126
Archipiélago de los Chonos	⬚	F7	126
Arco	•	D2	112
Arctic Bay	•	P2	108
Arctic Ocean	▬	(1)A1	128
Arda	✎	H3	62
Ardabīl	•	N4	84
Ardahan	•	K3	84
Ardennes	⬚	G4	48
Ardestan	•	F3	82
Ardila	✎	C6	54
Arequipa	•	C7	124
Arezzo	•	F5	58
Argenta	•	G6	56
Argentan	•	B6	48
Argentina	▲	H6	126
Argenton-sur-Creuse	•	G7	52
Argolikós Kólpos	✎	E7	62
Argos	•	E7	62
Árgos Orestikó	•	D4	62
Argostóli	•	C6	62
Argyll	⬚	G5	50
Århus	•	F8	42
Ari Atoll	⬚	B8	80
Arica	•	C7	124
Ariège	✎	G11	52
Arihge	✎	M2	54
Arinos	✎	F6	124
Aripuanã	✎	E5	124
Ariquemes	•	E5	124
Arizona	⬚	D2	118
Arkadelphia	•	C3	116
Arkalyk	•	M7	68
Arkansas	✎	C3	116
Arkansas	⬚	C3	116
Arkansas City	•	B2	116
Arkhalts'ikhe	•	K3	84
Arkhángel'sk	•	H2	64
Arkhipelag Nordenshel'da	⬚	R2	68
Arklow	•	F9	50
Arles	•	K10	52
Arlington, Tex., U.S	•	B3	116
Arlington, Va., U.S	•	E3	114
Armagh	•	F7	50
Armavir	•	J1	84
Armenia	▲	K3	84
Armentières	•	E4	48
Armidale	•	K6	102
Arnhem	•	H3	48
Arnhem Land	⬚	F2	102
Arno	✎	F7	56
Arnøya	⬚	L1	42
Arnsberg	•	L3	48
Arnstadt	•	F6	46
Arquipélago dos Bijagós	⬚	A2	94
Ar Ramādī	•	D3	82
Ar Rass	•	C7	86
Arran	⬚	G6	50
Ar Raqqah	•	H6	84
Arras	•	E4	48
Ar Riyād	■	E5	82
Ar Rutba	•	D3	82
Ärsandøy	•	G4	42
Arta, Greece	•	C5	62
Arta, Mallorca	•	P5	54
Artem	•	G2	74
Artesia	•	F2	118
Arthur's Town	•	F5	116
Artigas	•	K5	126
Artsyz	•	S4	60
Artux	•	P10	68
Artvin	•	J3	84
Artyk	•	Q4	70
Arua	•	E3	96
Aruba	⬚	K6	120
Arusha	•	F4	96
Arvayheer	•	C1	72
Arviat	•	N4	108
Arvidsjaur	•	K4	42
Arvika	•	G7	42
Aryta	•	M4	70
Arzamas	•	H3	64
Asahi-dake	▲	M2	74
Asahikawa	•	M2	74
Asansol	•	E4	80
Asbest	•	M3	64
Ascension	⬚	B6	88
Aschaffenburg	•	E7	46
Ascoli Piceno	•	H6	58
Åsela	•	F2	96
Åsele	✎	J4	42
Asenovgrad	•	G3	62
Asha	•	L3	64
Ashburton	✎	C6	104
Asherton	•	B4	116
Asheville	•	D3	114
Ashford	•	C3	48
Ash Fork	•	D1	118
Ashgabat	■	G2	82
Ashkhabad = Ashgabat	■	G2	82
Ashland, Ky., U.S	•	D3	114
Ashland, Mont., U.S	•	E1	112
Ashland, Wis., U.S	•	B1	114
Ashqelon	•	B5	86
Ash Shāriqah	•	F4	87
Ash Shihr	•	E7	82
Ashtabula	•	D2	114
Asia	✖	M5	66
Asilah	•	D1	92
Asinara	⬚	C7	58
Asino	•	R6	68
Asīr	⬚	H3	90
Aşkale	•	J4	84
Asmara	■	G4	90
Åsnes	•	J7	56
Āsosa	•	E1	96
Aspang Markt	•	M3	56
Aspermont	•	F2	118
As Sa'an	•	E1	86
Assab	•	H5	90
Assamakka	•	G5	92
Aş Şanamayn	•	D3	86
As Sarīr	⬚	D2	90
Assen	•	J2	48
Assens	•	E1	46
As Sidrah	•	C1	90
Assiniboine	✎	M7	108
Assis	•	L3	126
Assisi	•	G5	58
As Sulaymānīyah	•	L6	84
As Sulayyil	•	E5	82
As Suwaydā'	•	D4	86
As Suwayh	•	G5	82
Astana	■	N7	68
Astara	•	E2	82
Asti	•	D6	56
Astorga	•	D2	54
Astoria	•	B1	112
Astrakhan'	•	J5	64
Astypálaia	•	J8	62
Astypálaia	⬚	J8	62
Asunción	■	K4	126
Aswān	•	F3	90
Aswān Dam	⬚	F3	90
Asyūţ	•	F2	90
Aş Zaydīyah	•	H4	90
Atafu	⬚	J6	100
Atakpamé	•	E3	94
Atâr	•	C4	92
Atasu	•	N8	68
Atbara	•	F4	90
Atbara	✎	N4	64
Atbasar	•	N4	64
Atchison	•	B2	116
Aterno	✎	H6	56
Ath	•	F4	48
Athabasca	✎	J5	108
Athens = Athína	■	F7	62
Athens, Ga., U.S	•	E3	114
Athens, Oh., U.S	•	E2	114
Athens, Tenn., U.S	•	E2	114
Athens, Tex., U.S	•	B3	116
Athína	■	F7	62
Athlone	•	E8	50
Ath Thāyat	▲	D7	86
Athy	•	C5	90
Atiamuri	•	F4	104
Atikokan	•	B1	114
Åtka	✎	S4	70
Atka Island	⬚	(3)C1	118
Atlanta	□	E3	114
Atlantic	•	B1	116
Atlantic City	•	F3	114
Atlantic Ocean	▬	C2	52
Atlantic Ocean	▬	C7	88
Atlas Bogd	▲	B2	72
Atlas Mountains	⬚	N9	54
Atlasovo	✎	T5	70
Atlas Saharien	⬚	E2	92
Atlin	•	E5	108
Atmore	•	D3	116
Aţ Ţā'if	•	D5	82
Attapu	•	D4	76
Attawapiskat	✎	Q6	108
Attersee	✎	J3	56
Attu Island	⬚	(3)A1	118
At Turbah	•	H5	90
Atyrau	•	K5	64
Aubagne	•	L10	52
Aube	✎	K5	52
Auburn, Al., U.S.	•	D3	116
Auburn, Calif., U.S.	•	B3	112
Auburn, Nebr., U.S.	•	G2	112
Auch	•	F10	52
Auckland	•	C3	104
Auckland Island	⬚	(2)B1	104
Aude	✎	H10	52
Aue	•	H6	46
Auerbach	•	H6	46
Augathella	•	J5	102
Augsburg	•	F2	56
Augusta, Australia	•	C6	102
Augusta, Italy	■	K11	58
Augusta, Ga., U.S	•	E3	114
Augusta, Me., U.S	■	G2	114
Augustów	•	M4	44
Aurangābād	•	C5	80
Aurillac	•	H9	52
Aurora, Colo., U.S	•	C2	114
Aurora, Ill., U.S	•	C2	114
Aurora, Mo., U.S	•	C2	116
Aurukun	•	H2	102
Auschwitz = Oświęcim	•	J7	44
Austin, Minn., U.S	•	C3	114
Austin, Nev., U.S	•	C3	112
Austin, Tex., U.S	■	B3	116
Australia	▲	E4	102
Australian Alps	▲	E9	100
Australian Capital Territory	⬚	J7	102
Austria	▲	J3	56
Autun	•	K7	52
Auxerre	•	J6	52
Avalon	•	J6	52
Avam	✎	C7	70
Aveiro	•	B4	54

Name	Grid	Page
Avellino	J8	58
Avesta	J6	42
Aviemore	J4	50
Avignon	K10	52
Ávila	F4	54
Avilés	E1	54
Avion	E4	48
Avola	K12	58
Avranches	D5	52
Avrig	M4	60
Awat	Q9	68
Awatere	D5	104
Awbārī	B2	90
Awjilah	D2	90
Awka	F3	94
Ax-les-Thermes	G11	52
Ayacucho	C6	124
Ayaguz	Q8	68
Ayamonte	C7	54
Ayan	P5	70
Ayanka	V4	70
Aydin	B5	84
Aydıncık	R8	62
Ayers Rock = Uluru	F5	102
Aykino	H5	68
Aylesbury	B3	48
Aylmer Lake	K4	108
Ayr, Australia	J3	102
Ayr, U.K.	H6	50
Ayutthaya	Q7	60
Aytos	C4	76
Ayvalık	J5	62
Azaila	K3	54
Azaouâd	E5	92
A'zāz	G5	84
Azerbaijan	M3	84
Azores = Açores	(1)B2	92
Azov	G5	64
Azuaga	E6	54
Azul	K6	126
Az Zabadānī	D3	86
Az Zahrān	D3	87
Az Zāwiyah	B1	90
Az Zubayr	B1	87

B

Name	Grid	Page
Ba'albek	D2	86
Baardheere	G3	96
Babadag	R5	60
Babaeski	K3	62
Bāb al Mandab	D7	82
Babar	C4	79
Babo	D3	79
Babruysk	E4	64
Babura	F2	94
Babushkin	H6	70
Babuyan Islands	G3	76
Bacabal	J4	124
Bacan	C3	79
Bacău	P3	60
Bachu	L2	82
Bačka Palanka	G4	60
Bac Liêu	D5	76
Bacolod	G4	76
Badajoz	C6	54
Bad al Milh	K7	84
Bad Aussee	J3	56
Bad Bentheim	K2	48
Bad Doberan	G2	46
Bad Ems	K4	48
Baden-Baden	D2	56
Badgastein	J3	56
Badgingarra	C6	102
Bad Harzburg	F5	46
Bad Hersfeld	E6	46

Name	Grid	Page
Bad Homburg	D6	46
Bad Honnef	K4	48
Badin	A4	80
Bad Ischl	J3	56
Bādiyat ash Shām	D4	86
Bad Kreuznach	K5	48
Bad Lauterberg	F6	46
Bad Mergentheim	E7	46
Bad Neuenahr-Ahrweiler	F6	46
Bad Neustadt	D4	46
Bad Salzungen	F6	46
Bad Schwartau	F3	46
Bad Urach	E2	56
Bad Vöslau	D2	60
Bad Waldsee	E5	46
Bad Wildungen	E5	46
Baena	F7	54
Baffin Bay	J2	106
Baffin Island	R2	108
Bafoulabé	B2	94
Bafoussam	G3	94
Bafra	F3	84
Bafra Burun	G3	84
Bäft	G2	87
Bafwasende	D3	96
Baga	B5	90
Bagani	C3	98
Bagaroua	E2	94
Bagdad	D2	118
Bagdarin	J6	70
Bagé	L5	126
Baggs	E2	112
Baghdād	D3	82
Bagheria	H10	58
Baghlan	J2	82
Bagnols-sur-Cèze	K9	52
Baguio	G3	76
Baharampur	E4	80
Bahawalpur	B3	80
Bahía	J6	124
Bahía Blanca	J6	126
Bahía Blanca	J6	126
Bahía de Campeche	F4	120
Bahía de Santa Elena	A5	124
Bahía de Sechura	A5	124
Bahía Grande	H9	126
Bahía Kino	D6	110
Bahía Negra	K3	126
Bahir Dar	G5	90
Bahraich	D3	80
Bahrain	D4	87
Bahrat Hims	D2	86
Bahr el Abiad	F5	90
Bahr el Azraq	F5	90
Bahr el Ghazal	C5	90
Bahr el Ghazal	D2	96
Bahr el Jebe	E2	96
Bahr el Nîl = Nîle	F4	90
Baia de Marajó	H24	124
Baia do Bengo	G6	94
Baia Mare	L2	60
Baia Sprie	L2	60
Baião	H2	124
Baibokoum	B2	96
Baicheng, China	Q9	68
Baicheng, China	G1	72
Baie de la Seine	B5	48
Baie de la Somme	D4	48
Baie St. Paul	F1	114
Baile Átha Cliath = Dublin	K6	50
Baiji	F8	50
Bailleul	E4	48
Bainbridge	B2	98
Bainbridge	E3	116
Bairiki	H5	100
Bairin Yuoqi	F2	72

Name	Grid	Page
Bairin Zuoqi	F2	72
Bairnsdale	J7	102
Baja California	C5	110
Bakchar	Q6	68
Baker	J5	100
Baker, Calif., U.S	C3	112
Baker, Mont., U.S	F1	112
Baker, Oreg., U.S	C2	112
Baker Lake	M4	108
Baker Lake	N4	108
Bakersfield	C1	118
Bakhta	D4	70
Baki	E1	82
Bakkafjörður	(1)F1	42
Baku = Baki	E1	82
Balá	E4	84
Balabac	F5	76
Balabac Strait	F5	76
Balaghat	D4	80
Balaguer	L3	54
Balakava	E1	84
Balakovo	J4	64
Balashov	H4	64
Balassagyarmat	G1	60
Balaton	E3	60
Balatonfüred	E3	60
Balclutha	B8	104
Balearic Islands = Islas Baleares	N5	54
Bāleshwar	E4	80
Baley	K6	70
Bali	F4	78
Balige	B2	78
Balikesir	K5	62
Balikpapan	F3	78
Balimo	F4	79
Balingen	D2	56
Balkhash	N8	68
Ballarat	H7	102
Ballina, Australia	K5	102
Ballina, Republic of Ireland	C7	50
Ballinasloe	D8	50
Ballinger	G2	118
Balmazújváros	J2	60
Balotra	B3	80
Balranald	H6	102
Balsas	Z	120
Balta	S2	60
Bălţi	Q2	60
Baltic Sea	J8	42
Baltijsk	J3	44
Baltimore	E3	114
Baltrum	C3	46
Balykshi	K5	64
Bam	G4	82
Bamaga	H2	102
Bamako	C2	94
Bamba	E5	92
Bambari	C2	96
Bamberg	F7	46
Bambouk	C6	92
Bambouk Kaarta	B2	94
Bamenda	G3	94
Bāmiān	J3	82
Banaba	G6	100
Bañados del Izozog	E7	124
Banalia	D3	96
Banana	K4	102
Bananga	M6	62
Banaz	C3	94
Ban Ban	C3	76
Banda	D3	80
Banda Aceh	B5	76
Bandama	C3	94
Bandar-e 'Abbās	G3	87
Bandar-e Anzalī	E2	82
Bandar-e Deylam	D1	87

135

Place	Ref	Pg
Belize ▪	G5	120
Bellary •	C5	80
Belle Fourche ⌐	F2	112
Belle Île ▨	B6	52
Belleville •	E2	114
Bellingham •	B1	112
Bellingshausen Sea ▬	(2)JJ4	128
Belluno •	H4	56
Belmont •	E2	114
Belmonte, Brazil •	K7	124
Belmonte, Spain •	H5	54
Belmopan ▪	G5	120
Belmullet •	B7	50
Belo Horizonte. □	J7	124
Beloit, Kans., U.S. •	B2	116
Beloit, Wis., U.S. •	C2	114
Belomorsk •	F2	64
Belorechensk •	H1	84
Belo Tsiribihina •	G3	98
Belozersk •	Q6	68
Belyy Yar •	H4	46
Belzig •	H4	46
Bemidji •	A1	114
Bena Dibele •	C4	96
Benavente •	E3	54
Benebecula ▨	E4	50
Bend •	B2	112
Bender-Bayla •	J2	96
Bender Qaasim •	H1	96
Bene •	E3	98
Bešeňov •	D8	44
Benevento •	J7	58
Bengbu •	F4	72
Bengkulu •	C3	78
Benguela •	A2	98
Beni •	D3	96
Beni Abbès •	E2	92
Benidorm •	K6	54
Beni Mellal •	D2	92
Benin ▪ A	E2	94
Benin City •	F3	94
Beni Saf •	J9	54
Beni Slimane •	P8	54
Beni Suef •	F2	90
Ben More Assynt ▲	H3	50
Ben Nevis ▲	H4	50
Bensheim •	D7	46
Benson •	D7	46
Benteng •	B4	79
Benue ⌐	G3	94
Benxi •	G2	72
Beograd ▪	H5	60
Bepazari •	D3	84
Berat •	B4	62
Berber •	F4	90
Berbera •	H5	90
Berberati •	B3	96
Berchtesgaden •	J3	56
Berck •	D4	48
Berdyans'k •	G5	64
Bereeda •	J1	96
Berehove •	K1	60
Bererenes.. •	C2	54
Berettyóújfalu •	J2	60
Bereznik •	J2	60
Berezniki •	L3	64
Berezovo •	N2	64
Bergama •	E5	56
Bérgamo •	H1	54
Bergedorf •	F3	46
Bergen, Norway. •	C6	42
Bergen, Germany. •	J2	46
Bergen op Zoom •	G3	48
Bergerac •	F9	52
Bergisch Gladbach •	C6	46
Beringovskiy •	X4	70
Bering Sea ▬	(1)C4	118
Bering Strait ◑	(1)C2	118
Berkeley. •	B1	118
Berkner Island. ▨	(2)A2	128
Berlin, Germany. ▪	J4	46
Berlin, U.S. •	F2	114
Bermejillo •	F3	118
Bermejo ⌐	K4	126
Bermeo •	H1	54
Bermuda. ▨	H6	106
Bermeo •	C4	56
Bernay. •	C5	48
Bernburg •	G5	46
Berner Alpen ▲	C4	56
Berounka ⌐	J7	46
Berrouaghia •	N8	54
Berry Islands. ▨	F4	116
Bertoua •	G4	94
Berwick-upon-Tweed •	L6	50
Besalampy •	G3	98
Besançon •	J8	52
Beshneh •	F2	87
Bessemer •	D3	116
Bestuzhevo. •	H2	64
Bestyakh •	M4	70
Betanzos •	B1	54
Bêtdâmbâng •	C4	76
Bethany •	C5	86
Bethlehem, Israel. •	C5	86
Bethlehem, South Africa •	D5	98
Béthune •	E4	48
Betioky. •	G4	98
Betpak-Dala. ▨	M8	68
Betroka •	H4	98
Betzdorf. •	C6	46
Bey Dağları ▲	M8	62
Beyla •	J8	94
Beyneu •	P4	62
Beypazari •	C3	86
Beyrouth. ▪	C3	86
Beyşehir •	P7	62
Beyşehir Gölü ▨	P7	62
Béziers. •	J10	52
Bhadrakh •	E4	80
Bhagalpur •	E3	80
Bhairab Bazar •	F4	80
Bhakkar •	B2	80
Bhamo •	B2	76
Bharuch •	B4	80
Bhatpara •	E4	80
Bhavnagar •	B4	80
Bhawanipatna •	D5	80
Bhilwara •	B3	80
Bhind •	C3	80
Bhopal •	C4	80
Bhubaneshwar •	E4	80
Bhuj •	A4	80
Bhusawal •	C4	80
Bhutan ▪ A	E3	80
Biak •	E3	79
Biała ⌐	K8	44
Diała Podlaska •	N5	44
Białystok •	N4	44
Biarritz. •	D10	52
Biasca •	D4	56
Bibbiena •	G7	56
Bicaz •	P3	60
Bida. •	F3	94
Bidar •	C5	80
Bideford •	H10	50
Biedenkopf •	D6	46
Biel •	C3	56
Bielefeld •	D4	46
Biella •	D5	56
Bielsko-Biała •	J8	44
Bielsk Podlaski •	N5	44
Biên Hoa •	D4	76
Biga. •	K4	62
Bighorn Lake. ✶	E1	112
Bighorn Mountains ▲	E2	112
Bight of Bangkok •	C4	76
Bight of Benin ►	E3	94
Bight of Biafra... ►	F4	94
Big Lake. •	(1)H2	118
Bignona •	B6	92
Big Rapids •	C2	114
Big River •	K6	108
Big Sioux ⌐	G2	112
Big Spring •	F2	118
Big Sur. •	B1	118
Big Trout Lake. ✶	P6	108
Bihać •	L6	56
Bijapur •	M6	84
Bijeljina •	G5	60
Bijelo Polje •	G6	60
Bijie. •	D5	72
Bikaner •	B3	80
Bikin •	N7	70
Bikini ▨	G4	100
Bilaspur •	D4	80
Bilbao •	H1	54
Bileća •	F7	60
Bilecik •	M4	62
Bilhorod-Dnistrovs'kyy •	F5	64
Billings •	D1	112
Bill of Portland. ▨	K11	50
Bilma •	B4	90
Biloxi •	D3	116
Bimini Islands ▨	F4	116
Binghamton. •	E2	114
Bingöl •	J4	84
Bintulu •	E2	78
Bintuni •	D3	79
Binyang •	D2	76
Binzhou •	F3	72
Biograd •	L7	56
Birāk •	H3	92
Birao ⌐	D5	90
Bī'r Bazīrī •	E2	86
Birdsville •	G5	102
Bireun •	B1	78
Bîr Gifgâfa •	A6	86
Birjand ⌐	G3	82
Birmingham, U.K. •	L9	50
Birmingham, U.S. •	D3	116
Birnin-Gwari. •	F2	94
Birnin Kebbi •	E2	94
Birnin Konni. •	F2	94
Birnin Kudu •	F2	94
Birobidzhan. •	N7	70
Birżai. •	P1	44
Bisbee •	E2	118
Bischofshofen •	J3	56
Bishkek ▪	N9	68
Bishop •	C3	112
Bishop's Stortford •	C3	48
Biskra •	G2	92
Bismarck □	F2	110
Bismarck Sea ►	E6	100
Bissau ▪	B6	92
Bistrița •	M2	60
Bitburg •	J5	48
Bitola •	D3	62
Bitterfeld •	H5	46
Bitterroot Range ▲	C1	112
Biu •	G2	94
Biwa-ko ✶	H6	74
Bixby •	B3	114
Biysk •	R7	68
Bizerte •	G1	92
Bjelovar •	D4	60

Name	Grid	Page
Bjørnøya	B3	68
Black Hills	F2	112
Blackpool	J8	50
Black Range	E2	118
Black Rock Desert	C2	112
Black Sea	D2	84
Black Volta	D3	94
Blackwater	D9	50
Blagny-sur-Bresle	D5	48
Blagoevgrad	F3	62
Blagoveshchensk	M6	70
Blankenburg	F5	46
Blantyre	F3	98
Blaye-et-Sainte-Luce	C5	48
Blenheim	D5	104
Blida	F1	92
Bloemfontein	D5	98
Blois	G6	52
Bloomfield	D2	116
Bloomington, Ill., U.S	C2	114
Bloomington, Ind., U.S	C3	114
Bluefield	D3	114
Bluefields	H6	120
Blue Mountains	C2	112
Blue Nile = Bahr el Azraq	F5	90
Bluff, New Zealand	B8	104
Bluff, U.S	E1	118
Blythe	D2	118
Blytheville	D2	116
Bo	B3	94
Boac	G4	76
Boa Vista, Brazil	E3	124
Boa Vista, Cape Verde Islands	(D)B1	94
Bobbili	D5	80
Bobigny	E6	48
Bobo Dioulasso	D2	94
Bôca do Acre	E2	124
Boca Grande	E3	122
Bocaranga	B2	96
Bocholt	B5	46
Bodaybo	J5	70
Bode	G4	46
Bodélé	C4	90
Bodmin	H11	50
Bodø	H3	42
Bodrum	K7	62
Boe	D2	112
Boende	C4	96
Bogalusa	D3	116
Bognor Regis	B4	48
Bogor	E3	78
Bogotá	C3	124
Boguchany	F5	70
Bogué	C5	92
Bo Hai	F3	72
Böhmerwald	H7	46
Bohol	G5	76
Boiaçu	E4	124
Boise	C2	112
Boise City	F1	118
Bojnûrd	K10	68
Bokatola	B4	96
Boké	B2	94
Bolbec	C5	48
Bole, China	Q9	68
Bole, Ghana	D3	94
Bolechiv	N8	44
Boleslawiec	E6	44
Bolgatanga	D2	94
Bolhrad	R4	60
Bolivia	D7	124
Bollène	K9	52
Bollnäs	H6	42
Bolmen	G8	42
Bolnisi	L3	84
Bolobo	H5	94
Bologna	G6	56
Bol'shaya Pyssa	J2	64
Bol'sherech'ye	P3	64
Bol'shezemel'skaya Tundra	J4	68
Bolshoy Atlym	N2	64
Bolu	D3	84
Bolvadin	P6	62
Bolzano = Bozen	G4	56
Boma	G6	94
Bombay = Mumbai	B5	80
Bomili	D3	96
Bom Jesus da Lapa	J6	124
Bonaparte Archipelago	B2	102
Bondeno	G6	56
Bondo	C3	96
Bondoukou	D3	94
Bonganganda	C3	96
Bongor	H2	94
Bonifacio	D7	58
Bonn	C6	46
Bonners Ferry	C1	112
Bontoc	G3	76
Boone	D3	114
Boothia Peninsula	M2	108
Booué	G5	94
Bor, Sudan	E2	96
Bor, Turkey	S7	62
Bor, Yugoslavia	K5	60
Borah Peak	C3	112
Borås	G8	42
Borāzjān	D2	87
Bordeaux	E9	52
Borden Peninsula	Q2	108
Border Town	H7	102
Bordj Bou Arréridj	F1	92
Bordj Messaouda	G2	92
Bordj Mokhtar	F4	92
Bordj Omar Driss	G3	92
Borgarnes	(1)C2	42
Borger	F1	118
Borgomanero	D5	56
Borgo San Dalmazzo	C6	56
Borgosésia	D5	56
Bori Jenein	H2	92
Borisoglebsk	H4	64
Borkou	C4	90
Borkum	J1	48
Borlänge	H6	42
Bórmida	D6	56
Bormio	F4	56
Borneo	E3	78
Bornholm	H9	42
Borovichi	F3	64
Borriana	K5	54
Borroloola	G3	102
Borshchovochnyy Khrebet	J7	70
Borûjerd	E2	87
Borzya	K6	70
Bosa	C8	58
Bosanska Gradiška	E4	60
Bosanski Novi	D4	60
Bosanski Petrovac	D5	60
Bôsça	J4	60
Bose	D2	76
Bosilegrad	K7	60
Bosna	F5	60
Bosnia-Herzegovina	E5	60
Bosobolo	B3	96
Bosporus = Istanbul Boğazı	M3	62
Bossambélé	B2	96
Bossangoa	B2	96
Bosten Nı	R9	68
Boston, U.K	M9	50
Boston, U.S	F2	114
Botoşani	P2	60
Botrange	J4	48
Botswana	C4	98
Bou Ahmed	F9	
Bouaké	C3	94
Bouar	B2	96
Bouârfa	E2	92
Bougainville Island	F6	100
Bougouni	C2	94
Bou Ismaïl	N8	
Boujdour		
Bou Kadir	M8	
Boulder	E2	112
Boulder City	D1	118
Boulia	G4	100
Boulogne-sur-Mer	D4	
Bounty Islands	H10	100
Bourem	E5	
Bourg-en-Bresse	L7	52
Bourges	H6	52
Bourke	J6	100
Bournemouth	L11	50
Bousso	C5	
Bouzghaïa	M8	
Bowen	J4	100
Bowie	E2	118
Bowling Green, Fla., U.S	E4	116
Bowling Green, Ky., U.S	D2	114
Bowling Green, Mo., U.S	F1	114
Bowman	F1	112
Bowman Bay	R3	108
Boyang	F5	
Boyarka	F2	
Bozcaada	H5	
Boz Dağ	M7	
Bozeman	D1	112
Bozen	G4	
Bozkir	Q7	
Bra	C6	56
Brač	D6	
Bräcke	H5	
Brad	K3	
Bradford	L8	
Brady	B3	118
Braga	B1	
Bragança, Brazil	H4	124
Bragança, Portugal	D3	
Brahmapur	D5	
Brahmaputra	F3	
Brăila	Q4	
Brainerd	B1	114
Brake	L8	
Brampton	E2	114
Bramsche	D4	
Branco	E3	124
Brandberg	A4	98
Brandenburg	H4	
Braniewo	J3	
Brasília	H7	124
Braşov	N4	
Bratislava	G9	
Bratsk	F5	
Bratskoye Vodokhranilishche	G5	
Braţul	R4	
Braunau	J2	
Braunschweig	F4	46
Brazil	F4	124
Brazzaville	B4	
Brčko	F5	
Břeclav	F9	
Breda	B3	46
Bredasdorp	C6	98
Bredy	K5	
Bregenz	J7	
Breiðhafjörður	(1)A2	42
Bremen	D3	46
Bremerhaven	D3	
Bremervörde	E3	
Brenham	B3	118

Entry	Grid	Page
Breno.. .	F5	56
Bréscia	F5	56
Breslau = Wrocław	G6	44
Bressanone = Brixen	F2	58
Bressuire	E7	52
Brest, France	A5	52
Brest, Belarus	D4	64
Brest	E5	48
Bretten	D7	46
Breves	G4	124
Brewarrina	J5	102
Bria	C2	96
Briançon	B6	56
Briceni	Q1	60
Bridgeport, Calif., U.S.	C1	118
Bridgeport, Conn., U.S	F2	114
Bridgwater	J10	50
Brienzer See	C4	56
Brig	D2	112
Brigham City	B4	48
Brighton	D5	46
Brindisi	M8	58
Brinkley	C3	116
Brisbane	K5	102
Bristol, U.K.	K10	50
Bristol, U.S.	E2	116
Bristol Bay	(1)E4	118
Bristol Channel	H10	50
British Columbia	F5	108
Brive-la-Gaillarde	G8	52
Briviesca	G2	54
Brixen	G4	56
Brlik	N9	68
Brno	F8	44
Broadus	E1	112
Brockton	F2	114
Brockville	P2	108
Brodeur Peninsula	J4	44
Broken Hill	H6	102
Brokopondo	F2	124
Brooke's Point	C3	116
Brookhaven	B2	112
Brookings, Oreg., U.S.	B2	112
Brookings, S.D., U.S	G2	112
Brooks Range	(1)F2	118
Broome	D3	102
Brownfield	F2	118
Browning	D1	112
Brownsville	D2	116
Brownwood	B3	116
Bruck, Austria	L3	56
Bruck, Austria	M2	56
Bruck an der Mur	C2	60
Brugge	F3	48
Bruint	G3	80
Bruneck	G4	56
Brunei	E2	78
Brunsbüttel	E3	46
Brunswick	E3	116
Brush	F2	112
Brussels = Bruxelles	G4	48
Bruxelles	G4	48
Bryan	B3	116
Bryansk	F4	64
Brzeg	G7	44
Bucak	D5	84
Bucaramanga	C2	124
Buchanan	B3	94
Bucharest = Bucureşti	P5	60
Buchen	E7	46
Buchholz	E3	46
Buchy	M5	52
Buckeburg	E4	46
Bucureşti	P5	60
Budapest	G2	60
Budennovsk	L1	84
Büdingen	E6	46
Buea		
Buenaventura, Colombia	B3	124
Buenaventura, Mexico	E3	118
Buenos Aires	K5	126
Buffalo, N.Y., U.S.	E2	114
Buffalo, S.D., U.S.	F1	112
Buffalo, Tex., U.S.	B3	116
Buffalo, Wyo., U.S	E2	112
Buftea	N5	60
Bug	L5	44
Bugrino	H4	68
Buguruslan	K4	64
Buhayrat al Asad	H5	84
Buhayrat ath Tharthār	K6	84
Builth Wells	J9	50
Buir Nuur	F1	72
Bujumbura	D4	96
Bukachacha	K6	70
Bukavu	D4	96
Bukhara	H2	82
Bukittinggi	C3	78
Bukoba	E4	96
Bula..	D3	79
Bulawayo	D4	98
Bulgan	G7	70
Bulgaria	M7	60
Bulle	C4	56
Bullhead City	D1	118
Bulukumba	B4	79
Bumba	C3	96
Buna	F3	96
Bunbury	C6	102
Bundaberg	K4	102
Bunia	E3	96
Buôn Mê Thuột	D4	76
Bura	F4	96
Buranj	D2	80
Burao	H2	96
Buraq	D3	86
Buraydah	D4	82
Burco	J6	90
Burdur	D5	84
Burdur Gölü..	N7	62
Burë	G5	90
Burg	G4	46
Burgas	Q7	60
Burgaski Zaliv	Q7	60
Burgdorf.	C3	56
Burghausen	H2	56
Burglengenfeld	H7	46
Burgos	G2	54
Burgsvik	K8	42
Burhaniye	K5	62
Burhanpur.	C4	80
Burkina	D2	94
Burlin	K4	64
Burlington, Colo., U.S.	F1	118
Burlington, Ia., U.S.	B2	114
Burlington, Vt., U.S.	F2	114
Burma = Myanmar	B2	76
Burney	B2	112
Burnie	J8	102
Burns	C2	112
Burns Junction.	C2	112
Burqin	C3	62
Burrel	C3	62
Bursa	M4	62
Bür Safâga	F2	90
Bür Sa'îd	F1	90
Bur Sudan.	G4	90
Buru	C3	79
Burundi	D4	96
Bururi	D4	96
Buryatiya	J6	70
Bury St. Edmunds	C2	48
Büshehr	D2	87
Bushire = Būshehr	D2	87
Busira	C4	96
Bussum	H2	48
Busto Arsizio.	D5	56
Buta	C3	96
Butare	D4	96
Butembo.	D3	96
Buðardalur	(1)C2	42
Buton.	B3	79
Butte.	D1	112
Butuan	H5	76
Butzow.	G3	46
Buulobarde	H3	96
Buxton	A1	48
Buy	H3	64
Buynaksk	M2	84
Buzai Gumbad	K2	82
Buzău	P4	60
Buzuluk	K4	64
Byala Slatina	L6	60
Byarcza	N10	42
Bydgoszcz	H4	44
Bygland	D7	42
Bykovskiy	M2	70
Bylot Island.	R2	108
Bytatay..	N3	70
Bytom	H7	44
Bytów	G3	44

C

Entry	Grid	Page
Caballococha	C5	124
Cabanatuan.	G3	76
Cabano	G1	114
Cabañiquinta	E1	54
Cabinda	G6	94
Cabinda	G6	94
Cabo Beata.	K5	120
Cabo Catoche	G4	120
Cabo Corrientes, Colombia	B2	124
Cabo Corrientes, Mexico	C4	120
Cabo de Espichel	A6	54
Cabo de Gata	H8	54
Cabo de Hornos.	H10	126
Cabo de São Roque	K5	124
Cabo de São Vicente	A7	54
Cabo de Trafalgar	D8	54
Cabo Fisterra	A2	54
Cabo Frio	N3	126
Cabo Gracias á Dios.	H6	120
Cabo Mondego	A4	54
Cabo Norte.	H3	124
Cabo Ortegal.	B1	54
Cabo Peñas	E1	54
Caborca	D2	118
Cabo Roxo	A2	94
Cabo San Juan	F4	94
Cabo San Lucas	D7	110
Cabo Santa Elena.	J7	124
Cabot Strait	U7	108
Cabrera	N5	54
Čačak	H6	60
Cáceres, Brazil	F7	124
Cáceres, Spain	D5	54
Cachimbo	G5	124
Cacola	B2	98
Caconda	B2	98
Čadca	H8	44
Cadillac	C2	114
Cádiz	D8	54
Caen	B5	48
Caernarfon	H8	50
Cagayan de Oro.	G5	76
Cagli	H7	56

Name	Ref	Page
Caroline Island	L6	100
Caroline Islands	E5	100
Carpathian Mountains	J8	44
Carpati Meridionali	J4	60
Carpentras	L9	52
Carpi	F6	56
Carrabelle	E4	116
Carrara	F6	56
Carrington	G1	112
Carrizozo	E2	118
Carrollton, Ky., U.S.	D3	114
Carrollton, Mo., U.S.	C1	116
Çarşamba	G3	84
Carson City	C3	112
Cartagena, Colombia	B1	124
Cartagena, Spain	K7	54
Carthage	C3	116
Cartwright	V6	108
Caruaru	K5	124
Casablanca	D2	92
Casa Grande	D5	56
Casale Monferrato	D5	56
Casarano	N9	58
Cascade	C2	112
Cascade Range	B2	112
Cascavel	L3	126
Caserta	J7	58
Casino	K5	102
Caspe	K3	54
Casper	E2	112
Caspian Sea	J3	40
Cassino	H7	58
Castellane	B7	56
Castelló de la Plana	L3	54
Castelo Branco	C5	54
Castelsarrasin	G10	52
Castelvetrano	G11	58
Castlebar	C8	50
Castleford	L8	50
Castle Point	F5	104
Castres	H10	52
Castries	M6	120
Castrovillari	L9	58
Castuera	E6	54
Catamarca	H4	126
Catània	K11	58
Catanzaro	L10	58
Catanzaro Marina	L10	58
Catarman	G4	76
Catbalogan	F5	76
Cat Island	N6	108
Cauayan	G5	76
Caucasus	K2	84
Caudry	F4	48
Caura	E2	124
Causapscal	G1	114
Cavaillon	L10	52
Cave	C7	104
Cavinas	D6	124
Cavtat	F7	60
Caxias	J4	124
Caxias do Sul	L4	126
Caxito	G6	94
Cayenne	J4	124
Cayman Islands	H5	120
Cay Sal Bank	F5	120
Ceará	J4	124
Cebu	G4	76
Cedar City	D3	112
Cedar Falls	B2	114
Cedros	A2	118
Ceduna	F6	102
Ceerigaabo	H1	96
Cefalù	J10	58

Name	Ref	Page
Cegléd	G2	60
Celebes = Sulawesi	A3	79
Celebes Sea	B2	79
Celje	C3	60
Celle	F4	46
Celtic Sea	E10	50
Cento	G6	56
Central African Republic	C2	96
Centralia	B1	112
Central Range	F3	79
Central Siberian Plateau = Srednesibirskoye Ploskogor'ye	N2	66
Ceres, Argentina	J4	126
Ceres, Brazil	H7	124
Cerignola	K7	58
Çerkes	Q4	62
Cerritos	F4	118
Cerro Aconcagua	G5	126
Cerro Bonete	H4	126
Cerro de Pasco	B6	124
Cerro Marahuaca	D3	124
Cerro Murallón	G8	126
Cerro Nevado	H6	126
Cerro Pena Nevade	D4	120
Cerro San Valentin	G8	120
Cerro Yogan	H9	126
Certaldo	G7	56
Cervaro	K7	58
Cervia	H6	56
Cesena	H6	56
České Budějovice	K2	56
Český Krumlov	K2	56
Çeşme	J6	62
Cessano	J7	56
Cessnock	K6	102
Cetate	L5	60
Cetinje	F7	60
Ceuta	D1	92
Chachapoyas	B5	124
Chaco Boreal	K3	126
Chad	C5	90
Chadan	S7	68
Chadron	F2	112
Chāh Bahār	H4	82
Chalhuanca	C6	124
Chalki	K8	62
Chalkida	F6	62
Chalkidikí	F4	62
Challenger Deep	E4	100
Challis	D2	112
Châlons-sur-Marne	G6	48
Chalon-sur-Saône	K7	52
Cham	H7	46
Chama	E2	98
Chambal	C3	80
Chamberlain	G2	112
Chambéry	A5	56
Chamonix	B5	56
Champagne	C2	114
Champlitte	A3	56
Chañaral	G4	126
Chandigarh	C2	80
Chandler	D2	118
Chandrapur	C5	80
Changane	E4	98
Changara	E3	98
Changchun	C2	74
Changde	E5	72
Chang-hua	G6	72
Chang Jiang	D4	72
Changsha	E5	72
Changting	F5	72
Changzhi	E3	72
Changzhou	F4	72
Chania	G9	62
Channel Islands	K12	50

Name	Ref	Page
Channel-Port aux Basques	V7	108
Chanthaburi	C4	76
Chantilly	E5	48
Chanute	B2	116
Chao Phraya	C4	76
Chaoyang	G2	72
Chaozhou	F6	72
Chapada Diamantina	J6	124
Chapleau	D1	114
Chapra	D3	80
Chara	K5	70
Charcas	F4	118
Chardzhev	H2	82
Chari	C5	90
Chārīkār	J2	82
Charleroi	G4	48
Charleston, New Zealand	C5	104
Charleston, S.C., U.S.	F3	116
Charleston, W.Va., U.S.	E2	116
Charleville	D5	102
Charleville-Mézières	G5	48
Charlotte	E2	116
Charlottesville	F2	116
Charlottetown	U7	108
Charlton Island	Q6	108
Charsk	Q8	68
Charters Towers	J4	102
Chartres	G5	52
Chasel'ka	C3	70
Châteaubriant	D6	52
Châteaudun	G5	52
Château-Thierry	F5	48
Châtellerault	F7	52
Chatham	D2	114
Chatham Island	(1)B1	104
Chatham Islands	(1)B1	104
Châtillon-sur-Seine	K6	52
Chattanooga	F4	116
Chauk	H5	80
Chaumont	L5	52
Chauny	F5	48
Chaves	G4	124
Cheb	H6	46
Cheboksary	J3	64
Chechnya	L2	84
Cheduba Island	F5	80
Chegdomyn	N6	70
Cheju	D7	74
Cheju-do	D7	74
Chélif	L8	54
Chelkar	K8	68
Chełm	N6	44
Chełmno	H4	44
Chelmsford	C3	48
Cheltenham	L10	50
Chelyabinsk	M3	64
Chemnitz	H6	46
Chenab	B2	80
Chengde	F2	72
Chengdu	C4	72
Chennai	D6	80
Chenzhou	E5	72
Chepes	H5	126
Cher	G6	52
Cherbourg	D4	52
Cherchell	N8	54
Cheremkhovo	G6	70
Cherepovets	G3	64
Cherkasy	F5	64
Cherkessk	K1	84
Chernihiv	F4	64
Chernivtsi	E5	64
Chernyakhovsk	L3	44
Chernyshevskiy	J4	70
Chernyye Zemli	J5	64
Cherokee	A2	114

INDEX

Place	Ref	Page
Cherskiy	U3	70
Cherven Bryag	M6	60
Chesapeake	F2	116
Cheshskaya Guba	J1	64
Cheshunt	C3	48
Chester, U.K.	K8	50
Chester, U.S.	B2	112
Chesterfield Inlet	N4	108
Chetumal	G5	120
Che'w Bahir	F3	96
Cheyenne	F2	112
Cheyenne	F2	112
Cheyenne Wells	F1	118
Cheyne Bay	C6	102
Chhindwara	C4	80
Chhuka	E3	80
Chiang-Mai	B3	76
Chiang Rai	B3	76
Chiavari	E6	56
Chiavenna	E4	56
Chiba	L6	74
Chibougamau	S6	108
Chibuto	E4	98
Chicago	C2	114
Chicapa	C2	96
Chickasha	B3	116
Chiclayo	B5	124
Chico	H8	126
Chicoutimi	S7	108
Chiemsee	H3	56
Chieri	C5	56
Chiese	C5	56
Chieti	J6	58
Chifeng	F2	72
Chiganak	N8	68
Chigubo	E4	98
Chihuahua	E3	118
Chili	M9	68
Chilas	B1	80
Childress	F2	118
Chile	D8	122
Chile Chico	G8	126
Chillán	G6	126
Chillicothe	D3	114
Chilliwack	B1	112
Chiloquin	B2	112
Chi-lung	G5	72
Chimbay	K9	68
Chimborazo	B4	124
Chimbote	B5	124
Chimec	J1	60
Chimoio	E3	98
China	N6	66
Chincha Alta	B6	124
Chincilla de Monte-Aragón	J6	54
Chinde	F3	98
Chin do	C6	74
Chindwin	A2	76
Chingola	D2	98
Chinhoyi	E3	98
Chiniot	B2	80
Chinju	E6	74
Chinmen	F5	72
Chióggia	H5	56
Chios	J6	62
Chios	H6	62
Chipata	E2	98
Chippewa Falls	B2	114
Chipping Norton	A3	48
Chiromo	F3	98
Chirripó	H7	120
Chişinău	R2	60
Chita	J6	70
Chitato	C5	96
Chitembo	B2	98
Chitradurga	C6	80
Chitral	B1	80
Chitré	H7	120
Chittagong	F4	80
Chittaurgarh	B4	80
Chittoor	C6	80
Chitungwiza	E3	98
Chiume	C3	98
Chivasso	C5	56
Chizha	H1	64
Chojnice	G4	44
Chokurdakh	R2	70
Chókwé	E4	98
Cholet	E6	52
Choma	D3	98
Chomutov	C7	44
Ch'ŏngjin	E3	74
Ch'ŏngju	D6	74
Chŏngp'yŏng	D4	74
Chongqing	P7	66
Ch'ŏnju	D5	74
Chornobyl'	F4	64
Ch'osan	C3	74
Chōshi	L6	74
Choszczno	E4	44
Choteau	D1	112
Chott el Jerid	G2	92
Chott Melrhir	G2	92
Choybalsan	J7	70
Choyr	D1	72
Christchurch	D6	104
Christmas Island	D5	78
Chu	N9	68
Chubut	H7	126
Chūgoku-sanchi	J3	72
Chugwater	F2	112
Chukchi Sea	(1)C2	118
Chukotskiy Khrebet	W3	70
Chukotskiy Poluostrov	Z3	70
Chulucanas	A5	124
Chumikan	P6	70
Chum Phae	C3	76
Chumphon	B4	76
Ch'unch'ŏn	D5	74
Chundzha	P9	68
Chur	E4	56
Churchill	N5	108
Churchill	M5	108
Churchill Falls	U6	108
Churchill Peak	F5	108
Chusovoy	L3	64
Chute des Passes	S7	108
Chuvashiya	J3	64
Chuxiong	C2	76
Chuya	J5	70
Ciadir-Lunga	R3	60
Ciechanów	K5	44
Ciego de Ávila	J4	120
Cienfuegos	H4	120
Cieza	J6	54
Cilacap	D4	78
Cimarron	B2	116
Cinca	L3	54
Cincinnati	D3	114
Cine	L7	62
Cintalapa	F5	120
Circle	(1)U2	118
Cirebon	D4	78
Cirò Marina	M9	58
Cisterna	H3	58
Cittadella	H1	56
Città di Castello	H7	56
Ciucea	K3	60
Ciudad Acuña	F3	118
Ciudad Bolívar	E2	124
Ciudad Camargo	E3	118
Ciudad del Carmen	F5	120
Ciudad del Este	L4	126
Ciudad Delicias	E3	118
Ciudad del Maíz	E4	120
Ciudad Guayana	E2	124
Ciudad Juárez	E2	118
Ciudad Madero	G4	118
Ciudad Mante	E4	120
Ciudad Obregón	C3	120
Ciudad Real	G6	54
Ciudad-Rodrigo	D4	54
Ciudad Victoria	G7	110
Ciutadella	P4	54
Civita Castellana	G6	58
Civitanova Marche	H5	58
Civitavecchia	F6	58
Clairview	J4	102
Clamecy	J6	52
Clare Island	B8	50
Clarence	D6	104
Clarendon	F2	118
Clarkdale	D2	118
Clarksburg	E2	116
Clarksdale	C3	116
Clarksville	D2	116
Claveria	G3	76
Clayton	F1	118
Clearwater	C1	112
Clermont	J4	102
Clermont-Ferrand	J8	52
Cles	F4	56
Cleveland, Oh., U.S	D2	114
Cleveland, Tenn., U.S	B2	116
Clinton	B2	116
Clipperton Island	C6	120
Clonmel	E9	50
Cloppenburg	D4	46
Cloud Peak	E2	112
Clovis, Calif., U.S	C3	112
Clovis, N.Mex., U.S	F2	118
Cluj-Napoca	L3	60
Cluny	K7	52
Clyde	C7	108
Clyde River	T2	108
Coalville	C2	112
Coari	E4	124
Coast Mountains	E5	108
Coast Range	B3	112
Coats Island	Q4	108
Coatzacoalcos	F5	120
Cobán	F5	120
Cobija	D6	124
Cobourg Peninsula	F2	102
Cobue	E2	98
Coburg	F6	46
Cochabamba	D7	124
Cochin = Kochi	C7	80
Cochrane	D1	114
Coco	H6	120
Coco Channel	A4	76
Codajás	B4	124
Codigoro	H6	56
Codlea	N4	60
Codó	J4	124
Codroipo	J5	56
Coesfeld	C5	46
Coeur d'Alene	C1	112
Coffs Harbour	K6	102
Cofrents	J5	54
Cognac	E8	52
Cogne	C5	56
Coiba	C3	122
Coihaique	G8	126
Coimbatore	C6	80
Coimbra	B4	54
Colchester	C3	48
Colebrook	F1	114
Coll		50

D

Name		Coord	Page
Dili	■	C4	79
Dillingen	•	B7	46
Dillon	•	D1	112
Dilolo	•	C2	98
Dimapur		F3	80
Dimashq	■	D3	86
Dimitrovgrad, *Bulgaria*		N7	60
Dimitrovgrad, *Russia*		J4	64
Dimitrovgrad, *Yugoslavia*		K7	60
Dimona	•	C5	86
Dinagat		H4	76
Dinajpur		E3	80
Dinan	•	C5	52
Dinant	•	G4	48
Dinar	•	D4	84
Dinaric Alps		L6	56
Dindigul	•	C6	80
Dingle Bay	►	B9	50
Dingolfing	•	H2	56
Dingwall	•	H4	50
Dinkelsbühl	•	F7	46
Diomede Islands		AA3	70
Diourbel	•	B6	90
Dipolog	•	G5	76
Dir		B1	80
Diré Dawa	•	G2	96
Dirranbandi		J5	102
Disko = Qeqertarsuatsiaq		V2	108
Distrito Federal	a	H7	124
Dithmarschen		D2	46
Divândarreh	•	M6	84
Divinópolis		N3	126
Divriği	•	H4	84
Diyarbakır	•	J5	84
Djado		G4	94
Djakovo		H4	92
Djambala	•	G5	94
Djanet	•	G4	92
Djelfa	•	F2	92
Djéma	•	D2	96
Djibouti	▲	H5	90
Djibouti	■	H5	90
Djolu	•	C3	96
Djúpivogur	•	(1)F2	42
Dnieper	∠	F5	64
Dniester	∠	P1	60
Dnipro	•	H3	40
Dniprodzerzhyns'k	•	F5	64
Dnipropetrovs'k	•	F5	64
Dnister	∠	G3	40
Dno	•	E3	64
Doba	•	B2	96
Döbeln	•	J5	46
Doboj	•	F5	60
Dobrich	•	Q6	60
Dobryanka	•	L3	64
Dodecanese = Dodekanisos		J8	62
Dodge City	•	F3	112
Dodoma	■	F5	96
Doetinchem	•	J3	48
Dōgo		G5	74
Doha = Ad Dawhah	■	E2	94
Doha	•	D4	87
Dokka	•	F5	42
Dokkum	•	B3	46
Dolak		K4	79
Dolbeau	•	F1	114
Dole	•	A3	56
Dolgany	•	E2	70
Dolinsk	∠	Q7	70
Dollard	►	C3	46
Dolomiti	►	C4	56
Dolo Odo	•	G3	96
Dolores	•	K6	126
Dolphin and Union Strait	►	H3	108

Name		Coord	Page
Domažlice	•	H7	46
Dombås	•	E5	42
Dombóvár	•	F3	60
Dominica		E2	122
Dominican Republic		D1	122
Domodóssola	•	D4	56
Domžale	•	K4	56
Don	∠	H2	40
Donau = Danube	∠	H2	56
Donauwörth	•	F8	46
Don Benito	•	E6	54
Doncaster	•	L8	50
Dondra Head		D7	80
Donegal	•	D7	50
Donegal Bay	►	D7	50
Donets	∠	H3	40
Donets'k	•	G5	64
Dongfang	•	D3	76
Donggala	•	A3	79
Donggou	•	C4	74
Đông Hới	•	D3	76
Dongola	•	F4	90
Dongou	•	H4	94
Dongsha Qundao		F2	76
Dongsheng	•	E3	72
Đông Ujimqin Qi	•	F1	72
Donji Vakuf	•	N6	56
Donner Pass	•	B3	112
Donostia	•	J1	54
Dora	∠	C6	56
Dordrecht	•	G3	48
Dori	•	D2	94
Dorsten	•	J3	48
Dortmund	•	C5	46
Dos Hermanas	•	E7	54
Dosso	•	E2	94
Dothan	•	D3	116
Douai	•	F4	48
Douala	•	F4	94
Douarnenez	•	A5	52
Doubs	∠	B3	56
Douglas, *South Africa*	•	C5	98
Douglas, *U.K.*	•	H7	50
Douglas, *Ariz., U.S.*	•	E2	118
Douglas, *Ga., U.S.*	•	E3	116
Douglas, *Wyo., U.S*	•	E2	112
Doullens	•	E4	48
Dourados	•	L3	126
Douro	∠	B3	54
Dover, *U.K*	•	D3	48
Dover, *U.S*	•	F2	116
Dover, *Australia*		J8	102
Dowlatābād	•	E2	87
Drăgășani	•	M5	60
Draguignan	•	B7	56
Drakensberg	►	D6	98
Drake Passage	►	G10	126
Drama	•	G3	62
Drammen	•	F7	42
Drau	∠	J4	56
Drava	∠	E4	60
Dravograd	•	K2	58
Drawsko Pomorskie	•	J5	46
Dresden	•	J5	46
Dreux	•	D6	48
Drina	∠	G5	60
Drobeta-Turnu Severin.	•	K5	60
Drogheda	•	F8	50
Drohobych	•	N8	44
Drôme	∠	K9	52
Dronne	∠	F8	52
Dronning Maud Land		(2)F2	128
Drummondville.	•	F1	114
Dschang	•	G3	94
Dubai = Dubayy	•	F4	87
Dubāsari	•	S2	60

Name		Coord	Page
Dubawnt Lake	∠	L4	108
Dubayy	•	F4	87
Dubbo	•	J6	102
Dublin	■	F8	50
Dubois	•	D2	112
Du Bois	•	E2	114
Dubovskoye	•	H5	64
Dubrovnik	•	F7	60
Dubuque	•	B2	114
Ducie Island	•	P8	100
Dudelange	•	J5	48
Duderstadt	•	F5	46
Dugi Otok		B6	60
Duisburg	•	J3	48
Duiveland		F3	48
Duk Faiwil	•	E2	96
Dukhān	•	D4	87
Dukou	•	C5	72
Dulan	•	B3	72
Dulce	∠	E1	118
Dul'Durga	•	J6	70
Dülmen	•	C5	46
Dulovo	•	Q6	60
Duluth	•	B1	114
Dūmā	•	D3	86
Dumaguete	•	G5	76
Dumai	•	C2	78
Dumas	•	F3	112
Dumbier	▲	J9	44
Dumfries	•	J6	50
Dümmer	∠	D4	46
Dumont d'Urville Sea	≈	(2)U3	128
Dumyāt	•	F1	90
Duna = Danube	∠	D1	60
Dunaj = Danube	∠	G10	44
Dunărea = Danube	∠	K5	60
Dunaújváros	•	F3	60
Dunav = Danube	∠	J5	60
Dunbar	•	H3	102
Duncan.	•	B1	112
Duncan Passage	►	A4	76
Dundalk	•	F7	50
Dundee, *South Africa*	•	E5	98
Dundee, *U.K*	•	K5	50
Dunedin	•	C7	104
Dungarvan	•	E9	50
Dungeness		C4	48
Dunhua	•	E2	74
Dunhuang	•	A2	72
Dunkerque	•	E3	48
Dunkirk.	•	E2	114
Dún Laoghaire	•	F8	50
Dunnet Head		J3	50
Dunseith	•	G1	112
Durance	∠	L10	52
Durango, *Mexico*	•	F4	118
Durango, *Spain*	•	H1	54
Durant	•	B3	116
Durban	•	E5	98
Düren	•	J4	48
Durgapur	•	E4	80
Durham, *U.K*	•	L7	50
Durham, *U.S.*	•	F2	116
Durrës	•	B3	62
Dursunbey	•	L5	62
D'Urville Island	•	D5	104
Dushanbe	■	J2	82
Düsseldorf	•	J3	48
Duyun	•	D5	72
Düzce	•	P4	62
Dvina	∠	H2	40
Dvinskaya Guba	►	J1	64
Dwarka	•	A4	80
Dyersburg.	•	D2	116
Dyje	∠	M2	56

Dzerzhinsk . . . . ● H3 64
Dzhambeyty . . . . ● K4 64
Dzhankoy . . . . ● F5 64
Dzhardzhan . . . . ● L3 70
Dzhetygara . . . . ● M4 64
Dzhezkazgan . . . . ● N5 64
Dzhizak . . . . ● M9 68
Dzhusaly . . . . ● M5 64
Działdowo . . . . ● K4 44

E

Eagle Pass . . . . ● F3 118
East Antarctica . . . . . . ◙ (2)P2 128
Eastbourne . . . . ● C4 48
East Cape . . . . ◙ A4 123
East China Sea . . . . ▬ H4 72
Easter Island . . . . ● Q8 100
Eastern Cape . . . . ◙ D6 98
Eastern Ghats . . . . ▲ C6 80
East Falkland . . . . ● K9 126
Eastleigh . . . . ● A4 48
East London . . . . ● D6 98
Eastmain . . . . ● R6 108
Eastmain . . . . ∕ S6 108
East Point . . . . ● E3 116
East Retford . . . . ● B1 48
East St. Louis . . . . ● B3 114
East Siberian Sea =
    Vostochno-Sibirskoye
    More. . . . . ▬ U2 70
East Timor . . . . A C4 79
Eau Claire . . . . ● B2 114
Ebersberg . . . . ● J4 46
Eberswalde . . . . ● J4 46
Éboli . . . . ● K8 58
Ebolowa . . . . ● G4 94
Eceabat . . . . ● J4 62
Ech Chélif . . . . ● F1 92
Echo Bay . . . . ● H3 108
Écija . . . . ● E7 54
Eckernförde . . . . ● E2 46
Ecuador . . . . A B4 124
Ed . . . . ● H5 90
Ed Damazin . . . . ● F5 90
Ed Debba . . . . ● F4 90
Ed Dueim . . . . ● F5 90
Ede, Netherlands . . . . . . ● H2 48
Ede, Nigeria . . . . ● E3 94
Edéa . . . . ● G4 94
Eden, Australia . . . . ● J7 102
Eden, U.S. . . . . ● G2 118
Edendale . . . . ● B8 104
Eder . . . . ∕ E5 46
Edessa . . . . ● E4 62
Edinburgh . . . . ▫ J6 50
Edirne . . . . ● J3 62
Edmonds . . . . ● B1 112
Edmonton . . . . ▫ J6 108
Edmundson . . . . ● N2 110
Edmundston . . . . ● G1 114
Edolo . . . . ● F4 56
Edremit . . . . ● J5 62
Edremit Körfezi . . . . ◙ H5 62
Edwards Plateau . . . . . . ◙ F2 118
Éfaté . . . . ◙ G7 100
Eferding . . . . ● D9 44
Effingham . . . . ● D2 116
Eger . . . . ● H2 60
Eggenfelden . . . . ● H2 56
Egilsstaðir . . . . ● (1)F2 42
Eğridir . . . . ● N7 62
Eğridir Gölü . . . . ◙ N6 62
Egvekinot . . . . ● Y3 70
Egypt . . . . A E2 90
Ehingen . . . . ● E2 56

Eibar . . . . ● H1 54
Eichstätt . . . . ● G2 56
Eider . . . . ▬ D2 46
Eidsvoll . . . . ● F6 42
Eifel . . . . ◙ J4 48
Eigg . . . . ◙ F5 50
Eight Degree Channel . . . ▬ B7 80
Einbeck . . . . ● E5 46
Eindhoven = ... ● H3 48
Eirunepé . . . . ● D5 124
Eiseb . . . . ∕ C4 98
Eisenach . . . . ● F6 46
Eisenerz . . . . ● K3 56
Eisenhüttenstadt . . . . . . ● D5 44
Eisenstadt . . . . ● M3 56
Eisleben . . . . ● G5 46
Eivissa . . . . ● M5 54
Eivissa . . . . ◙ M6 54
Ejea de los Caballeros . . . ● J2 54
Ejin Qi . . . . ● C2 72
Ejmiadzin . . . . ● L3 84
Ekenäs . . . . ● M7 42
Ekibastuz . . . . ● P7 68
Ekimchan . . . . ● N6 70
El Aaiún . . . . ▫ C3 92
El 'Alamein . . . . ● E1 90
El Amria . . . . ● J9 54
El 'Arîsh . . . . ● A5 86
Elat . . . . ● B7 86
Elazığ . . . . ● H4 84
El Azraq . . . . ● D5 86
Elba . . . . ◙ E6 58
Elbasan . . . . ● C3 62
Elbeuf . . . . ● D5 48
Elbistan . . . . ● G4 84
Elblag . . . . ● J3 44
Elbrus . . . . ▲ K2 84
El Cajon . . . . ● C2 118
El Centro . . . . ● C2 118
El Cerro . . . . ● E7 124
Elch . . . . ● K6 54
Elda . . . . ● K6 54
Eldorado . . . . ● L4 126
El Dorado, Ark., U.S. . . . ● C3 116
El Dorado, Kans., U.S. . . ● B2 116
El Dorado, Venezuela . . . ● E2 124
Eldoret . . . . ● F3 96
Elefsina . . . . ● F6 62
Eleuthera . . . . ◙ L6 110
El Fahs . . . . ● D12 58
El Faiyûm . . . . ● F2 90
El Fasher . . . . ● E5 90
El Geneina . . . . ● D5 90
Elgin, U.S. . . . . ● J4 50
Elgin, Ill., U.S . . . . ● C2 114
Elgin, N.D., U.S. . . . . . . ● F1 112
El Gîza . . . . ● F1 90
El Goléa . . . . ● F2 92
El Iskandarîya . . . . ● E1 90
Elista . . . . ▫ H5 64
Elizabeth City . . . . ● F2 116
El Jadida . . . . ● D2 92
El Jafr . . . . ● D6 86
El Jafr . . . . ◙ D6 86
Elk . . . . ● M4 44
Elk . . . . ∕ M4 44
El Kala . . . . ● C12 58
Elk City . . . . ● G1 118
El Kef . . . . ● C12 58
El Kelaâ des Srarhna . . . . ● D2 92
El Khârga . . . . ● F2 90
Elkhart, Ind., U.S . . . . . . ● C2 114
Elkhart, Kans., U.S. . . . . ● A2 116
El Khartum . . . . ▫ F4 90
El Khartum Bahri . . . . . . ● F4 90
Elkhovo . . . . ● J2 62
Elko, Canada . . . . ● C1 112

Elko, U.S . . . . ● C2 112
El Kuntilla . . . . ● B7 86
Ellendale . . . . ● G2 110
Ellensburg . . . . ● B1 112
Ellesmere Island . . . . . . ◙ K1 106
Ellice Islands . . . . ◙ H6 100
Elliot . . . . ● D6 98
Elliot Lake . . . . ● D4 98
Elliston . . . . ● F6 102
Ellora . . . . ● G2 114
Ellwangen . . . . ● F2 56
Elmadağ . . . . ● R5 62
Elmali . . . . ● M8 62
El Mansûra . . . . ● F1 90
El Minya . . . . ● F2 90
Elmira . . . . ● E2 114
El Muglad . . . . ● E5 90
El Obeid . . . . ● F5 90
El Oued . . . . ● G2 92
El Paso . . . . ● E2 118
El Prat de Llobregat . . . . ● N3 54
El Qâhira . . . . ▫ F1 90
El Reno . . . . ● B2 116
El Salvador . . . . A F6 120
Elster . . . . ∕ H5 46
Elsterwerda. . . . . ● J5 46
El Sueco . . . . ● E3 118
El Suweis . . . . ● F2 90
El Tarf . . . . ● C12 58
El Thamad . . . . ● B7 86
El Tigre . . . . ● E2 124
El Turbio . . . . ● G9 126
Eluru . . . . ● D5 80
Elvas . . . . ● C6 54
Ely, U.K. . . . . ● N9 50
Ely, U.S. . . . . ● D3 112
Emba . . . . ● L5 64
Embalse de Alcántara Uno . ∕ D5 54
Embalse de Almendra . . . ∕ D3 54
Embalse de Contreras . . . ∕ J5 54
Embalse de Gabriel y Galán . ∕ D4 54
Embalse de Garcia Sola . . ∕ E5 54
Embalse de la Serena . . . ∕ E5 54
Embalse del Ebro . . . . . . ∕ G1 54
Embalse del Río Negro . . ∕ F7 122
Embalse de Negratmn . . . ∕ G7 54
Embalse de Ricobayo . . . ∕ E3 54
Embalse de Santa Teresa . ∕ E4 54
Emden . . . . ● C3 46
Emerald . . . . ● J4 102
Emi Koussi . . . . ▲ C4 90
Emin . . . . ● Q8 68
Emirdağ . . . . ● P5 62
Emmen. . . . . ● J2 48
Emmerich . . . . ● J3 48
Emory Peak . . . . ▲ F3 118
Empangeni . . . . ● E5 98
Empoli . . . . ● F7 56
Emporia . . . . ● B2 116
Empty Quarter =
    Rub' al Khālī. . . . . ◙ E6 82
Ems. . . . . ∕ J1 48
Ems-Jade-Kanal . . . . . . ∕ C3 46
Enafors . . . . ● B2 64
Encarnación . . . . ● K4 126
Ende . . . . ● B4 79
Enderby Island . . . . . . ◙ (2)B1 104
Enewetak . . . . ◙ F7 100
Enez . . . . ● J4 62
Engel's. . . . . ● J4 64
Enggano . . . . ◙ C4 78
England . . . . ◙ L9 50
English Channel . . . . . . ▬ J12 50
Enid . . . . ● B2 116
Enna . . . . ● J11 58
En Nahud . . . . ● E5 90
Ennis . . . . ● D1 114

Enniskillen	•	E7	50
Enns	⌀	K3	56
Enschede	•	J2	48
Ensenada	•	C2	118
Enshi	•	D4	72
Entebbe	•	E3	96
Entrevaux	•	B7	56
Entroncamento	•	B5	54
Enugu	•	F3	94
Enurmino	•	Z3	70
Epanomi	•	E4	62
Epernay	•	J4	52
Epinal	•	B2	56
Epsom	•	B3	48
Equatorial Guinea	A	F4	94
Erbach	•	D7	46
Erciş	•	K4	84
Érd	•	F2	60
Erdek	•	K4	62
Erding	•	G2	56
Erechim	•	L4	126
Ereğli, Turkey	•	D3	84
Ereğli, Turkey	•	F5	84
Erenhot	•	E2	72
Erfurt	•	G6	46
Ergani	•	H4	84
Erg Chech	⊠	D4	92
Erg du Ténéré	⊠	H5	92
Erg Iguidi	⊠	D3	92
Erie	•	D2	114
Erimo-misaki	•	M3	74
Eritrea	A	G4	90
Erlangen	•	G7	46
Ermenek	•	E5	84
Ermoupoli	•	G7	62
Er Rachidia	•	E2	92
Er Ruseifa	•	D4	86
Erskine	•	A1	114
Ertai	•	S8	68
Ertix	⌀	S9	68
Erzgebirge	⌀	H6	46
Erzin	•	S7	68
Erzincan	•	H4	84
Erzurum	•	J4	84
Esashi, Japan	•	L3	74
Esashi, Japan	•	M1	74
Esbjerg	•	E9	42
Escanaba	•	C1	114
Esch	•	J5	48
Escondido	•	C2	118
Esfahán	•	F3	82
Eskilstuna	•	J7	42
Eskişehir	•	D4	84
Esla	⌀	E3	54
Eslamshahr	•	F2	82
İsler Dağ	▲	M7	62
Esmeraldas	•	B3	124
Espalion	•	H9	52
Española, Canada	•	D1	114
Española, U.S.	•	E3	112
Espelkamp	•	D4	46
Esperance	•	D6	102
Espinho	•	B4	54
Espírito Santo	a	J7	124
Espíritu Santo	⊠	U9	100
Espoo	•	N6	42
Espungabera	•	E4	98
Esquel	•	D2	92
Essaouira	•	C3	92
Es Semara	•	C3	92
Essen	•	K3	48
Essequibo	⌀	F2	124
Esslingen	•	E8	54
Estepona	•	E8	54
Esteros	•	C5	42
Estonia	A	M7	42
Estoril	•	A6	54
Estrecho de Magallanes	▶	G9	126
Estrela	▲	C4	54
Estremoz	•	C6	54
Estuario do Rio Amazonaz.	▶	H3	124
Esztergom	•	F2	60
Étain	•	H5	48
Étampes	•	H5	52
Étang de Berre	⌀	L10	52
Étaples	•	D4	48
Etawah	•	C3	80
Ethiopia	A	G5	88
Etosha Pan	⌀	B3	98
Ettelbruck	•	B7	46
Eucla	•	E6	102
Euclid	•	D2	114
Eufaula	•	D3	116
Eugene	•	B2	112
Euphrates	⌀	D3	82
Euphrates = Firat	⌀	H4	84
Eure	⌀	D6	48
Eureka, Calif., U.S.	•	B2	112
Eureka, Mont., U.S.	•	C1	112
Eureka, Ut., U.S.	•	D3	112
Europe	✕	F3	40
Europoort	•	F3	48
Euskirchen	•	B6	46
Evanston, Ill., U.S.	•	C2	114
Evanston, Wyo., U.S.	•	D2	112
Evansville	•	D2	116
Evaz	•	F3	87
Everett	•	B1	112
Everglades City	•	E4	116
Evergreen	•	D3	116
Évora	•	C6	54
Évreux	•	D5	48
Evros	⌀	J3	62
Evvoia	⊠	F6	62
Ewo	•	G5	94
Exeter	•	J11	50
Exmouth	•	B4	102
Eyl	•	H2	96
Eyre Peninsula	⊠	G2	102
Ezine	•	J5	62

F

Faadippolu Atoll	⊠	B8	80
Fåborg	•	F1	46
Fabriano	•	H7	56
Fada Ngourma	•	E2	94
Faenza	•	G6	56
Faeroes	⊠	D1	40
Făgăraş	•	M4	60
Fagernes	•	E6	42
Fairbanks	•	(1)H3	118
Fair Isle	⊠	B1	50
Fairmont	•	B2	114
Faisalabad	•	B2	80
Faith	•	B2	112
Faizabad	•	D3	80
Fakfak	•	D3	79
Fakse Bugt	▶	G9	42
Falaise	•	B6	48
Falaise de Tiguidit	⊠	G5	92
Falcon Lake	⌀	B4	116
Fălești	•	Q2	60
Falfurrias	•	B4	116
Falkense	•	J4	46
Falkland Islands	⊠	K9	126
Fallon	•	C3	112
Falls City	•	G3	110
Falster	⊠	H2	46
Falun	•	H6	42
Famagusta = Ammochostos	•	A1	86
Fangzheng	•	H1	72
Fano	•	J7	56
Fana	•	D1	46
Fanø Bugt	▶	D1	46
Faradje	•	D3	96
Farafangana	•	H4	98
Farāh	•	H3	82
Farah Rud	⌀	H3	82
Fargo	•	G2	110
Farmington	•	E1	118
Farnborough	•	B3	48
Fårö	⊠	K8	42
Faro, Brazil	•	F4	124
Faro, Portugal	•	C7	54
Farrāshband	•	E2	87
Farson	•	E2	112
Fasā	•	E2	87
Fáurei	•	Q4	60
Favara	•	H11	58
Faversham	•	C3	48
Favignana	⊠	G11	58
Faxaflói	▶	(1)B2	42
Faya	•	C4	90
Fayette	•	D3	116
Fayetteville, Ark., U.S.	•	C2	116
Fayetteville, N.C., U.S.	•	D3	114
Fayetteville, Tenn., U.S.	•	D2	116
Fderik	•	C4	92
Featherston	•	E5	104
Fécamp	•	C5	48
Federated States of Micronesia	A	E5	100
Fedorovka	•	M4	64
Fehmarn	⊠	G2	46
Feijó	•	C5	124
Feilding	•	E5	104
Feira de Santana	•	K6	124
Feistritz	⌀	L3	56
Feldbach	•	L4	56
Feldkirch	•	E3	56
Feldkirchen	•	K4	56
Felixstowe	•	D3	48
Feltre	•	G4	56
Femund	⌀	F5	42
Fengning	•	F2	72
Feng Xian	•	D4	72
Fenyang	•	E3	72
Feodosiya	•	F1	84
Fergana	•	K1	82
Fergus Falls	•	G2	110
Ferkessédougou	•	C3	94
Fermo	•	H5	58
Fernandópolis	•	L3	126
Ferrara	•	G6	56
Ferreira do Alentejo	•	B7	54
Ferrol	•	B1	54
Fès	•	E2	92
Festus	•	B3	114
Feteşti	•	Q5	60
Fethiye	•	M8	62
Fetisovo	•	F1	82
Feyzābād	•	K2	82
Fianarantsoa	•	H4	98
Fianga	•	B2	96
Fiché	•	F2	96
Fidenza	•	F6	56
Fier	•	B4	62
Figueira da Foz	•	B4	54
Figueres	•	N2	54
Fiji	A	H8	100
Filadélfia	•	J3	126
Filiași	•	L5	60
Filicudi	⊠	J10	58
Finale Ligure	•	D6	56
Findlay	•	D2	114
Fingoè	•	E3	98
Finike	•	N8	62
Finland	A	P3	42
Finnsnes	•	K2	42
Finsterwalde	•	J5	46

147

Firat H4 84
Firenze G7 56
Firozabad C3 80
Firozpur B2 80
Firth of Clyde . . . G6 50
Firth of Forth K5 50
Firth of Lorn G5 50
Firth of Thames . . E3 104
Fish B5 98
Fisher Strait Q4 108
Fishguard H9 50
Fiskenæsset
 = Qeqertarsuatsiaat . . W4 108
Fitzroy Crossing . . E3 102
Fivizzano F6 56
Fizi D4 96
Flaming Gorge Reservoir . E2 112
Flamingo E4 116
Flannan Islands . . . E3 50
Flåsjön H4 42
Flathead Lake D1 112
Flensburg E2 46
Flensburg Fjorde . . E2 46
Flers B6 48
Flinders Island . . . J7 102
Flinders Ranges . . G6 102
Flinders Reefs . . . J3 102
Fin Flon L6 108
Flint D2 114
Flint Island L7 100
Florac J9 52
Florence = Firenze, Italy . G7 56
Florence, Al., U.S. . . D3 116
Florence, S.C., U.S . . F3 116
Florencia B3 124
Florennes G4 48
Flores, Azores . . . (1)A2 92
Flores, Indonesia . . . B4 79
Floresti R2 60
Floriano J5 124
Florida E4 116
Florida K5 126
Florida Keys K7 106
Florina D4 62
Flora C6 42
Fly F4 79
Foča F6 60
Focşani Q4 60
Fòggia K7 58
Fogo . . . . (1)B1 94
Fohnsdorf K3 56
Föhr D2 46
Foleyet D1 114
Foligno G6 58
Folkestone D3 48
Follónica E6 58
Fond du Lac C2 114
Fondi H7 58
Fongafale H6 100
Fontainebleau . . . H5 52
Fonte Boa D4 124
Fontenay-le-Comte . E7 52
Fontur . . . . (1)F1 42
Forbach J5 48
Forchheim G7 46
Forestville G1 114
Forges-les-Eaux . . D5 48
Forks B1 112
Forlì H6 56
Formentera M6 54
Formosa, Brazil . . H7 124
Formosa, Paraguay . K4 126
Forssa M6 42
Fortaleza K4 124
Fort Bayne C4 114
Fort Beaufort . . . D6 98
Fort Benton D1 112

Fort Chipewyan . . . J5 108
Fort Collins E2 112
Fort Dodge B2 114
Forte dei Marmi . . F7 56
Fort Frances B1 114
Fort George R6 108
Fort Good Hope . . F3 108
Forth H5 50
Fort Kent G1 114
Fort Lauderdale . . E4 116
Fort Liard G4 108
Fort Macleod D1 112
Fort McMurray . . . J5 108
Fort McPherson . . (1)L2 118
Fort Myers E4 116
Fort Nelson G5 108
Fort Norman . . . . (1)M3 108
Fort Payne D3 116
Fort Pierce E4 116
Fort Portal E3 96
Fort Providence . . H4 108
Fortrose B8 104
Fort Rupert R6 108
Fort St. John G5 108
Fort Scott C2 116
Fort Severn P5 108
Fort Shevchenko . . J9 68
Fort Simpson . . . G4 108
Fort Smith, Canada . J4 108
Fort Smith, U.S. . . C2 116
Fort Stockton . . . F2 118
Fortuna F1 112
Fort Vermilion . . . H5 108
Fort Wayne D1 116
Fort William G5 50
Fort Worth B3 116
Fossano C6 56
Fougamou G5 94
Fougères D5 52
Foula K1 50
Foulness C3 48
Foumban G3 94
Fournies G4 48
Fournoi J7 62
Fouta Djallon . . . B2 94
Foveaux Strait . . . A8 104
Foxe Basin R3 108
Foxe Channel . . . R4 108
Foxe Peninsula . . R4 108
Fox Islands . . . . (1)D5 118
Foz do Cunene . . A3 98
Foz do Iguaçu . . . L4 126
Fraga L3 54
Francavilla M8 58
France G7 52
Franceville G5 94
Francistown D4 98
Francs Peak E2 112
Frankenthal D7 46
Frankfort E2 116
Frankfurt, Germany . K4 46
Frankfurt, Germany . D6 46
Franklin D. Roosevelt Lake . C1 112
Franz Josef Glacier . . C6 104
Franz Josef Land =
 Zemlya Frantsa-Iosifa . . J2 68
Fraser G6 108
Fraserburgh L4 50
Fraser Island . . . K5 102
Frederick, Md., U.S . . E3 114
Frederick, Okla., U.S . . B3 116
Fredericksburg, Tex., U.S. . B3 116
Fredericksburg, Va., U.S. . E3 114
Fredericton T7 108
Frederikshåb = Paamiut . . X4 108
Frederikshavn . . . F8 42

Fredrikstad F7 42
Freeport, Ill., U.S. . . C2 114
Freeport, Tex., U.S. . B4 116
Freeport City . . . F4 116
Freer B4 116
Free State D5 98
Freetown B3 94
Freiberg J6 46
Freiburg C3 56
Freilassing H3 56
Freising G2 56
Fréjus M10 52
Fremantle C6 102
Fremont B1 118
Frenchglen C2 112
French Guiana . . G3 124
French Polynesia . L7 100
Fresnillo D4 120
Fresno C1 118
Fribourg C4 56
Friedrichshafen . . E3 56
Friesach K4 56
Frisian Islands . . H1 48
Fritzlar E5 46
Frobisher Bay . . . T4 108
Frolovo H5 64
Frosinone H7 58
Frýdek Místek . . . H8 44
Fudai L4 74
Fuente E3 54
Fuentesauco . . . C3 92
Fuerteventura . . C3 92
Fuhai R8 68
Fuji-san. K6 74
Fuji-san. H6 74
Fukuchiyama . . . E7 74
Fukue E7 74
Fukue-jima. . . . E7 74
Fukui J5 74
Fukuoka F7 74
Fukushima L5 74
Fukuyama G6 74
Fulda E6 46
Fulda E6 46
Fuling D5 72
Fulton D2 116
Funabashi. L6 74
Funafuti H6 100
Funchal B2 92
Furneaux Group . F2 94
Fürstenfeldbruck . G2 56
Fürstenwalde. . . K4 46
Fürth F7 46
Furukawa L4 74
Fushun. B3 74
Fusong. D2 74
Füssen F3 56
Fuxhou. F5 72
Fuyang. F4 72
Fuyu G1 72
Fuzhou. F1 76
Fyn F1 46

G

Gaalkacyo H2 96
Gabes H2 92
Gabon G5 94
Gaborone D4 98
Gabrovo N7 60
Gacko F6 60
Gäddede. H4 42
Gadsden. D3 116
Găeşti N5 60
Gaeta. H7 58

Gafsa — ● G2 92
Gaggenau — ● D2 56
Gagnoa — ● C3 94
Gagra — ● J2 84
Gainesville, *Fla., U.S.* — ● E4 116
Gainesville, *Ga., U.S.* — ● E3 116
Gainesville, *Tex., U.S* — ● B3 116
Gai Xian — ● B3 74
Galana — ∕ F4 96
Galanta — ● N2 56
Galápagos Islands = Islas Galápagos — ⬡ (1)B1 124
Galashiels — ● K6 50
Galați — ● R4 60
Galdhøpiggen — ▲ D6 42
Galena — ● (1)F3 118
Galesburg — ● B2 114
Galich — ● H3 64
Gallabat — ● G5 90
Galle — ● D7 80
Gällivare — ● L3 42
Gallup — ● E1 118
Galtat Zemmour — ● C3 92
Galveston Bay — ⊢ G6 110
Galway — ● C8 50
Galway Bay — ⊢ C8 50
Gambēla — ● E2 96
Gambier Islands — ⬡ N8 100
Gambona — ● B4 96
Gamboula — ● B3 96
Ganado — ● E1 118
Gäncä — ● M3 84
Gander — ● W7 108
Gändhīdhām — ● B4 80
Gandhinagar — ● B4 80
Gandia — ● K6 54
Ganganagar — ● B3 80
Gangdise Shan — ▲ D2 80
Ganges — ∕ E3 80
Gangi — ● J11 58
Gangtok — ● E2 80
Gannett Peak — ▲ E2 112
Ganzhou — ● E5 72
Gao — ● E5 92
Gaoual — ● C6 92
Gap — ● B6 56
Garanhuns — ● K5 124
Garbsen — ● E4 46
Gardelegen — ● G4 46
Garden City — ● F3 112
Gardēz — ● J3 82
Garissa — ● F4 96
Garmisch-Partenkirchen — ● G3 56
Garonne — ∕ E9 52
Garoowe — ● H2 96
Garoua — ● G3 94
Garoua Boulai — ● G3 94
Garry Lake — ⊢ L3 108
Garut — ● D4 78
Garyarsa — ● D2 80
Garzê — ● B4 72
Gasan Kuli — ● F2 82
Gashua — ● G2 94
Gastonia — ● E2 116
Gatchina — ● F3 64
Gauja — ∕ N8 42
Gauteng — [a] D5 98
Gavdos — ● G10 62
Gävle — ● J6 42
Gawler — ● G6 102
Gaya — ● E4 80
Gaylord — ● D1 114
Gayndah — ● K5 102
Gayny — ● K2 64
Gaza — ● B5 86
Gazandzhyk — ● K10 68
Gaza Strip — [a] B5 86

Gaziantep — ● G5 84
Gbarnga — ● C3 94
Gdańsk — ● H3 44
Gdov — ● P7 42
Gdyel — ● K9 54
Gdynia — ● H3 44
Gebel el Tîh — ▲ A7 86
Gebel Katherina — ▲ F2 90
Gebel Yi'allaq — ▲ A6 86
Gebze — ● M4 62
Gedaref — ● G5 90
Gediz — ∕ K6 62
Gedser — ● G2 46
Geel — ● H3 48
Geelong — ● H7 102
Geesthacht — ● F3 46
Geilenkirchen — ● J4 48
Geita — ● E6 96
Geislingen — ● E2 56
Gejiu — ● C2 76
Gela — ● J11 58
Geladī — ● H2 96
Geleen — ● H4 48
Gelendzhik — ● H1 84
Gelibolu — ● J4 62
Gelibolu Yarimadasi — ◫ J4 62
Gembloux — ● G4 48
Gembu — ● G4 94
Gemena — ● B3 96
Gemlik — ● M4 62
Gemona del Friuli — ● J4 56
Genalē Wenz — ∕ G2 96
General Alvear — ● H6 126
General Roca — ● H6 126
General Santos — ● H5 76
Geneva — ● E2 114
Genève — ● B4 56
Genk — ● H4 48
Genoa = Genova — ● D6 56
Genova — ● D6 56
Gent — ● F3 48
Genthin — ● H4 46
George Town, *Australia* — ● J8 102
George Town, *Malaysia* — ● C1 78
George Town, *U.S* — ● F5 116
Georgetown, *Gambia* — ● B2 92
Georgetown, *Guyana* — ■ F2 124
Georgetown, *U.S.* — ● B3 116
George West — ● B4 116
Georgia — [a] K2 84
Georgia — ● E3 116
Georgian Bay — ⊢ D1 114
Gera — ● H6 46
Geraldine — ● C7 104
Geraldton, *Australia* — ● B5 102
Geraldton, *Canada* — ● J2 110
Gérardmer — ● B2 56
Gerede — ● H3 82
Gereshk — ● H3 82
Gerik — ● C5 76
Gerlach — ● C2 112
Germantown — ● J4 116
Germany — [A] E6 46
Gerolzhofen — ● F7 46
Gêrzê — ● D2 80
Geser — ● J8 79
Getafe — ● G4 54
Gettysburg — ● F2 114
Gevas — ● K4 84
Gewanē — ● H5 90
Geyik Dağı — ▲ Q8 62
Geyser — ● D1 112
Ghadāmis — ● G2 92
Ghadir Minqār — ∕ E3 86
Ghana — [A] D3 94
Ghanzi — ● C4 98

Gharandal — ● C6 86
Ghardaïa — ● F2 92
Gharyän — ● H2 92
Ghāt — ● B2 90
Ghaziabad — ● C3 80
Ghazn — ● J3 82
Gheorgheni — ● N3 60
Ghotāru — ● B3 80
Giannitsa — ● E4 62
Gibraltar — ● E8 54
Gibson Desert — ⬡ D4 102
Gien — ● H6 52
Gießen — ● D6 46
Gifhorn — ● F4 46
Gifu — ● J6 74
Giglio — ● E6 58
Gijón — ● E1 54
Gila — ∕ E2 118
Gila Bend — ● D2 118
Gilan Garb — ● L6 84
Gilbert Islands — ⬡ H5 100
Gilbués — ● H5 124
Gilf Kebir Plateau — ⬡ E3 90
Gilgandra — ● J6 102
Gilgit — ● B1 80
Gilgit — ∕ K2 82
Gillam — ● N5 108
Gillette — ● E2 112
Gillingham — ● C3 48
Gills Rock — ● C1 114
Gīmbī — ● F2 96
Gīnīr — ● F2 96
Gioia del Colle — ● L8 58
Gioura — ∕ F5 62
Giresun — ● H3 84
Girona — ● N3 54
Gironde — ∕ E8 52
Gisborne — ● G4 104
Gitega — ● D4 96
Giurgiu — ● N6 60
Givet — ● G4 48
Giyon — ● F2 96
Gizhiga — ● U4 70
Gjirokastër — ● C4 62
Gjøvik — ● F6 42
Glacier Peak — ▲ B1 112
Gladstone — ● K4 102
Glan — ∕ C1 79
Glarner Alpen — ▲ D4 56
Glasgow, *U.K* — ● H6 50
Glasgow, *Ky., U.S* — ● C3 114
Glasgow, *Mont., U.S.* — ● E1 112
Glazov — ● J6 68
Gleisdorf — ● L3 56
Glendale, *Ariz., U.S* — ● D2 118
Glendale, *Calif., U.S.* — ● C2 118
Glendive — ● F1 112
Glennallen — ● (1)H3 118
Glenn Innes — ● K5 102
Glens Falls — ● F2 114
Glenwood, *Ark., U.S* — ● B4 114
Glenwood, *N.Mex., U.S.* — ● E2 118
Glenwood Springs — ● E3 112
Gliwice — ● H7 44
Głogów — ● F6 46
Glomma — ∕ F5 42
Glorieuses — ⬡ H7 88
Gloucester — ● K10 50
Głuchołazy — ● G7 44
Gmünd, *Austria* — ● J4 56
Gmünd, *Austria* — ● L2 56
Gmunden — ● J3 56
Gniezno — ● G5 44
Gnjilane — ● D2 62
Goalpara — ● F3 80
Goba — ● F2 96
Gobabis — ● B4 98

Name	Ref	Page
Gobi Desert	C2	72
Goch	J3	48
Godbout	G1	114
Goderich	D2	114
Godhåb = Nuuk	G2	60
Godöllö	W4	108
Goes	F3	48
Gogama	D1	114
Goiânia	H7	124
Goiás	G6	124
Goiás	G7	124
Gökçeada	E4	62
Gökova Körfezi	K8	62
Goksun	G5	84
Golan Heights	C3	86
Golbåf	G2	87
Gôlbasi	G5	84
Gol'chikha	Q3	68
Goldap	M3	44
Gold Coast	K5	102
Golden Bay	D5	104
Goldendale	B1	112
Goldsboro	E3	114
Goleniów	D4	44
Golestānak	F1	87
Golfe d'Ajaccio	C7	58
Golfe de Gabès	H2	92
Golfe de Sagone	C6	58
Golfe de Saint-Malo	C5	52
Golfe de Tunis	E11	58
Golfe de Valinco	C7	58
Golfe du Lion	J10	52
Golfo de Almería	H8	54
Golfo de Cádiz	C7	54
Golfo de California	B3	120
Golfo de Corcovado	F7	126
Golfo de Guayaquil	A4	124
Golfo de Honduras	G5	120
Golfo del Darién	B2	124
Golfo de los Mosquitos	J7	54
Golfo de Mazarrón	H4	54
Golfo de Panamá	J7	120
Golfo de San Jorge	H8	126
Golfo de Santa Clara	D2	118
Golfo de Tehuantepec	E5	120
Golfo de València	L5	54
Golfo de Venezuela	C1	124
Golfo di Catánia	K11	58
Golfo di Gaeta	H7	58
Golfo di Gela	J11	58
Golfo di Génova	C4	58
Golfo di Manfredonia	L7	58
Golfo di Oristano	C9	58
Golfo di Orosei	D8	58
Golfo di Policastro	K9	58
Golfo di Salerno	J8	58
Golfo di Sant'Eufemia	K10	58
Golfo di Squillace	L10	58
Golfo di Táranto	L8	58
Golfo di Trieste	J5	58
Golfo San Matías	J6	126
Goma	D4	96
Gombe	G2	94
Gombi	G2	94
Gómez Palacio	F3	118
Gonder	G5	90
Gondia	D4	80
Gönen	E5	62
Gongga Shan	C5	72
Gonghe	C3	72
Gongliu	Q9	68
Gongpoquan	B2	72
Gongshan	B1	76
Goodland	F3	112
Goolgowi	J6	102
Goomalling	C6	102
Goondiwindi	K5	102
Goose Lake	B2	112
Göppingen	E2	56
Gora Bazardyuzi	H5	84
Gora Kamen	S4	68
Gorakhpur	D3	80
Gora Ledyanaya	W4	70
Gora Pobeda	R4	70
Gora Yenashimskiy Polkan	S6	68
Goražde	F6	60
Gore	B8	104
Gorgān	F2	82
Gorgona	E7	56
Gori	L2	84
Gorinchem	H3	48
Goris	M4	84
Gorizia	J5	56
Gorki	N1	64
Gorlice	L8	44
Görlitz	D6	44
Gorna Oryakhovitsa	N6	60
Gorno-Altaysk	R7	68
Gorodets	H3	64
Gory Belukha	R8	68
Gory Ulutau	N5	64
Gorzów Wielkopolski	E5	44
Goslar	F5	46
Gospić	K4	58
Gostivar	C3	62
Göteborg	F8	42
Gotha	F6	46
Gothèye	E2	94
Gotō-rettō	E7	74
Gotska Sandön	K7	42
Göttingen	E5	46
Gough Island	B10	88
Goundam	E5	92
Gourdon	E4	52
Gournay-en-Bray	D5	48
Governador Valadares	J7	124
Governor's Harbour	F4	116
Goya	K4	126
Gozo = Gwardex	J12	58
Graaff-Reinet	C6	98
Gračac	L6	56
Gračanica	F5	60
Grafton, Australia	K5	102
Grafton, U.S.	G1	112
Grajaú	H5	124
Grajewo	M4	44
Gram	E1	46
Grampian Mountains	H5	50
Granada, Nicaragua	G6	120
Granada, Spain	G7	54
Granby	F1	114
Gran Canaria	B3	92
Gran Bahama	B4	116
Grand Ballon	J2	52
Grand Bank	V7	108
Grand Canyon	D3	112
Grande	J6	124
Grande Prairie	H5	108
Grand Erg de Bilma	H5	92
Grand Erg Occidental	E3	92
Grand Erg Oriental	F3	92
Grand Falls, N.B., Canada	G1	114
Grand Falls, Nfld., Canada	V7	108
Grand Forks, Canada	C2	110
Grand Forks, U.S.	G1	112
Grand Island	G2	112
Grand Junction	E3	112
Grand Marais, Mich., U.S.	C1	114
Grand Marais, Minn., U.S.	B1	114
Grand-Mère	F1	114
Grândola	B6	54
Grand Portage	C1	114
Grand Rapids, Canada	M6	108
Grand Rapids, Mich., U.S.	C2	114
Grand Rapids, Minn., U.S.	B1	114
Grand Teton	D2	112
Gran Paradiso	C5	56
Grants	E1	118
Grants Pass	B2	112
Granville	D5	52
Gräsö	K6	42
Grasse	B7	56
Gravelines	E3	48
Gravesend	C3	48
Gravina in Puglia	L8	58
Grayling	D2	114
Grays	C3	48
Grayville	C3	114
Graz	L3	56
Great Abaco	F4	116
Great Artesian Basin	H4	102
Great Australian Bight	E6	102
Great Bahama Bank	J4	120
Great Barrier Island	E3	104
Great Barrier Reef	J2	102
Great Basin	G1	118
Great Bend	G1	118
Great Dividing Range	J4	102
Greater Antilles	J5	120
Great Exhibition Bay	L7	104
Great Exuma	D1	116
Great Falls	D1	112
Great Inagua	K4	120
Great Karoo	C6	98
Great Nicobar	F7	80
Great Ouse	N9	50
Great Plains	F2	112
Great Rift Valley	E5	96
Great Salt Lake	D2	112
Great Salt Lake Desert	D2	112
Great Sand Sea	D2	92
Great Sandy Desert	D4	102
Great Slave Lake	N3	106
Great Victoria Desert	E5	102
Great Wall	C3	72
Great Yarmouth	P9	50
Greece	D5	62
Greeley	F2	112
Green	D3	112
Green Bay	C2	114
Greenland	G2	108
Greenland Sea	B2	106
Greenock	H6	50
Green River, Wyo., U.S.	E2	112
Green River, Ut., U.S.	D3	112
Greensboro	E2	114
Greensburg, Ind., U.S.	D2	114
Greensburg, Pa., U.S.	E2	114
Greenvale	J3	102
Greenville, Liberia	C3	94
Greenville, Fla., U.S.	E3	114
Greenville, Miss., U.S.	C3	114
Greenville, N.C., U.S.	E3	114
Greenville, S.C., U.S.	E3	114
Greenwood, Miss., U.S.	C3	114
Greenwood, S.C., U.S.	E3	114
Gregory	G2	112
Greifswald	J2	44
Greifswalder Bodden	J2	44
Greiz	H6	46
Grenada	E12	120
Grenoble	L8	52
Greve in Chianti	G7	56
Greven	K2	48
Grevena	D4	62
Greybull	E2	112
Greymouth	C5	104
Grey Range	H5	102

Name	Grid	Page
Grigoriopol	S2	60
Grimma	H5	46
Grimmen	J2	46
Grimsby	M8	50
Grimsey	(1)D1	42
Grímsvötn	(1)E2	42
Grindsted	E9	42
Grodzisk Wielkopolski	F5	44
Gronau	C4	46
Groningen	B3	46
Groote Eylandt	G2	102
Grootfontein	B3	98
Großer Arber	J7	46
Grosser Beerberg	F6	46
Grosseto	F6	58
Groß-Gerau	D7	46
Großglockner	H3	56
Groswater Bay	V6	108
Grozny	L2	84
Grudovo	K2	62
Grudziądz	H4	44
Gryazovets	H3	64
Gryfice	E4	44
Grytviken	P9	126
Gstaad	C4	56
Guadalajara, Mexico	D4	120
Guadalajara, Spain	G4	54
Guadalcanal	F7	100
Guadalquivir	E7	54
Guadalupe	E3	120
Guadalupe	A3	120
Guadeloupe	E2	122
Guadiana	C7	54
Guadix	G7	54
Guajará Mirim	D6	124
Guam	E4	100
Guanambi	J6	124
Guangshui	E4	72
Guangyuan	D4	72
Guangzhou	E2	76
Guantánamo	J4	120
Guanyun	F4	72
Guapore	C4	54
Guarda	C4	54
Guasave	E6	110
Guatemala	F5	120
Guatemala	F6	120
Guaviare	D3	124
Guayaquil	B4	124
Guaymas	D3	118
Guba, Democratic Republic of Congo	D6	96
Guba, Ethiopia	G5	90
Guba Buorkhaya	N2	70
Guban	G2	96
Gúbbio	H7	56
Gubin	D6	44
Gudbransdalen	E6	42
Gudermes	M2	84
Gudvangen	B7	52
Guéret	B7	52
Guernsey	F2	112
Guernsey	C4	57
Guerrero Negro	D3	118
Gugë	F2	96
Gúh Kúh	G4	82
Guiana	L7	120
Guiana Highlands	F3	124
Guider	G3	94
Guiglo	C3	94
Guildford	M10	50
Guilianova	H6	58
Guilin	E1	76
Guillaumes	B6	56
Guillestre	B6	56
Guimarães	B3	54
Guinea	B2	94
Guinea-Bissau	A2	94
Güines	H4	120
Guingamp	B5	52
Güira	E1	124
Guiyang	D5	72
Gujarat	B2	80
Gulbarga	C5	80
Gulbene	P8	42
Gulf of Aden	E7	82
Gulf of Alaska	(1)H4	118
Gulf of Aqaba	C4	86
Gulf of Boothia	N2	108
Gulf of Bothnia	K6	42
Gulf of Carpentaria	G2	102
Gulf of Finland	M7	42
Gulf of Gdansk	H3	44
Gulf of Guinea	D4	94
Gulf of Mannar	C7	80
Gulf of Martaban	B3	76
Gulf of Mexico	F3	120
Gulf of Oman	G4	87
Gulf of Riga	M8	42
Gulf of St. Lawrence	U7	108
Gulf of Thailand	C4	76
Gulf of Tongking	D3	76
Gulf of Venice	H5	56
Gulfport	D3	116
Gulu	E3	96
Gülübovo	H2	62
Gümüshane	H3	84
Guna	C4	80
Guna Terara	G5	90
Gungu	B5	96
Gunnbjørns Fjeld	(1)U2	128
Gunnedah	K6	102
Gunnison	E3	112
Gunong Kinabalu	F1	78
Gunong Korbu	C3	78
Gunong Kerinci	C3	78
Gunong Kwoka	D3	79
Gunong Leuser	C3	78
Gunong Mekongga	B3	79
Gunong Mulu	E2	78
Gunungsitoli	B2	78
Günzburg	F2	56
Gunzenhausen	F7	46
Gürün	G4	84
Gurupi	H4	124
Gusau	F2	94
Gusev	M3	44
Gushgy	H2	82
Güssing	M3	56
Güstrow	B4	44
Gütersloh	D5	46
Guthrie, Okla., U.S.	G3	112
Guthrie, Tex., U.S	F2	118
Guwahati	F3	80
Guyana	F2	124
Guymon	F1	118
Guyuan	D3	72
Gwadar	H4	82
Gwalior	C3	80
Gwanda	D4	98
Gwardejsk	L3	44
Gwardafuy	H4	82
Gweru	D3	98
Gyangzê	E3	80
Gyaring Hu	B4	72
Gydanskiy Poluostrov	P3	68
Gympie	K5	102
Gyomaendröd	H3	60
Gyöngyös	G2	60
Györ	E2	60
Gypsumville	M6	108
Gyula	J3	60
Gyumri	K3	84

H

Name	Grid	Page
Haapajärvi	N5	42
Haapsalu	M7	42
Haar	G2	56
Haarlem	G2	48
Haast	B6	104
Habbán	E7	82
Habirag	F2	72
Habomai-Shoto	R8	70
Hachijō-jima	K7	74
Hachinohe	L3	74
Hachiōji	K6	74
Hadadong	Q9	68
Hadejia	G2	94
Hadejia	F2	94
Hadera	B4	86
Haderslev	E1	46
Hadhramaut	E6	82
Haeju	C4	74
Haenam	D6	74
Hafar al Bátin	A2	87
Hafnarfjördur	(1)C2	42
Haft Gel	C1	87
Hagen	K3	48
Hagerstown	E3	114
Haguenau	K6	48
Haicheng	B3	74
Haïl	B4	86
Ha'il = Ḥefa		
Haikou	D4	82
Haïlai	D4	82
Hailar	K7	70
Hailong	C2	74
Hailuoto	N4	42
Hainan	D3	76
Hai Phong	D2	76
Haiti	K5	120
Haiya	G4	90
Hajdúböszörmény	J2	60
Hajdúhadház	J2	60
Hajmah	E7	82
Hajnówka	N5	44
Haka	F4	80
Hakkâri	K5	84
Hakodate	L3	74
Halaib	G3	90
Halba	D2	86
Halberstadt	G5	46
Halifax	U8	108
Hall	G4	48
Hall Beach	Q3	108
Halle	G4	48
Hallein	J3	56
Halls Creek	E3	102
Halmahera	C2	79
Halmahera Sea	C3	79
Halmstad	B1	44
Haltern	K3	48
Hamada	E3	82
Hamadán	E3	82
Hamāh	G6	84
Hamamatsu	J6	74
Hamar	F6	42
Hamatonbetsu	M1	74
Hamburg, Germany	E3	46
Hamburg, U.S.	E2	114
Hämeenlinna	N6	42
Hameln	E4	46
Hamersley Range	B4	102
Hamhüng	D3	74
Hami	S9	68
Hamilton, Bermuda	M2	120
Hamilton, Canada	E2	114

Ilorin	E3	94
Ilwaco	B1	112
Ilych	L2	64
Imabari	G6	74
Imatra	Q6	42
Imeni Polinyosipenko	P6	70
Imese	B3	96
Imī	G2	96
Imisli	N4	84
Immenstadt	F3	56
Imola	G6	56
Imotski	E6	60
Imperatriz	H5	124
Impéria	D7	56
Imperial	F2	112
Impfondo	B3	96
Imphal	F4	80
Inangahua	C5	104
Inanwatan	D3	79
Iñapari	D6	124
Inarijärvi	P2	42
Inca	N5	54
Ince Burun	F2	84
Inch'ŏn	D5	74
Indalsälven	H5	42
India	C4	80
Indiana	J3	110
Indianapolis	D2	116
Indian Ocean	D8	80
Indianola	B2	114
Indiga	J1	64
Indio	C2	118
Indonesia	D3	78
Indore	C4	80
Indramayu	D4	78
Indre	G6	52
Indus	K3	82
Inebolu	E3	84
In Ekker	G4	90
Ineu	J3	60
Ingeniero Jacobacci	H7	126
Ingham	J3	102
Ingolstadt	G2	56
Ingräj Bäzär	E3	80
Ingushetiya	L2	84
Inhambane	F4	98
Inner Hebrides	F5	50
Inner Mongolia = Nei Monggol	E2	72
Innisfail	J3	102
Innsbruck	G3	56
Inongo	B4	96
Inowrocław	H5	44
In Salah	F3	92
Insein	B3	76
Inta	K4	68
Interlaken	C4	56
International Falls	B1	114
Inukjuak	R5	108
Inuvik	(1)L2	118
Invercargill	B8	104
Inverness	H4	50
Ioannina	C5	62
Iola	B2	116
Iona	F5	50
Ionian Sea	B6	62
Ionioi Nísoi	B5	62
Ios	H6	62
Iowa	H3	110
Iowa City	B2	114
Ipatovo	H5	64
Ipiales	B3	124
Ipoh	C2	78
Iporá	G7	124
Ipsala	J4	62
Ipswich	P9	50
Iqaluit	T4	108
Iquique	G3	126
Iquitos	C4	124
Irakleio	H9	62
Iraklion = Irakleio	G4	40
Iran	F3	82
Iranshahr	H4	82
Irapuato	D4	120
Iraq	D3	82
Irbid	C4	86
Irbit	M3	64
Irgiz	M5	64
Iringa	F5	96
Iriri	G4	124
Irish Sea	G8	50
Irkutsk	G6	70
Iron Mountain	C1	114
Ironwood	B1	114
Irrawaddy	F5	80
Irta	J2	64
Irtysh	P3	64
Irtyshsk	P7	68
Irvine	H6	50
Irving	G2	118
Ísafjörður	(1)B1	42
Isahaya	J4	72
Isar	G3	56
Ischia	H8	58
Ise	J6	74
Isel	H4	56
Isère	B5	56
Iserlohn	K3	48
Isernia	J7	58
Isetskoye	N3	64
Ishikari-wan	L2	74
Ishim	N3	64
Ishim	N4	64
Ishinomaki	L4	74
Isiolo	F3	96
Isiro	D3	96
Iskår	M6	60
Iskenderun	G5	84
Isla Clarión	B5	120
Isla de Alborán	G9	54
Isla de Bioco	F4	94
Isla de Chiloé	G7	126
Isla de Coco	G7	120
Isla de Cozumel	G4	120
Isla de la Juventud	H4	120
Isla de los Estados	J9	126
Isla de Malpelo	A3	124
Isla de Margarita	E1	124
Isla de Providencia	H6	120
Isla de San Andrés	H6	120
Isla Fernandina	(1)A2	124
Isla Grande de Tierra del Fuego	H9	126
Isla Isabela	(1)A2	124
Isla La Tortuga	D1	124
Islamabad	B2	80
Isla Marchena	(1)A1	124
Island Lake	M6	108
Isla San Benedicto	B5	120
Isla San Cristóbal	(1)B2	124
Isla San Salvador	(1)A2	124
Isla Santa Cruz	(1)A2	124
Isla Santa Maria	(1)A2	124
Islas Baleares	N5	54
Islas Canarias	B3	92
Islas Canarias	A3	88
Islas Columbretes	L5	54
Islas de la Bahía	G5	120
Islas de los Desventurados	E4	126
Islas Galápagos	(1)B1	124
Islas Juan Fernández	E5	126
Islas Los Roques	D1	124
Islas Marías	C4	120
Isla Socorro	B5	120
Islas Revillagigedo	B5	12
Islas Wellington	F8	12
Islay	F6	5
Isle	F8	5
Isle	H7	5
Isle of Man	H7	5
Isle of Wight	L11	5
Isle Royale	C1	11
Isles of Scilly	F12	5
Ismâ'îlîya	F1	9
Isna	F2	9
Isoka	E2	9
Isola di Pantelleria	G12	5
Isole Égadi	F11	5
Isole Lípari	J10	5
Isole Ponziane	H8	5
Isole Trémiti	K6	5
Isparta	N7	6
Íspica	J12	5
Israel	B5	8
Issoire	J8	5
Issoudun	H7	5
Istanbul	C3	8
Istanbul Boğazı	C3	8
Istiaía	F6	6
Istra	J5	5
Istres	K10	5
Itabuna	K6	12
Itacoatiara	F4	12
Itaituba	F4	12
Itajaí	M4	12
Italy	D3	5
Itanagar	F3	8
Itapicuru	K4	12
Itarsi	C4	8
Ithaca	E2	11
Itháki	C6	6
Itumbiara	H7	12
Ituri	D3	9
Itzehoe	E3	4
Ivalo	P2	4
Ivangrad	G6	6
Ivanhoe, Australia	H6	10
Ivanhoe, U.S.	A2	11
Ivano-Frankivs'k	D5	6
Ivanovo	H3	6
Ivdel'	M2	6
Ivittuut	X4	10
Ivosjön	D1	4
Ivrea	C5	5
Ivujivik	R4	10
Iwaki	L5	7
Iwaki	L2	7
Iwamizawa	L2	7
Iwo	E3	9
Izhevsk	K3	6
Izhma	K1	6
Izki	G5	8
Izmayil	R4	6
Izmir	B4	8
Izmir Körfezi	J6	6
Iznik	C3	8
Iznik Gölü	C3	8
Izra'	D4	8
Izumo	G6	7
Izu-shotō	K6	7

J

Jabal ad Durüz	D4	8
Jabal Akhdar	G5	8
Jabal al Nusayrïyah	D1	8
Jabal an Nabî Shu'ayb	H4	9
Jabal Ash Sham	G5	8
Jabalpur	C4	8
Jabal Shammar	G2	9
Jabal Thamar	J5	9
Jabiru	F2	10

INDEX

Name	Grid	Page
Jablah ●	C1	86
Jaca ●	K2	54
Jackman ●	F1	114
Jacksboro ●	B3	116
Jackson, Miss., U.S. □	C3	116
Jackson, Oh., U.S. ●	E2	116
Jackson, Tenn., U.S. ●	D2	116
Jackson Head ☒	B6	104
Jacksonville, Fla., U.S. ●	E5	116
Jacksonville, Ill., U.S. ●	B3	114
Jacksonville, N.C., U.S. ●	B3	116
Jacobabad ●	A3	80
Jacobina ●	J6	124
Jacupiranga ●	M3	126
Jadebusen ►	D3	46
Jaén ●	B5	124
Jaffna ●	D7	80
Jagdalpur ●	D5	80
Jagst ⌒	C1	46
Jahrom ●	E2	87
Jaipur ●	C3	80
Jaisalmer ●	B3	80
Jajce ●	E5	60
Jakarta ●		
Jakobshavn = Iluissat ●	W3	108
Jakobstad ●	M5	42
Jalalabad ●	B2	80
Jalandhar ●	C2	80
Jalgaon ●	C4	80
Jalingo ●	G3	94
Jalna ●	C5	80
Jalpaiguri ●	E3	80
Jalula ●	L6	84
Jamaica ▲	H5	120
Jambi ●	C3	78
James Bay ►	G2	112
Jamestown, N.Y., U.S. ●	E2	114
Jamestown, N.D., U.S. ●	G1	112
Jammu ●	B2	80
Jammu and Kashmir ☒	C2	80
Jamnagar ●	B4	80
Jamsa ●	N6	42
Jamshedpur ●	E4	80
Janakpur ●	E3	80
Jandaq ●	F3	82
Jane Peak ▲	B7	104
Janesville ●	C2	114
Jan Mayen ☒	C2	106
Janow Lubelski ●	M7	44
Japan ▲	L5	74
Japan Trench ☒	F2	100
Japurá ⌒	D4	124
Jarash ●	C4	86
Jaroslaw ●	M7	44
Jarpen ●	G5	42
Jarvis ●	K6	100
Jask ●	G4	87
Jasper ●	E3	116
Jastrebarsko ●	L5	56
Jaszbereny ●	G2	60
Jatai ●	G7	124
Jaunpur ●	D3	80
Java = Jawa ☒	E4	78
Jawa ☒	E4	78
Jawhar ●	H3	96
Jayapura ●	F3	79
Jazirat Farasan ☒	H4	90
Jazirat Bubiyan ●	C2	87
Jazireye Khark ☒	D2	87
Jebel Bou Naceur ▲	E2	92
Jebel Toubkal ▲	D2	92
Jebba ●	E3	94
Jebel el Ata'ita ▲	C6	86
Jebel el Batra ▲	C7	86
Jebel-esh Sharqi ►	C3	86
Jebel Gimbala ▲	D5	90
Jebel Ithriyat ▲	D6	86
Jebel Liban ►	C3	86
Jebel Mubrak ▲	C6	86
Jebel Ram ▲	C7	86
Jebel Uweinat ▲	E3	90
Jedda = Jiddah ●	C5	82
Jedrzejow ●	K7	44
Jega ●	E2	94
Jekabpils ●	N8	42
Jelgava ●	M8	42
Jena ●	G6	46
Jequie ●	J6	124
Jerez de la Frontera ●	D8	54
Jerez de los Caballeros ●	D6	54
Jericho ●	C5	86
Jersey ☒	C4	52
Jerusalem = Yerushalayim ●	C5	86
Jesenice ●	B3	60
Jesenik ●	G7	44
Jesi ●	E2	56
Jesup ●	E3	116
Jeziora Sniardwy ●	D4	44
Jezioro Sniardwy ●	L4	44
Jhang Maghiana ●	B2	80
Jhansi ●	C3	80
Jhelum ●	B2	80
Jialing Jiang ⌒	D4	72
Jiamusi ●	J1	72
Ji'an ●	E5	72
Jiangling ●	E4	72
Jiangmen ●	E6	72
Jiaozou ●	E3	72
Jiayuguan ●	B3	72
Jiddah ●	C5	82
Jiesjavrre ●	N2	42
Jihlava ●	E8	44
Jilib ●	G3	96
Jilin ●	D2	72
Jima ●	F2	96
Jimbolia ●	H4	60
Jiménez ●	F3	118
Jinan ●	F3	72
Jinchang ●	C3	72
Jincheng ●	E3	72
Jingdezhen ●	F5	72
Jinggu ●	C6	72
Jinghe ●	Q9	68
Jinghong ●	C6	72
Jingmen ●	E4	72
Jingxi ●	D6	72
Jinhua ●	F5	72
Jining, China ●	E2	72
Jining, China ●	F3	72
Jinja ●	E3	96
Jinsha ●	E5	72
Jinsha ⌒	C5	72
Jinshi ●	E5	72
Jinta ●	B2	72
Jinxi ●	G2	72
Jinxi ●	G2	72
Jinzhou ●	G2	72
Jiroft ●	G2	87
Jishou ●	D5	72
Jiu ⌒	L4	60
Jiujiang ●	F5	72
Jixi ●	F1	74
Jizan ●	H4	90
J. J. Castelli ●	D4	124
João Pessoa ●	L5	124
Jodar ●	G7	54
Jodhpur ●	B3	80
Joensuu ●	E2	64
Joetsu ●	K5	74
Jogeva ●	P7	42
Johannesburg □	D5	98
John Day ⌒	C2	112
John o' Groats ●	J3	50
Johnson ●	A2	116
Johnston Island ☒	J4	100
Johor Bahru ●	C2	78
Joigny ●	J5	52
Joinville ●	M4	126
Jokkmokk ●	K3	42
Jolfa ●	L4	84
Joliet ●	J3	110
Joliette ●	F1	114
Jolo ●	B1	79
Jonava ●	P2	44
Jonesboro ●	B3	114
Jonglei Canal ⌒	E2	96
Jonkoping ●	H8	42
Jonquiere ●	F1	114
Joplin ●	C2	116
Jordan ▲ A	D5	86
Jordan ⌒	E1	112
Jorhat ●	F3	80
Jos ●	F3	94
Jose de San Martin ●	G7	126
Joseph Bonaparte Gulf ►	E2	102
Jounie ●	C2	86
Juan de Nova ☒	G3	98
Juàzeiro do Norte ●	K5	124
Juba ●	E3	96
Jubba ⌒	G3	96
Jucar ⌒	J5	54
Juchitan ●	F5	120
Judenburg ●	K3	56
Juist ●	B3	46
Juiz de Fora ●	N3	126
Julesburg ●	F2	112
Juliaca ●	C7	124
Juliana Top ▲	F3	124
Jülich ●	J4	48
Jumilla ●	J6	54
Junction City ●	B2	116
Juneau □	(1)L4	118
Jungfrau ▲	C4	56
Junggar Pendi ►	R8	68
Jun Xian ●	E4	72
Jura ►	B4	56
Jura ▲	G5	50
Jurbarkas ●	M2	44
Jurf ed Darawish ●	C6	86
Jürmala ●	M8	42
Jürmala ●	D3	64
Jutai ⌒	D5	124
Ju Xian ●	F3	72
Jüyom ●	F2	87
Jylland ►	E8	42
Jyvaskyla ●	E2	64
Jyväskylä ●	N5	42

K

Name	Grid	Page
K2 ▲	C1	80
Kaarta ☒	C6	92
Kabaena ☒	B4	79
Kabala ●	B3	94
Kabale ●	E4	96
Kabalo ●	D5	96
Kabardino-Balkariya ☒	K2	84
Kabongo ●	D5	96
Kabul ●	J3	82
Kabwe ●	D2	98
Kachikattsu ●	M4	70
Kachug ●	H6	70
Kadama ☒	B6	80
Kadañ ●	C7	44
Kadinhani ●	Q6	62
Kadirli ●	G5	84
Kadoka ●	F2	112
Kadoma ●	D3	98
Kadugli ●	E5	90

Name		Grid	Page	Name		Grid	Page	Name		Grid	Page
Kaduna	•	F2	94	Kamina	•	C5	96	Karasuk	•	P7	
Kaédi	•	C5	92	Kamloops	•	G6	108	Karatobe	•	K5	
Kaesŏng	•	D5	74	Kampala	•	E3	96	Karaton	•	K5	
Kaffrine	•	A2	94	Kampen	•	H2	48	Karbalā'	•	D3	
Kåfjord	•	N1	42	Kampong Cham	•	D4	76	Karcag	•	H2	
Kafr el Sheikh	•	F1	90	Kam'yanets'-Podil's'kyy	•	E5	64	Karditsa	•	D5	
Kafue	⟋	D3	98	Kamyshin	•	J4	64	Kareliya	▨	R4	
Kagoshima	•	F8	74	Kananga	•	C5	96	Karepino	•	L2	
Kahemba	•	B5	96	Kanazawa	•	J5	74	Karesuando	•	M2	
Kahnûj	•	G3	87	Kanbalu	•	G4	80	Kargalinskaya	•	M2	
Kahraman Maraş	•	G5	84	Kanchipuram	•	C6	80	Kargasok	•	Q6	
Kaifeng	•	E4	72	Kandahār	•	J3	82	Kargopol'	•	G2	
Kaikohe	•	D2	104	Kandalaksha	•	S3	42	Kariba	•	D3	
Kaikoura	•	D6	104	Kandalakshskiy Zaliv	►	F1	64	Kariba Dam	◉	D3	
Kailua	•	(2)D2	118	Kandi	•	E2	94	Karibib	•	B4	
Kailua Kona	•	(2)E4	118	Kandira	•	N3	62	Karimata	▨	D3	
Kaimana	•	D3	79	Kandy	•	D7	80	Karimnagar	•	C5	
Käina	•	M7	42	Kangaatsiaq	•	W3	108	Karkaralinsk	•	P8	
Kainji Reservoir	⟋	E2	94	Kangal	•	G4	84	Karlik Shan	▲	A2	
Kaipara Harbour	•	D3	104	Kangān	•	E3	87	Karlovac	•	C4	
Kairouan	•	H1	92	Kangaroo Island	▨	G7	102	Karlovo	•	G2	
Kaiserslautern	•	C7	46	Kangchenjunga	▲	E3	80	Karlovy Vary	•	H6	
Kaitaia	•	D2	104	Kangetet	•	F3	96	Karlshamn	•	D1	
Kaiyuan	•	C2	76	Kangiqsualujjuaq	•	T5	108	Karlskoga	•	H7	
Kajaani	•	P4	42	Kangmar	•	E3	80	Karlskrona	•	H8	
Kakamega	•	E3	96	Kangnŭng	•	E5	74	Karlsruhe	•	D8	
Kakata	•	B3	94	Kaniama	•	C5	96	Karlstad, Norway	•	G7	
Kakhovs'ke Vodoskhovshche	⟋	F5	64	Kankakee	•	C2	114	Karlstad, U.S.	•	A1	11
Käkinäda	•	D5	80	Kankan	•	C2	94	Karlstadt	•	E7	
Kalabagh	•	B2	80	Kankossa	•	C5	92	Karmay	⟋	F4	
Kalabahi	•	B4	79	Kano	•	F2	94	Karnafuli Reservoir	⟋	F4	
Kalach	•	H4	64	Kanoya	•	F8	74	Karnal	•	C3	
Kalach-na-Donu	•	H5	64	Kanpur	•	D3	80	Karnische Alpen	▲	H4	
Kalahari Desert	▨	C4	98	Kansas	▨	A2	116	Karonga	•	E5	
Kalakan	•	K5	70	Kansas	⟋	B2	116	Karpathos	•	K9	
Kalamata	•	E7	62	Kansas City, Kans., U.S.	•	C2	116	Karpathos	▨	K9	
Kalamazoo	•	C2	114	Kansas City, Mo., U.S.	•	C2	116	Karrabük	•	E3	
Kalaotoa	▨	B4	79	Kansk	•	T6	68	Kars	•	K3	
Kalaupapa	•	(2)E2	118	Kao-Hsiung	•	F6	72	Karshi	•	J2	
Kalavryta	•	E6	62	Kaolack	•	B6	92	Karskoye More	▨	L3	
Kalemie	•	D5	96	Kaoma	•	C2	98	Kartaly	•	M4	
Kalevala	•	R4	42	Kapanga	•	C5	96	Karufa	•	D3	
Kalewa	•	F4	80	Kap Arkona	►	C3	44	Karumba	•	H3	1
Kalgoorlie	•	D6	102	Kapchagay	•	P9	68	Karvina	•	H8	
Kalibo	•	G4	76	Kap Farvel = Uummannarsuaq	►	Y5	108	Karwar	•	B6	
Kalima	•	D4	96	Kapit	•	E2	78	Karystos	•	G6	
Kalimantan	•	E2	78	Kapoeta	•	E3	96	Kasai	⟋	B4	
Kaliningrad	•	K3	44	Kaposvár	•	E3	60	Kasaji	•	C2	
Kaliningradskij Zaliv	⟋	J3	44	Kapsan	•	E3	74	Kasama	•	E2	
Kalispell	•	D1	112	Kapuskasing	•	K2	110	Kasenga	•	D2	
Kalisz	•	H6	44	Kapuvár	•	E2	60	Käshän	•	F3	
Kalixälven	⟋	M3	42	Kara	⟋	M4	68	Kashi	•	L2	
Kalkan	•	M8	62	Kara, Russia	•	M4	68	Kasimov	•	H4	
Kallavesi	⟋	P5	42	Kara, Togo	•	E3	94	Kasli	•	M3	
Kallsjön	⟋	G5	42	Kara-Balta	•	N9	68	Kasongo	•	D4	
Kalmar	•	J8	42	Karabutak	•	M5	64	Kasos	▨	K9	
Kalmykiya	▨	M1	84	Karacabey	•	L4	62	Kaspiysk	•	M2	
Kalmykovo	•	K5	64	Karacaköy	•	L3	62	Kassala	•	G4	
Kalocsa	•	F3	60	Karacal Tepe	▲	Q8	62	Kassel	•	E5	
Kalpakio	•	C5	62	Karachayevo-Cherkesiya	▨	J2	84	Kastamonu	•	E3	
Kaluga	•	G4	64	Karachi	•	J5	82	Kastelli	•	F9	
Kalyan	•	B5	80	Karaganda	•	N8	68	Kastoria	•	D4	
Kalymnos	•	J8	62	Karaginskiy Zaliv	⟋	V5	70	Kasur	•	B2	
Kalymnos	▨	J7	62	Karaj	•	F2	82	Katerini	•	E4	
Kama	•	D4	96	Karak	•	C5	86	Katha	•	G4	
Kama	⟋	K1	40	Kara-Kala	•	G2	82	Katherine	•	F2	1
Kamaishi	•	L4	74	Karakol	•	P9	68	Kathiawar	•	K5	
Kamande	•	D4	96	Karakoram	▨	L6	66	Kathmandu	■	E3	
Kambo Ho.	▲	A3	94	Karaman	•	E5	84	Katihar	•	E3	
Kamchatka	▨	U6	70	Karamay	•	R8	68	Katonga	⟋	J7	
Kamenka	•	H1	64	Karamea	•	D5	104	Katowice	•	F2	
Kamen'-na-Obi	•	Q7	68	Karamea Bight	►	C5	104	Katsina	•	F2	
Kamensk-Ural'skiy	•	M3	64	Karapınar	•	R7	62	Katsina-Ala	•	F3	
Kamenz	•	D6	44	Kara-Say	•	P9	68	Kattavia	•	K9	
Kamet	▲	C2	80	Karasburg	•	B5	98	Kattegat	⟋	F8	
Kamiiso	•	L3	74	Kara Sea = Karskoye More	▨	L3	68	Kauai	▨	(2)B1	11

oynas	•	J2	64	Küh-e Hormoz	▲	F3	87	Kutu	•	H5	94
ozani	•	D4	62	Küh-e Kalat	▲	G3	82	Kutum	•	D5	90
ozhikode	•	C6	80	Küh-e Kührän	▲	H3	87	Kuujjuaq	•	T5	108
palimé	•	E3	94	Küh-e Masähün	▲	F1	87	Kuujjuarapik	•	R5	108
agujevac	•	H5	60	Küh-e Safidär	▲	E2	87	Kuusamo	•	E1	64
aków	•	J7	44	Küh-e Sahand	▲	M5	84	Kuvango	•	B2	98
aljevo	•	H6	60	Kühestak	▲	G3	87	Kuwait	▲	A B2	87
amators'k	•	G5	64	Küh-e Taftän	▲	H4	82	Kuwait = Al Kuwayt	•	C2	87
amfors	•	J5	42	Kühhä-ye Kashäkerd	▲	G3	87	Kuybyshev	•	P6	68
anj	•	B3	60	Kühhä-ye Zägros	▲	D1	87	Kuygan	•	N8	68
asino	•	J3	68	Kuhmo	•	Q4	42	Kuytun	•	R9	68
ăslava	•	P9	42	Kuito	•	B2	98	Kuznetsk	•	J4	64
aśnik	•	M7	44	Kukës	•	H7	60	Kuzomen'	•	G1	64
asnoarmeysk	•	N4	64	Kula	•	K6	60	Kvaløya	🏝	J2	42
asnodar	•	G5	64	Kulandy	•	K8	68	Kwale	•	F4	96
asnokamensk	•	K6	70	Kuldïga	•	L8	42	Kwangju	•	D6	74
assosel'kup	•	C3	70	Kügera	•	F5	102	Kwango	🌊	B5	96
asnotur'insk	•	M3	64	Kulmbach	•	G6	46	Kwazulu Natal	🌊	E5	98
asnoufimsk	•	L3	64	Külob	•	J2	82	Kwekwe	•	D3	98
asnovishersk	•	L2	64	Kul'sary	•	K5	64	Kwilu	🌊	H5	94
asnoyarsk	•	E5	70	Kulunda	•	P7	68	Kyakhta	•	H6	70
asnoyarskoye Vodokhranilishche	🌊	S6	68	Kuma	🌊	N3	64	Kyancutta	•	G6	102
asnystaw	•	N7	44	Kumamoto	•	F7	74	Kyeburn	•	C7	104
asny Chikoy	•	H6	70	Kumanovo	•	J7	60	Kyklades	🌊	G7	62
asny Yar	•	J5	64	Kumara	•	M6	70	Kyle of Lochalsh	•	G4	50
atovo	•	E2	62	Kumasi	•	D3	94	Kyll	🌊	J4	48
efeld	•	J3	48	Kumba	•	F4	94	Kyllini	•	D7	62
emenchuk	•	F5	64	Kumbakonam	•	C6	80	Kymi	•	G6	62
emmling	•	E2	112	Kumertau	•	L4	64	Kyōto	•	H6	74
etinga	•	L2	56	Kumluca	•	N8	62	Kyparissia	•	D7	62
ishna	🌊	C5	80	Kumo	🌊	G3	94	Kyparissiakos Kolpos	►	C7	62
istiansand	•	E7	42	Kumta	•	B6	80	Kyra Panagia	🌊	G5	62
istianstad	•	H1	84	Kunene	🌊	A3	98	Kyrgyzstan	▲ A	N9	68
istiansund	•	D5	42	Kungrad	•	K9	68	Kyritz	•	H4	46
istinestad	•	L5	42	Kungur	•	K5	64	Kyshtovka	•	P6	68
iti	•	H10	62	Kunming	•	B2	76	Kystatyam	•	L3	70
ázevci	•	D3	60	Kunlun Shan	▲	D1	80	Kythira	•	E8	62
k	•	K5	56	Kunming	•	C6	72	Kythira	🌊	F8	62
k	🌊	K5	56	Kunsan	•	D6	74	Kythnos	🌊	G7	62
onach	•	G6	46	Kuolavarvi	•	Q3	42	Kyūshū-sanchi	▲	F7	74
óng Kaôh Kông	•	C4	76	Kuopio	•	E2	64	Kyustendil	•	E2	62
onotskiy Zaliv	►	U6	70	Kupang	•	B2	102	Kyusyur	•	M2	70
oonstadt	•	D5	98	Kuqa	•	Q9	68	Kyyiv	■	F4	64
oper	•	H3	58	Kura	🌊	L2	84	Kyzyl	□	S7	68
osno	•	L8	44	Kurashiki	•	G6	74	Kyzyl-Dzhar	•	N5	64
uge	•	B3	62	Kurchum	•	Q8	68	Kyzyl-Orda	•	N6	64
ui	•	C4	78	Kürdämir	•	N3	84	Kyzyltu	•	N7	68
umbach	•	F2	56	Kurduvadi	•	C5	80				
ung Thep	•	C4	76	Kürdzhali	•	H3	62	**L**			
uševac	•	J6	60	Kure	•	G6	74				
ym'	•	E1	84	Kuressaare	•	M7	42	Laascaanood	•	H2	96
ymsk	•	H1	84	Kurgal'dzhinskiy	•	N7	68	La Bañeza	•	E2	54
ynica	•	L8	44	Kurgan	•	N3	64	Labé	•	B2	94
ntiko Pelagos	🌊	G9	62	Kuril Islands				Labin	•	K5	56
vvy Rih.	•	F5	64	Kuril'skiye Ostrova	🌊	S7	70	Labrador	🌊	U6	108
ena	🌊	N5	44	Kuril'skiye Ostrova	🌊	S7	70	Labrador City	•	T6	108
ar el Boukhari	•	N9	54	Kuril Trench	V5	66		Labrador Sea	►	V4	108
ala Kerai	•	C1	78	Kurmuk	•	F5	90	Lábrea	•	E5	124
ala Lipis	•	C2	78	Kurnool	•	C5	80	Labuha	•	C3	79
ala Lumpur	•	C2	78	Kurow	•	C7	104	Laç	•	G8	60
ala Terengganu	•	C1	78	Kuršėnai	•	M1	44	Lac à l'Eau Claire	🌊	R5	108
andian	•	C3	78	Kursk	•	G4	64	La Carolina	•	G6	54
antan	🌊	C2	78	Kuršumlija	•	J6	60	Laccadive Islands	🌊	B6	80
acadasi	•	K7	62	Kuruman	•	C5	98	Lac d'Annecy	🌊	B5	56
ševo	•	J5	60	Kurume	•	F7	74	Lac de Bizerte	🌊	D11	58
ching	•	E2	78	Kurumkan	•	J6	70	Lac de Kossou	🌊	C3	94
dat	•	F1	78	Kushimoto	•	H7	74	Lac de Lagdo	🌊	G3	94
dymkar	•	K3	64	Kushiro	•	N2	74	Lac de Neuchâtel	🌊	B4	56
fstein	•	H3	56	Kuskokwim	►	(1)E4	118	Lac de Retenue de la Lufira	🌊	D6	96
hbonän	•	G1	87	Kuskokwim Mountains	▲	(1)F3	118	Lac de St-Croix	🌊	B7	56
hdasht	•	K5	87	Kustanay	•	M4	64	Lac des Bois	🌊	G3	108
he Bül	▲	E1	87	Kütahya	•	C4	84	Lac de Sélingue	🌊	C2	94
he Dinär	▲	D1	87	K'ut'aisi	•	L2	84	Lacepede Bay	►	G7	102
he Fürgun	▲	G3	87	Kutchan	•	M2	74	Lac Fitri	🌊	C5	90
he Hazärän	▲	G2	87	Kutina	•	D4	60	La Charité-sur-Loire	•	J6	52
				Kutno	•	J5	44	Lac La Biche	•	J6	108

Entry	Grid	Page
Lac Léman = Lake Geneva	B4	56
Lac Mai-Ndombe	B4	96
Lac Minto	R5	108
Lac Nzilo	D6	96
Láconi	D9	58
Laconia	F2	114
La Crosse	B2	114
Lac St-Jean	F1	114
Lac St. Joseph	N6	108
Lac Seul	N6	108
Lac Tumba	B4	96
Lacul Brateş	Q4	60
Lacul Razim	R5	60
Lacul Sinoie	R5	60
Ladozhskoye Ozero	F2	64
Ladysmith	D5	98
Ladyzhenka	N4	64
La Esmeralda	D3	124
Læsø	F8	42
Lafayette, Ind., U.S.	C2	114
Lafayette, La., U.S.	C3	116
Lafia	F3	94
La Flèche	E6	52
Laft	F3	87
Lagan		
Lågen	E6	42
Lage's		
Laghouat	F2	92
Lagoa dos Patos	L5	126
Lagoa Mirim	L5	126
Lago de Cahora Bassa	E3	98
Lago de Maracaibo	C2	124
Lago de Nicaragua	G6	120
Lago de Poopó	D7	124
Lago di Como	E4	56
Lago di Garda	F5	56
Lago di Lecco	E5	56
Lago di Lugano	E5	56
Lago d'Iseo	E5	56
Lago di Verano	K7	58
Lago Maggiore	D5	56
Lagos, Nigeria	E3	94
Lagos, Portugal	B7	54
Lago Titicaca	D7	124
Lago Trasimeno	G5	58
La Goulette	E12	58
La Grande	C1	112
La Grange		
Laguna Madre	B4	116
Laguna Mar Chiquita	F7	122
La Habana	H4	120
Lahad Datu	F5	76
Lahat	C3	78
Lāhījān	F2	82
Lahn	C4	48
Lahnstein	K4	48
Lahore	B2	80
Lahr	C2	56
Lahti	N6	42
Lai	B2	96
Lai Chau	C2	76
L'Aigle	C6	48
Laingsburg	C6	98
Lajes	L4	126
La Junta	F3	112
Lake Abbe	G1	96
Lake Abitibi	E1	114
Lake Albert	D3	96
Lake Amadeus	F4	102
Lake Athabasca	K5	108
Lake Balkhash = Balkhash	L5	66
Lake Bangweulu	E2	98
Lake Barlee	C5	102
Lake Benmore	C7	104
Lake Carey	D5	102
Lake Carnegie	D5	102
Lake Chad	B5	90
Lake Charles	C3	116
Lake Chelan	B1	112
Lake Chilwa	F3	98
Lake City	E3	116
Lake Constance	E3	56
Lake Diefenbaker	K6	108
Lake Disappointment	D4	102
Lake District	J7	50
Lake Dojran	E3	62
Lake Edward	D4	96
Lake Erie	D2	114
Lake Eyasi	E4	96
Lake Eyre	D8	100
Lake Eyre Basin	G5	102
Lake Eyre North	G5	102
Lake Eyre South	G5	102
Lake Francis Case	G2	112
Lake Frome	H6	102
Lake Gairdner	G6	102
Lake Geneva	B4	56
Lake Grace	C6	102
Lake Harbour	T4	108
Lake Hudson	B2	116
Lake Huron	D1	114
Lake Kariba	D3	98
Lake Kyoga	D4	96
Lake Ladoga = Ladozhskoye Ozero	F2	64
Lakeland	E4	116
Lake Macdonald	E4	102
Lake Mackay	E4	102
Lake Macleod	B4	102
Lake Manapouri	A7	104
Lake Manitoba	M6	108
Lake Mead	D3	112
Lake Melville	U6	108
Lake Michigan	C2	114
Lake Murray	F4	79
Lake Mweru	D5	96
Lake Nasser	F3	90
Lake Natron	E4	96
Lake Nipigon	P6/7	108
Lake Nipissing	E1	114
Lake Nyasa	E2	98
Lake Oahe	F2	112
Lake of the Woods	B1	114
Lake Okeechobee	E4	116
Lake Onega = Onezhskoye Ozero	H1	40
Lake Ontario	E2	114
Lake Peipus	P7	42
Lake Placid	E4	116
Lake Powell	D3	112
Lake Prespa	D4	62
Lake Pskov	P7	42
Lake Rotorua	F4	104
Lake Rukwa	E5	96
Lake Sakakawea	F1	112
Lake Scutari	G7	60
Lake Simcoe	E2	114
Lake Superior	C1	114
Lake Tahoe	B3	112
Lake Tanganyika	D5	96
Lake Taupo	E4	104
Lake Te Anau	A7	104
Lake Tekapo	C6	104
Lake Tekapo	C6	104
Lake Texoma	B3	116
Lake Torrens	G6	102
Lake Turkana	F3	96
Lake Victoria	E4	96
Lakeview	B2	112
Lake Volta	D3	94
Lake Waikaremoana	F4	104
Lake Wakatipu	B7	10
Lake Wanaka	B7	10
Lake Winnipeg	M6	10
Lake Winnipegosis	L6	10
Lakewood	E3	11
Lake Xau	C4	9
Lakhdaria	P8	5
Lakin	A2	11
Lakonikos Kólpos	E8	6
Lakota	G1	11
Lalín	B2	5
La Línea	E8	5
Lalitpur	C4	8
La Loche	K5	10
La Louvière	G4	4
La Maddalena	D7	5
Lamar	F1	11
Lamard	E3	8
Lambaréné	G5	9
Lamesa	F2	11
Lamia	E6	6
Lamone	G6	5
Lampang	B3	7
Lampasas	G2	11
Lampedusa	H1	5
Lamu	G4	9
Lanai	(2)D3	11
Lancang	B2	7
Lancaster, U.K	K7	5
Lancaster, Mo., U.S	B2	11
Lancaster, Pa., U.S	E2	11
Lancaster Sound	Q2	10
Lanciano	J6	5
Landau, Germany	L5	4
Landau, Germany	H2	5
Landeck	F3	5
Lander	E2	11
Landerneau	A5	5
Land's End	F11	5
Landshut	H2	5
Landskrona	B2	4
Langarüd	N5	8
Langdon	G1	11
Langeland	F2	4
Langenhagen	E4	4
Langeoog	C3	4
Langjökull	(1)C2	4
Langkawi	B5	5
Langon	E9	5
Langøya	H2	4
Langreo	E1	5
Langres	A3	5
Langsa	B6	7
Langtry	F3	11
Lankaran	N4	8
Lannion	B5	5
Lansing	D2	11
Lanya	E2	9
Lanzarote	C3	9
Lanzhou	G3	6
Laoag	G3	7
Lao Cai	C2	7
Laon	F5	4
Laos	C3	7
La Palma	J7	12
La Palma	B3	9
La Paragua	E2	11
La Paz, Bolivia	D7	11
La Paz, Mexico	B4	12
La Pedrera	D4	11
La Pérouse Strait	L1	
La Pesca	B5	11
La Pine	F1	11
La Plata	K5	11
Lappajärvi	M5	
Lappeenranta	Q6	

Name	Coord	Page		Name	Coord	Page		Name	Coord	Page
Lappland	M2	42		Layton	D2	112		Leszno	F6	44
Laptev Sea = More Laptevykh	L1	70		Lazarev	Q6	70		Lethbridge	D1	112
Lapua	M5	42		Lázaro Cárdenas	D5	120		Lethem	F3	124
Lapy	M5	44		Leavenworth	B1	112		Leticia	D4	124
L'Aquila	H3	126		Lebach	J5	48		Letterkenny	E7	50
La Quiaca	H6	58		Lebanon	C3	86		Leutkirch	F3	56
Lär	F3	87		Lebork	G3	44		Levanzo	G10	58
Larache	D1	92		Lebrija	D8	54		Levashi	M2	84
Laramie	E2	112		Lecce	N8	58		Leverkusen	J3	48
Larantuka	B4	79		Lecco	E5	56		Levice	H9	44
Larat	D4	79		Leck	D2	46		Levin	E5	104
Larba	P8	54		Le Creusot	K7	52		Lévis	F1	114
Laredo, Spain	G1	54		Łęczyca	J5	44		Levski	N6	60
Laredo, U.S	G3	118		Leeds	L8	50		Lewis	F3	50
Largo	E4	116		Leer	K1	48		Lewis and Clark Lake	G2	112
L'Ariana	E12	58		Leesburg	E4	116		Lewiston, Id., U.S.	C1	112
La Rioja	H4	126		Leeston	D6	104		Lewiston, Me., U.S.	F2	114
Lárisa	E5	62		Leesville	C3	116		Lewistown, Mont., U.S	E1	112
Larkana	J4	82		Leeuwarden	H1	48		Lewistown, Pa., U.S.	E2	114
Larnaka	A2	86		Leeward Islands	M5	120		Lexington, Ky., U.S.	D3	114
Larne	G7	50		Lefkada	C6	62		Lexington, Nebr., U.S.	G2	112
La Rochelle	D7	52		Lefkada	C6	62		Leyte	G4	76
La Roche-sur-Yon	D7	52		Lefkosia	R9	62		Lezhë	G8	60
La Roda	H5	54		Legaspi	G4	76		Lhasa	F3	80
La Romana	K5	108		Legionowo	K5	44		Lhaza	E3	80
La Ronge	E1	114		Legnago	G5	56		Lhokseumawe	B5	76
La Sarre	E2	118		Legnica	F6	44		Lian Xian	E2	76
Las Cruces	G4	126		Leh	C2	80		Liaocheng	F3	72
La Serena	D9	52		Le Havre	C5	48		Liao He	B3	74
La Seu d'Urgell	M2	54		Leiah	C4	82		Liaoyang	B3	74
La Seyne-sur-Mer	L10	52		Leibnitz	L4	56		Liaoyuan	C2	74
Lashio	B2	76		Leicester	A2	48		Liard River	F5	108
Lashkar Gäh	H3	82		Leiden	G2	48		Libenge	B3	96
Las Lomitas	J3	126		Leie				Liberal	A2	116
Las Palmas	B3	92		Leine				Liberec	E7	44
La Spézia	E6	56		Leipzig	H5	46		Liberia	B3	94
Last Chance	F3	112		Leiyang	E5	72		Libjo	H4	76
Lastovo	D7	60		Lek	G3	48		Libourne	E9	52
Las Vegas, Nev., U.S	C3	112		Lelystad	H2	48		Libreville	F4	94
Las Vegas, N.Mex., U.S	E1	118		Le Mans	F6	52		Libya	C2	90
La Teste	D9	52		Lemberg	D8	46		Libyan Desert	D2	90
Latina	G7	58		Lemesos	Q10	62		Libyan Plateau	E1	90
La Tuque	F1	114		Lemmer	H2	48		Licata	H11	58
Latur	C5	80		Lemmon	F1	112		Lich	D6	46
Latvia	M8	42		Lena	E1	54		Lichinga	F2	98
Lauenburg	F3	46		Lena	L4	70		Lichtenfels	G6	46
Lauf	G7	46		Leninsk-Kuznetskiy	R7	68		Lida	N10	42
Lau Group	J7	100		Lenmalu	D3	79		Lido di Óstia	G7	58
Launceston, Australia	J8	102		Lenne	K3	48		Lidzbark Warmiński	K3	44
Launceston, U.K	H11	50		Lennestadt	L3	48		Liechtenstein	E3	56
La Union	K7	54		Lens	E4	48		Liège	H4	48
Laupheim	E2	56		Lensk	K4	70		Lienz	H5	56
Laura	H3	102		Lenti	M4	56		Liepāja	L1	44
Laurel	D3	116		Lentini	J11	58		Liezen	K3	56
Lausitz	K8	58		Leo	D2	94		Ligurian Sea	D7	56
Lausanne	B4	56		Leoben	L3	56		Lihue	B2	118
Laut, Indonesia	F3	78		León, Mexico	D4	120		Lijiang	C1	76
Laut, Malaysia	D2	78		León, Nicaragua	G6	120		Likasi	D6	96
Laut Banda	C3	79		León, Spain	E2	54		Lille	F4	48
Lauterbach	E4	46		Leonberg	E2	56		Lillehammer	F6	42
Laut Flores	A4	79		Leonora	D5	102		Lilongwe	E2	98
Laut Java	E4	78		Lepsy	P8	68		Lima	G5	76
Laut Molucca	C2	79		Le Puy	J8	52		Lima, Peru	B6	124
Laut Sawu	B4	79		Lér	G3	94		Lima, Mont., U.S	D2	112
Laut Seram	C3	79		Leros	J7	62		Lima, Oh., U.S.	D2	114
Lava	L3	44		Lerwick	L1	50		Limassol = Lemesos	Q10	62
Laval, Canada	F1	114		Lesbos = Lesvos	H5	62		Limerick	D9	50
Laval, France	E5	52		Leshan	C5	72		Limni Trichonida	D6	62
A Vall d'Uixó	K5	54		Leshukonskoye	J2	64		Limni Vegoritis	D4	62
Lavant	K4	56		Leskovac	J7	60		Limni Volvi	F4	62
Lávrio	G7	62		Lesosibirsk	S6	68		Límnos	H5	62
Lawdar	D5	90		Lesotho	D5	98		Limoges	G8	52
Lawrence	B7	104		Les Sables-d'Olonne	D7	52		Limon	F3	112
Lawton	B3	116		Les Sept Îles	B5	52		Limón	H7	120
Laya	L1	64		Lesser Antilles	L6	120		Limoux	H10	52
Laylä	J3	90		Lesser Slave Lake	J5	108		Limpopo	D4	98
				Lesvos	H5	62				

INDEX

Name	Ref	Pg		Name	Ref	Pg		Name	Ref	Pg		Name	Ref	Pg
Limpopo	D4	98		Lobito	A2	98		Losheim	J5	48				
Linares, Chile	G6	126		Locarno	D4	56		Lošinj	K6	56				
Linares, México	G4	118		Lochinver	G3	50		Los Mochis	C3	120				
Linares, Spain	G6	54		Loch Lomond	H5	50		Los Teques	D1	124				
Lincang	C2	76		Loch Ness	H4	50		Lost Trail Pass	D1	112				
Linchuan	F5	72		Lockhart	B4	116		Lotte	K2	48				
Lincoln, U.K	B1	48		Locri	L10	58		Louang Namtha	C2	76				
Lincoln, U.S	G2	112		Lodève	J10	52		Louangphrabang	C3	76				
Lindesnes	D8	42		Lodi	E5	56		Loudomo	C5	94				
Lindi	F6	96		Lodja	C4	96		Loudéac	C5	52				
Lindi	D3	96		Łódź	J6	44		Louga	A1	94				
Lindos	L8	62		Loei	C3	76		Loughborough	A2	48				
Line Islands	L5	100		Lofoten	G3	42		Lough Corrib	C8	50				
Linfen	E3	72		Logan, Ia., U.S	A2	114		Lough Derg	C8	50				
Lingen	K2	48		Logan, N.Mex., U.S	F1	118		Lough Foyle	E6	50				
Lingga	C3	78		Logan, Ut., U.S	D2	112		Lough Mask	C8	50				
Linguere	A1	94		Logansport	C2	114		Lough Neagh	F7	50				
Linhal	G5	72		Logroño	H2	54		Lough Ree	E8	50				
Linhares	J7	124		Loikaw	B3	76		Louisiade Archipelago	K2	102				
Linhe	D2	72		Loir	F6	52		Louisiana	C3	116				
Linjiang	D3	74		Loire	D6	52		Louis Trichardt	D4	98				
Linköping	H7	42		Loja, Ecuador	B4	124		Louisville, Ga., U.S.	E3	116				
Linkou	F1	74		Loja, Spain	F7	54		Louisville, Ky., U.S.	D2	116				
Linosa	G13	58		Lokan tekojärvi	P3	42		Louisville, Miss., U.S.	D3	116				
Lins	M3	126		Lokoja	F3	94		Loukhi	S3	42				
Linton	F1	112		Lolland	G2	46		Loup	G2	112				
Linxia	C3	72		Lollondo	F4	96		Louth	E10	52				
Linyi	F3	72		Lom	L6	60		Louth	J6	102				
Linz	K2	56		Lomami	C4	96		Louviers	D5	48				
Lipari	J10	58		Lomas de Zamora	K5	126		Lovech	M6	60				
Lipari	J10	58		Lomblen	B4	79		Lovell	E2	112				
Lipetsk	G4	64		Lombok	F4	78		Lovelock	C2	112				
Lipno	J5	44		Lomé	E3	94		Lovosice	K6	46				
Lippe	L3	48		Lomela	C4	96		Lowa	D4	96				
Lippstadt	L3	48		Lomela	C4	96		Lowell	F2	114				
Lipu	E2	76		Lommel	H3	48		Lower Hutt	E5	104				
Liqeni i Fierzës	H7	60		Lomonosovka	N4	64		Lower Lough Erne	E7	50				
Lira	E3	96		Lompoc	B2	118		Lowestoft	D2	48				
Lisala	C3	96		Łomża	M4	44		Loyalty Islands	G8	100				
Lisboa	A6	54		London, Canada	D2	114		Loyno	K3	64				
Lisbon = Lisboa	A6	54		London, U.K	B3	48		Loznica	G5	60				
Lisburn	G7	50		London, U.S	E2	116		Lu'an	F4	72				
Liscannor Bay	C9	50		Londonderry	E6	50		Luanda	A5	96				
Lisieux	C5	48		Londrina	L3	126		Luangwa	E3	98				
Liski	G4	64		Long Bay	C2	116		Luangwa	E2	98				
Litang	C5	72		Long Beach	C2	118		Luarca	D1	54				
Litani	G3	124		Longford	E8	50		Luau	C2	98				
Litchfield	B1	114		Long Island	F2	114		Lubango	A2	98				
Lithgow	K6	102		Longmont	E2	112		Lubao	D5	96				
Lithuania	L9	42		Long Prairie	B1	114		Lübben	J5	46				
Little Abaco	F4	116		Longview, Tex., U.S	C3	116		Lubbock	F2	118				
Little Andaman	F6	80		Longview, Wash., U.S	B1	112		Lübeck	F3	46				
Little Barrier Island	E3	104		Longwy	H5	48		Lubilash	C5	96				
Little Current	D1	114		Long Xuyên	D4	76		Lubin	F6	44				
Little Falls	B1	114		Longyan	F1	76		Lublin	M6	44				
Little Karoo	C6	98		Löningen	K2	48		Lubliniec	H7	44				
Little Minch	E4	50		Lons-le-Saunier	A4	56		Lubny	F5	44				
Little Nicobar	F7	80		Lookout Pass	C1	112		Lubudi	D5	96				
Little Ouse	C2	48		Loop Head	B9	50		Lubuklinggau	C3	78				
Little Rock	C3	116		Lopez	G4	76		Lubumbashi	D6	98				
Litvinov	J6	46		Lop Nur	S9	68		Lubutu	D4	96				
Liupanshui	C5	72		Lopphavet	L1	42		Lucala	B5	96				
Liuzhou	D6	72		Loptyuga	J2	64		Lucca	F7	56				
Liverpool	K8	50		Lora del Río	D3	54		Lucena, Philippines	G4	76				
Livingston	D1	112		Lorain	D2	114		Lucena, Spain	F7	54				
Livingstone	D3	98		Loralai	A2	80		Lucero	E2	118				
Livno	E6	60		Lorca	J7	54		Lucira	A2	98				
Livorno	F7	56		Lord Howe Island	L6	102		Luckenwalde	J4	46				
Liwale	F5	96		Lordsburg	E2	118		Lucknow	D3	80				
Lizard Point	G12	50		Loreto	B3	120		Lucusse	C2	98				
Ljubljana	K4	56		Lorient	B6	52		Lüdenscheid	K3	48				
Ljusdal	J6	42		Lörrach	C3	56		Lüderitz	B5	98				
Llanos	C2	124		Lorraine	B6	52		Ludhiana	C2	80				
Lleida	L3	54		Los Alamos	E1	118		Ludington	C2	114				
Llucmajor	N5	54		Los Angeles, Chile	G6	126		Ludlow	C2	118				
Loano	D6	56		Los Angeles, U.S.	C2	118		Ludogori	P6	60				
Lobatse	D5	98						Luduş	M3	60				

Name		Grid	Page
Ludvika	•	H6	42
Ludwigsburg	•	E2	56
Ludwigshafen	•	L5	48
Ludwigslust	•	G3	46
Ludza	•	P8	42
Luebo	•	C5	96
Luena	•	B2	98
Lufeng	•	F2	76
Lufira	∕	D6	96
Lufkin	•	C3	116
Luga	∕	E3	64
Lugano	•	D4	56
Lugenda	∕	F2	98
Lugo	•	G6	56
Lugoj	•	J4	60
Lugovoy	•	N9	68
Luhans'k	•	G5	64
Luilaka	∕	B4	96
Luino	•	C2	56
Lukow	•	M6	44
Lukulu	•	C2	98
Lukuni	•	B5	96
Luleå	•	M4	42
Lüleburgaz	•	K3	60
Lulua	∕	D5	96
Lumbala Kaquengue	•	C2	98
Lumberton	•	F3	116
Lumbrales	•	D2	56
Lumsden	•	B7	104
Lund	•	C2	44
Lundazi	•	E2	98
Lüneburg	∕	F3	46
Lüneburger Heide	⌂	F4	46
Lünen	•	K3	48
Lunéville	∕	C3	56
Lungau	∕	J3	56
Luntai	•	Q9	68
Luohe	•	E4	72
Luoyang	•	E4	72
Lúrio	∕	F2	98
Lusaka	■	C5	96
Lusambo	•	B5	72
Lushui	•	G3	72
Lutherstadt Wittenberg	•	H5	46
Luton	•	B3	48
Luts'k	•	E4	64
Luverne	•	A2	114
Luvua	∕	D5	96
Luwuk	•	B3	79
Luxembourg	A	H5	48
Luxembourg	■	J5	48
Luxeuil-les-Bains	∕	B3	56
Luxor	•	F2	90
Luza	•	J2	64
Luzern	•	D3	56
Luzhou	•	D5	72
Luznice	∕	K1	56
Luzon	•	G2	76
Luzon Strait	⊢	G2	76
L'viv	•	N8	44
Lyapin	•	M2	64
Lynchburg	•	E3	114
Lynn Lake	•	L5	108
Lyon	•	K8	52
Lys	∕	L3	64
Lys'va	•	L3	64
Lysychans'k	•	D6	104
Lyttelton	•	D6	104

M

Name		Grid	Page
Ma'ān	•	C6	86
Maasin	•	G4	76

Name		Grid	Page
Maastricht	•	H4	48
Mabalane	•	E4	98
Mabanza-Ngungu	•	G6	94
Mablethorpe	•	C1	48
Macapá	⌂	G3	124
Macas	•	B4	124
Macau, Brazil	•	K5	124
Macau, China	•	E2	76
Macdonnell Ranges	▲	F4	102
Macedonia	A	C3	62
Maceió	•	K5	124
Macerata	•	J7	56
Machakos	•	F4	96
Machala	•	B4	124
Macheng	•	F4	72
Machilipatnam	•	D5	80
Machiques	•	C1	124
Mack	•	E1	118
Mackay	•	J4	102
Mackay Lake	∕	J4	108
Mackenzie	∕	G4	108
Mackenzie Bay	⊢	D3	108
Mackenzie Mountains	▲	E3	108
Mackinaw City	•	D1	114
Macmillan Pass	∕	F4	108
Macomer	•	C8	58
Macon, Ga., U.S	•	E3	116
Macon, Mo., U.S	•	C2	116
Macuba	•	K7	52
Mädabä	•	C5	86
Madadeni	•	H3	98
Madaoua	•	F2	94
Madeira	∕	E5	124
Madeira	⌂	B2	94
Madikeri	•	C6	80
Madison	•	C2	114
Madison, Minn., U.S	•	A1	114
Madison, S.D., U.S	•	Q2	112
Madiun	•	E4	78
Mado Gashi	•	F3	96
Madoi	•	B4	72
Madona	•	P8	42
Madras = Chennai	•	D6	80
Madre de Dios	∕	C6	124
Madrid	■	G4	54
Madura	•	E4	78
Madurai	•	C6	80
Maebashi	•	K5	74
Mae Hong Son	•	B3	76
Mae Sariang	•	B3	76
Maevatanana	•	H3	98
Mafeteng	•	D5	98
Mafia Island	•	G5	96
Mafraq	•	D4	86
Magadan	•	S5	70
Magadi	•	F4	96
Magdagachi	•	M6	70
Magdalena	∕	C2	124
Magdalena, Bolivia	•	E6	124
Magdalena, Mexico	•	D2	118
Magdalena, U.S	•	E2	118
Magdeburg	•	G4	46
Magelang	•	E4	78
Magerøya	⌂	N1	42
Magnitogorsk	•	L4	64
Magu	•	E4	96
Magwe	•	A2	76
Mahābād	•	L5	84
Mahajanga	•	H3	98
Mahanoro	•	H3	98
Mahasamund	•	D4	80
Mahbubnagar	•	D5	80
Mahé Island	•	(2)C1	98
Mahenge	•	F5	96
Mahesāna	•	B4	80
Mahia Peninsula	•	F4	104
Mahilyow	•	F4	64

Name		Grid	Page
Mahnomen	•	A1	114
Mahón	•	Q5	54
Mahuva	•	K5	82
Maicao	•	C1	124
Maidstone	•	C3	48
Maiduguri	•	G2	94
Mai Gudo	▲	F2	96
Maimédy	•	B6	46
Main	∕	E7	46
Mainburg	•	G2	56
Main-Donau-Kanal	∕	G7	46
Maine	•	G1	114
Maine	⌂	G1	114
Maine Soroa	•	G2	94
Maingkwan	•	B1	76
Mainland, Orkney Is., U.K	⌂	J2	50
Mainland, Shetland Is., U.K	⌂	L1	50
Maintirano	•	G3	98
Mainz	•	D6	46
Maio	⌂	(1)B1	94
Majene	•	A3	79
Majuro	•	H5	100
Makamba	•	D4	96
Makarora	•	B7	104
Makarov	•	Q7	70
Makarska	•	E6	60
Makassar	•	A4	79
Makat	•	K5	64
Makeni	•	B3	94
Makgadikgadi	∕	C4	98
Makhachkala	•	H2	64
Makindu	•	F4	96
Makinsk	•	P4	64
Makiyivka	•	G5	64
Makkah	•	G3	90
Makó	•	H3	60
Makokou	•	G4	94
Makorako	▲	F4	104
Makoua	•	G4	94
Makran	⌂	G4	82
Makumbako	•	E5	96
Makurazaki	•	F8	74
Makurdi	•	F3	94
Makūyeh	•	E2	87
Malabar Coast	⌂	B6	80
Malabo	■	F4	94
Malack	•	F9	44
Malad City	•	D2	112
Maladzyechna	•	E4	64
Málaga	•	F8	54
Malaita	⌂	G6	100
Malakal	•	E2	96
Malamala	•	B3	79
Malang	•	E4	78
Malanje	•	B5	96
Malanville	•	E2	94
Malaryta	•	P6	44
Malatya	•	H4	84
Malawi	A	E2	98
Malaya Vishera	•	F3	64
Malaybalay	•	H5	76
Malay Peninsula	⌂	C6	76
Malaysia	A	C2	78
Malbork	•	J3	44
Maldives	A	B8	80
Male	■	B8	80
Male Atoll	⌂	B8	80
Mali	A	E5	92
Malindi	•	G4	96
Malin Head	⌂	E6	50
Malkara	•	J4	62
Mallaig	•	G4	50
Mallawi	•	F2	90
Mallorca	⌂	P5	54
Malmédy	•	J4	48
Malmö	•	C2	44
Måløy	•	C6	42

INDEX

Malozemel'skaya Tundra .. ◎	K1 64
Malta .... A	J13 58
Malta .... ●	E1 112
Malta Channel	J12 58
Maltahöhe .... ●	B4 98
Malvern .... ●	B4 114
Mama .... ●	J5 70
Mambasa .... ●	D3 96
Mamburao .... ●	G4 76
Mamonovo .... ●	J3 44
Mamoré .... ⌀	D6 124
Mamou .... ●	B2 94
Mamoudzou .... ●	H2 98
Mamuju .... ●	A3 79
Ma'mūl .... ●	G6 82
Mamuno .... ●	C4 98
Man .... ●	C3 94
Manacapuru ...... ●	E4 124
Manacor .... ●	P5 54
Manado .... ●	B2 79
Managua .... ◎	G6 120
Manali .... ●	C2 80
Mananara Avaratra . ●	H3 98
Mananjary .... ●	H4 98
Manaus .... ▫	E4 124
Manavgat .... ●	P8 62
Manbij .... ●	G5 84
Manchester, U.K .. ●	K8 50
Manchester, Ky., U.S .. ●	D3 114
Manchester, Vt., U.S. . ●	F2 114
Mand .... ●	H4 82
Mandalay .... ▪	B2 76
Mandalgovĭ ...... ●	D1 72
Mandan .... ●	F1 112
Mandera .... ●	G3 96
Manding .... ▲	D6 92
Mandla .... ●	D4 80
Mandsaur .... ●	C4 80
Manduria .... ●	C6 102
Mandvi .... ●	M8 58
Mandya .... ●	A4 80
Manfredonia ...... ●	C6 80
Manga .... ◎	K7 58
Mangalia .... ●	G2 94
Mangalia .... ●	R6 60
Mangalore .... ●	B6 80
Mangaweka .... ▲	F4 104
Mangnai .... ●	C3 79
Mangokyo. .... ◎	S10 68
Mangole .... ●	C3 79
Mangonui .... ●	D2 104
Manhattan .... ●	B2 116
Manhuaçu .... ●	J8 124
Mania .... ⌀	H3 98
Manicoré .... ●	E5 124
Maniitsoq .... ●	W3 108
Manila .... ■	G4 76
Manisa .... ●	K6 62
Manitoba .... ▪	M6 108
Manitoulin Island . ◎	D1 114
Manitowoc .... ●	C2 114
Maniwaki .... ●	E1 114
Manizales .... ●	B2 124
Manja .... ●	G4 98
Mankato .... ●	B2 114
Manlleu .... ●	N3 54
Manna .... ●	C3 78
Mannheim .... ●	L5 48
Manokwari .... ●	D3 79
Manono .... ●	D5 96
Manosque .... ●	L10 52
Manp'o .... ●	D3 74
Manresa .... ●	M3 54
Mansa .... ●	D2 98
Mansel Island ... ◎	Q4 108
Mansfield, U.K. ... ●	A1 48
Mansfield, U.S. ... ●	D2 114

Manta .... ●	A4 124
Mantes-la-Jolie ... ●	D5 48
Mántova .... ●	F5 56
Manturovo .... ●	H3 64
Manū .... ●	C6 124
Manujan .... ●	G3 87
Manukau .... ●	E3 104
Manukau Harbour . ►	E3 104
Manyinga .... ●	C2 98
Manyoni .... ●	E5 96
Manzanares ...... ●	G5 54
Manzanillo ...... ●	J4 120
Manzhouli .... ●	K7 70
Mao .... ●	C5 90
Maoming .... ●	E2 76
Mapi .... ●	E4 79
Mapinhane .... ●	F4 98
Maple Creek ..... ●	E2 110
Mapuera .... ⌀	E4 124
Maputo .... ◎	E5 98
Maquela do Zombo . ●	B5 96
Maquinchao ...... ●	H7 126
Maraba .... ●	H5 124
Maracaibo .... ●	C1 124
Maracay .... ●	D1 124
Maradi .... ●	F2 94
Marāgheh .... ●	M5 84
Marand .... ●	L4 84
Maranhão .... ▪	H5 124
Marañón .... ⌀	B4 124
Mārāsesti .... ●	Q4 60
Marathon, Canada . ●	C1 114
Marathon, U.S. ... ●	F2 118
Marbella .... ●	F8 54
Marche .... ▪	H4 48
Marchena .... ●	E7 54
Mardan .... ●	B2 80
Mar del Plata. ... ●	K6 126
Mardin .... ●	J5 84
Mareeba .... ●	J3 102
Marettimo .... ◎	F11 58
Margate .... ●	D3 48
Marghita .... ●	K2 60
Marianas Trench . ◎	E4 100
Marianna .... ●	D3 116
Mariánská Lázně . ●	H7 46
Mariazell .... ●	L3 56
Marîb .... ●	J4 90
Maribor .... ●	L4 56
Maridi .... ●	D2 96
Marie Byrd Land . ◎	(2)FF2 128
Mariehamn .... ●	K6 42
Marienberg ...... ●	J6 46
Mariental .... ●	B4 98
Marietta .... ●	B3 116
Mariinsk .... ●	R6 68
Marijampole ..... ●	N3 44
Marília .... ●	M3 126
Marín .... ●	B2 54
Marinette .... ●	C1 114
Maringá .... ●	L3 126
Marion, Ill., U.S . ●	C3 114
Marion, Ind., U.S . ●	C2 114
Marion, Oh., U.S . ●	D2 114
Maritime Alps ... ▲	C6 56
Mariupol' .... ●	G5 64
Marīvān .... ●	M6 84
Mariy El .... ▪	J3 64
Marjayoûn .... ●	C3 86
Marka .... ●	G3 96
Markam .... ●	B5 72
Markaryd .... ●	C1 44
Markermeer ...... ◢	H2 48
Markham .... ●	E2 114
Markit .... ●	P10 68
Markkleeberg .... ●	H5 46
Markovo .... ●	W4 70

Marktredwitz .... ●	H7 46
Marla .... ●	F5 102
Marle .... ●	F9 52
Marmande .... ●	E7 52
Marmara Adasi ... ◎	K4 62
Marmara Denizi .. ▬	L4 62
Marmaris .... ●	L8 62
Marmolada .... ▲	G4 56
Marne .... ⌀	F5 48
Maroantsetra .... ●	H3 98
Marolambo .... ●	H4 98
Maroni .... ⌀	G3 124
Maroua .... ●	G2 94
Marquesas Islands . ◎	M6 100
Marquette .... ●	C1 114
Marrakech .... ●	D2 92
Marree .... ●	G5 102
Marrupa .... ●	F2 98
Marsa Alam. ..... ●	F2 90
Marsabit .... ●	F3 96
Marsala .... ●	G11 58
Marsberg .... ●	L3 48
Marsden .... ●	J6 102
Marseille .... ●	L10 52
Marshall, Ill., U.S . ●	D2 116
Marshall, Tex., U.S . ●	C3 116
Marshall Islands . A	G4 100
Marshalltown .... ●	B2 114
Marsh Harbour ... ●	F4 116
Marsh Island .... ◎	C4 116
Martapura .... ●	E3 78
Martha .... ⌀	C4 56
Martigues .... ●	L10 52
Martin .... ●	H8 44
Martina Franca . ●	M8 58
Martinique ...... ◎	M6 120
Marton .... ●	E5 104
Martos .... ●	G7 54
Mary .... ●	H2 82
Maryborough .... ●	K5 102
Maryland .... ▪	E3 114
Marysville ...... ●	B2 114
Maryville .... ●	B2 114
Masai Steppe .... ◎	F4 96
Masaka .... ●	E4 96
Masalembu Besar. . ◎	E4 78
Masali .... ●	N4 84
Masan .... ●	E6 74
Masasi .... ●	F6 96
Masbate .... ●	G4 76
Masbate .... ◎	G4 76
Maseru .... ■	D5 98
Mashhad .... ●	G2 82
Masindi .... ●	E3 96
Masĭrah .... ◎	H5 82
Maskanah .... ●	H5 84
Mason .... ●	B3 116
Mason City ...... ●	B2 114
Masqat .... ▪	H5 87
Massa .... ●	F6 56
Massachusetts ... ▪	F2 114
Massachusetts Bay . ►	G2 114
Massafra .... ●	M8 58
Massawa .... ●	G4 90
Massena .... ●	F2 114
Massena .... ●	E6 108
Massif Central .. ▲	H8 52
Massif de l'Air .. ▲	G5 92
Massif des Écrins. ▲	B5 56
Massif du Tsaratanana . ▲	H2 98
Massif Ennedi ... ▲	D4 90
Massinga .... ●	F4 98
Masteksay .... ●	K5 64
Masterton .... ●	E5 104
Mastung .... ●	J4 82
Masvingo .... ●	E4 98
Masyāf .... ●	D1 86
Matadi .... ●	A5 96

Entry	Grid	Page
Matagami	E1	114
Matagorda Island	B4	116
Matam	B1	94
Matamoros	G3	118
Matane	G1	114
Matanzas	K7	110
Matara	D7	80
Mataram	F4	78
Mataranka	F3	102
Mataró	N3	54
Matawai	F4	104
Matehuala	F4	118
Matera	L8	58
Mateszalka	K2	60
Mateur	D11	58
Matheson	D1	114
Mathura	C3	80
Mati	H5	76
Matlock	A1	48
Mato Grosso	F6	124
Mato Grosso	F6	124
Mato Grosso do Sul	F7	124
Matosinhos	B3	54
Matrûh	E1	90
Matsu	G5	72
Matsue	G6	74
Matsumae	L3	74
Matsumoto	J5	74
Matsusaka	J6	74
Matsuyama	C5	74
Matterhorn	C5	56
Maubeuge	F4	48
Maui	(2)F3	118
Maun	C3	98
Maun	K6	56
Mauna Kea	(2)F4	118
Mauna Loa	(2)F4	118
Mauritania	(1)B2	98
Mauritius	C5	52
Mauron	H4	56
Mauthen	A2	76
Mawlaik	D3	78
Maya	K4	120
Mayaguana	H1	96
Maydh	E5	52
Mayenne	E5	52
Maykop	B1	84
Mayn	W4	70
Mayor Island	F3	104
Mayotte	H2	98
Mayskiy	M6	70
Mayya	N4	70
Mazagão	G4	124
Mazagran	K4	52
Mazama	B1	112
Mazamet	H10	52
Mazara del Vallo	G11	58
Mazâr-e Sharîf	J2	82
Mazatlán	C4	120
Mazeikiai	M1	44
Mazomora	F5	96
Mazyr	E4	64
Mazzarino	J11	58
Mbabane	E5	98
Mbaïki	E5	96
Mbale	E5	96
Mbalmayo	G4	94
Mbandaka	B3	96
M'banza Congo	A5	96
Mbarara	E4	96
Mbeya	E5	96
Mbomou	C3	96
Mbour	A2	94
Mbuji-Mayi	C5	96
McAlester	B3	116
McBride	G6	108
McCammon	D2	112
McClintock	N5	108
McClintock Channel	L2	108
McComb	C3	116
McCook	F2	112
McDermitt	C3	116
McGehee	(1)F3	118
McGrath	F1	112
McLaughlin	H5	108
McLennan	B2	116
McPherson	K6	108
Meadow Lake	D2	114
Meaux	E6	48
Mecca = Makkah	G3	90
Mechelen	G3	48
Mecklenburger Bucht	G2	46
Mecula	F2	98
Medak	C5	80
Medan	B2	78
Médéa	N8	54
Medellín	B2	124
Medenine	H2	92
Medford	B2	112
Medgidia	M3	60
Medicine Bow	E2	112
Medicine Hat	J7	108
Medicine Lodge	B2	116
Medina = Al Madînah	G3	90
Medinaceli	H3	54
Medina de Campo	F3	54
Medina Sidonia	E8	54
Mediterranean Sea	E4	40
Mednogorsk	L4	64
Medvezh'yegorsk	F2	64
Meekatharra	C5	102
Meeker	E2	112
Meerut	C3	80
Megara	F6	62
Megisti	M8	62
Mehrân	M7	84
Meiktila	B2	76
Meiningen	F6	46
Meizhou	F2	76
Mejez El Bab	D12	58
Mékambo	G4	94
Mek'elê	G5	90
Meknès	D2	92
Mekong	D4	76
Melaka	C2	78
Melanesia	F5	100
Melbourne, Australia	H7	102
Melbourne, U.S.	E4	116
Melchor de Mencos	G5	120
Melfi	C5	90
Melfi	K8	58
Melilla	H9	54
Melita	F1	112
Melitopol'	G5	64
Melk	L2	56
Melkosopochnik	N8	68
Mělník	K6	46
Melo	L5	126
Melton Mowbray	B2	48
Melun	F5	90
Melut	F2	90
Melville Island, Australia	F2	102
Melville Island, Canada	N2	106
Melville Peninsula	P3	108
Memboro	A4	79
Memmert	J1	48
Memmingen	F3	56
Mempawah	D2	78
Memphis	C3	114
Mena	C3	116
Ménaka	F5	92
Mendawai	E3	78
Mende	J9	52
Mendoza	H5	126
Menemen	K6	62
Menen	F4	48
Menggala	D3	78
Mennonitee	C1	114
Menongue	B2	98
Menorca	Q4	54
Mentok	D3	78
Menyuan	C3	72
Menzel Bourguiba	D11	58
Menzel Temime	E12	58
Meppel	J2	48
Meppen	K2	48
Merano = Merano	G4	56
Meråker	F4	79
Mercato Saraceno	H7	56
Merced	B3	112
Mercedes, Argentina	H5	126
Mercedes, Argentina	K4	126
Mercedes, U.S.	B4	116
Mercedes, Uruguay	K5	126
Mercury Islands	E3	104
Mergenevo	K5	64
Mergui	B4	76
Mergui Archipelago	A4	76
Mérida, Mexico	G4	120
Mérida, Spain	D6	54
Mérida, Venezuela	K7	120
Meridian	D3	116
Meriruma	G3	124
Merowe	F4	90
Merredin	C6	102
Merriman	F2	112
Mers el Kébir	K9	54
Mersin = Icel.	J8	50
Mersin = Içel	S8	62
Merthyr Tydfil	J10	50
Meru	F3	96
Merzifon	F3	84
Mesa	D2	118
Mesa de Yambi	C3	124
Mesagne	M8	58
Mesolóngi	D6	62
Mesopotamia	K6	84
Messina, Italy	K10	58
Messina, South Africa	D4	98
Messini	E7	62
Messiniakós Kólpos	D8	62
Mestre	H5	56
Meta	C2	124
Metairie	J4	126
Metangula	E2	98
Meteor Depth	J19	122
Metković	A1	86
Metlaoui	D6	62
Metlika	D5	62
Metz	J5	48
Metzingen	J5	48
Meulaboh	B2	76
Meuse	G4	48
Mexicali	C2	118
Mexican Hat	E1	118
México	D4	120
México	E5	120
Meymaneh	H2	82
Mezdra	L6	60
Mézen'	H1	64
Mezenskaya Guba	H1	64
Mézőkövesd	H2	60
Mezőtúr	H2	60
Miami	E4	116
Miàndowâb	M5	84

Name		Grid	Page
Miandrivazo	●	H3	98
Mäneh		M5	84
Mianwali	●	B2	80
Manyang		C4	72
Miass	●	M4	64
Michalovce		L9	44
Michigan	ⓐ	C1	114
Michipicoten Island	●	C1	114
Michurinsk	●	H4	64
Micronesia		F4	100
Mid-Atlantic Ridge		G1	122
Middelburg, *Netherlands*	●	F3	48
Middelburg, *South Africa*		D6	98
Middelkerke	●	E3	48
Middle Andaman		A4	76
Middlesboro	●	D3	114
Middlesbrough	●	L7	50
Middletown	●	F2	114
Midland, *Canada*	●	E2	114
Midland, *Mich., U.S*		D2	114
Midland, *Tex., U.S*	●	F2	118
Midway Islands		J3	100
Midwest City	●	B2	116
Midzor		K6	60
Miechów	●	K7	44
Mielec	●	L7	44
Miercurea-Ciuc		N3	60
Mieres	●	E1	54
Miesbach	●	G3	56
M'eso	●	G2	96
Miging		F3	80
Mikhaylovka	●	H4	64
Mikhaylovskiy		P7	68
Mikkeli	●	P6	42
Mikuni-sammyaku		K5	74
Miladhunmadulu Atoll	●	B7	80
Milan = Milano, *Italy*	●		
Milan, *U.S*		D2	116
Milano	●	E5	56
Milas	●	K7	62
Milazzo	●	K10	58
Miles		K5	102
Miles City	●	E1	112
Milford, *Del., U.S*	●	E3	114
Milford, *Ut., U.S*		D3	112
Milford Sound	▲	A7	104
Miliana		N8	54
Millau	●	J9	52
Millbank		G1	112
Millerovo	●	H5	64
Miloro		E5	96
Milos		G8	62
Milton	●	B8	104
Milton Keynes	●	B2	48
Milwaukee	●	C2	114
Mimizan-Plage		D9	52
Mināb		G3	87
Minas Gerais	ⓐ	H7	124
Minas Novas	●	J7	124
Minatitlán		F5	120
Mindanao		G5	76
Mindelheim		F2	56
Mindelo	●	(1)B1	94
Minden	●	L2	48
Mindoro		G4	76
Mindoro Strait		G4	76
Mineola	●	B3	116
Minfeng		Q10	68
Mingäçevir		M3	84
Mingäçevir Su Anbarı	✦	M3	84
Mingulay		D5	50
Minicoy	●	B7	80
Minna	●	F3	94
Minneapolis	●	A1	114
Minnesota	ⓐ		
Miño	✦	C2	54
Minot	●	F1	112

Name		Grid	Page
Minsk	●	E4	64
Minturn	●	E3	112
Minusinsk	●	S7	68
Min Xian		C4	72
Min'yar	●	L3	64
Miquelon		E1	114
Miraflores	●	C3	124
Miranda de Ebro		H2	54
Miranda do Douro		D3	54
Mirandela		C3	54
Mirbāt	●	D6	74
Mirnyy		J4	70
Mirpur Khas	●	A3	80
Mirtoö Pelagos		F7	62
Mirzapur	●	D3	80
Miskolc	●	H1	60
Misoöl		D3	79
Mişrātah	●	C1	90
Mission	●	F12	112
Mississippi	ⓐ	D3	116
Mississippi	✦	D2	116
Mississippi River Delta	▬	D4	116
Missoula	●	D1	112
Missouri	ⓐ	B3	114
Missouri	✦	F1	112
Mistelbach	●	M2	56
Mitchell	●	G2	112
Mithymna		J5	62
Mito	●	L6	74
Mits'iwa		C6	82
Mittellandkanal	✦	K2	48
Mittersill	●	H3	56
Mitú	●	C3	124
Miyake-jima		K6	74
Miyako		L4	74
Miyakonojō		F8	74
Miyazaki		F8	74
Miyoshi		G6	74
Mizan Teferī		F2	96
Mizdah	●	H2	92
Mizen Head	🖫	B10	50
Mizil	●	P4	60
Mizpe Ramon		B6	86
Mjøsa	♪	F6	42
Mkuze		E5	98
Mladá Boleslav	●	D7	44
Mladenovac	●	H5	60
Mława	●	K4	44
Mljet	●	E7	60
Mmabatho	◻	D5	98
Moa	🖫	H2	102
Moanda		G5	94
Moapa	●	D3	112
Moba	●	C3	96
Mobayi-Mbongo	●	B2	96
Moberly	●	B3	114
Mobile	●	D3	116
Moçambique	●	G3	98
Mochudi		D4	98
Mocímboa da Praia		G2	98
Mocuba		F3	98
Modane		B5	56
Módena		F6	56
Modesto	●	B3	112
Mödling	●	M2	56
Modowi		D3	79
Modrıča	●	F5	60
Moenkopi		D1	118
Moffat	●	J6	50
Moffat Peak	▲	B7	104
Mogadishu = Muqdisho	■	H3	96
Mogocha		K6	70
Mogok	●	F7	76
Mohács	●	F4	60
Mohammadia		L9	54
Mohe	●	L6	70

Name		Grid	Page
Mohembo	●	C3	98
Mohoro	●	F5	96
Mohyliv-Podil's'kyy		Q1	60
Moincêr		D2	80
Moineşti	●	P3	60
Mo i Rana		H3	42
Mojave	●	C2	118
Mojave Desert	🖫	C2	118
Mokau		E4	104
Mokolo		G2	94
Mokpo		D6	74
Mola di Bari	●	M7	58
Molat		K6	56
Molde	●	F2	42
Moldova	◼	R2	60
Moldova	✦	P2	60
Moldova Nouă		J5	60
Molepolole		C4	98
Molfetta	●	L7	58
Molina de Aragón		J4	54
Moline	●	B2	114
Moll	✦	A4	56
Mollendo	●	C7	124
Molokai		(2)D2	118
Molopo	✦	C5	98
Molsheim	●	C5	52
Moma	●	F3	98
Mombasa	●	G4	96
Monaca		H2	46
Monaco	A	C7	56
Monaco	■	C7	56
Monbetsu, *Japan*		M1	74
Monbetsu, *Japan*		M2	74
Moncalieri	●	C5	56
Monchegorsk		S3	42
Mönchengladbach	●	J3	48
Monclova		F3	118
Mondoví		C6	56
Mondovì		J5	56
Monforte de Lemos	●	C3	54
Monfredónia	●	K7	58
Monga	●	C3	96
Mongo	●	C5	90
Mongolia	◼	B2	72
Mongonu	●	G2	94
Mongu	●	C3	98
Mong Yai	●	B2	76
Mong Yu	●	B2	76
Monkoto	●	C3	96
Mono Lake		C3	112
Monopoli	●	M8	58
Monor		J10	44
Monowai		A7	104
Monroe, *La., U.S*	●	C3	116
Monroe, *N.C., U.S*	●	E3	116
Monroe, *Wash., U.S*	●	B1	112
Monrovia	■	B3	94
Mons	●	F4	48
Monschau	●	J4	48
Monsélice	●	G5	56
Montabaur	●	K4	48
Montague Island	●	J9	122
Montalbán		K4	54
Montana	ⓐ	E1	112
Montana	●	L6	60
Montargis		G10	52
Mont aux Sources	▲	D5	98
Montbard	●	K6	52
Montbéliard	●	B3	56
Mont Blanc	▲	B5	56
Montblanc	●	M3	54
Mont Cameroun	▲	F4	94
Montceau-les-Mines	●	K7	52
Mont-de-Marsan	●	E10	52
Monte Alegre	●	G4	124
Monte Azul	●	J7	124

Montebelluna . . . . • H5 56
Monte Calvo . . . . • K7 58
Monte Cinto . . . . ▲ C6 58
Montecristo. E6 58
Monte Etna J11 58
Montego Bay J5 120
Montélimar . . . . • K9 52
Monte Limbara . . . . • D8 58
Montemorelos . . . . • B4 116
Monte Namuli . . . . ▲ F3 98
Montenegro = Crna Gora. . ▪ F7 60
Monte Perdino . . . . ▲ L2 54
Monte Pollino . . . . ▲ L9 58
Montepuez . . . . • F2 98
Montepulciano . . . . • F5 58
Montereau-faut-Yonne . . . . • H5 52
Monterey E3 114
Montería B2 124
Monte Rosa. . . . . ▲ C5 56
Monterrey . . . . • F3 118
Montes Claros . . . . • J7 124
Montesilvano Marina J6 58
Montevarchi . . . . • G7 56
Montevideo, U.S A1 114
Montevideo, Uruguay . . . . ■ K5 126
Monte Viso . . . . ▲ C6 56
Monte Vista. . . . . • E1 118
Montgomery . . . . □ D3 116
Monticello . . . . • E3 112
Mont Joli G1 114
Mont-Laurier . . . . • E1 114
Montluçon H7 52
Montmagny . . . . • F1 114
Montmédy . . . . • H5 48
Montoro . . . . • K9 52
Mont Pelat . . . . ▲ F6 54
Montpelier, Id., U.S . . . . • M9 52
Montpelier, Vt., U.S . . . . ■ F2 114
Montpellier . . . . • J10 52
Montréal F1 114
Montreux . . . . • B4 56
Montrose E3 112
Monts Bagzane . . . . ▲ G5 92
Montserrat . . . . ▫ M5 120
Monts Nimba . . . . ▲ C3 94
Mont Tahat . . . . ▲ A2 76
Monywa . . . . • E5 56
Monza . . . . • L3 54
Monzón . . . . • F2 112
Moorcroft . . . . • A1 114
Moorhead G1 56
Moosburg . . . . ▲ Q6 108
Moosonee . . . . • E6 92
Mopti . . . . • F2 60
Mór . . . . • F2 60
Móra . . . . • B6 54
Moradabad . . . . • C3 80
Moramanga . . . . • H3 98
Moran . . . . • D2 112
Morava . . . . ✦ G8 44
Moravské Budějovice . . . . • L1 56
Morawhanna . . . . F? 124
Moray Firth . . . . ► J4 50
Morbach . . . . • K5 48
Mordoviya. . . . . ▪ H4 64
Moree . . . . • J5 102
More Laptevykh . . . . ▪ L1 70
Morelia. . . . . ● D5 120
Morella. . . . . ▲ K4 54
Morgan. . . . . • G6 102
Morgantown. . . . . ● D3 114
Mori. L2 74
Morioka. . . . . • L4 74
Morokoka. . . . . ▪ J4 70
Morlaix. . . . . • B5 52
Morocco. . . . . A C2 88

Morogoro . . . . • F5 96
Moro Gulf . . . . ► G5 76
Morombe . . . . • F8 98
Morondava . . . . • G7 70
Morón . . . . • G2 98
Morón de la Frontera . . . . • E7 54
Moroni . . . . ■ G2 98
Morotai . . . . ⬟ C2 79
Morris . . . . • G1 112
Morristown . . . . • E2 116
Mors . . . . ⬟ E8 42
Morwell . . . . • J7 102
Mosby . . . . • D1 112
Moscow = Moskva. . . . . . ■ G3 64
Mosel. . . . . ✦ J6 48
Moselle . . . . ✦ G6 48
Moses Lake . . . . • C1 112
Mosgiel . . . . • C7 104
Moshi . . . . • F4 96
Mosjøen . . . . • G4 42
Moskva . . . . ■ G3 64
Monmagyarórszág . . . . . ▪ N3 56
Moss . . . . • F7 42
Mossburn . . . . • B7 104
Mossbaai C6 98
Mosselbaai . . . . • C6 98
Mossoró . . . . • K5 124
Most . . . . • J6 46
Mostaganem . . . . • L9 54
Mostar . . . . • E6 60
Møsvatn . . . . ✦ E7 42
Mot'a . . . . • G5 90
Motherwell . . . . • J6 50
Motril . . . . • E8 54
Motygino . . . . • S6 68
Moudros . . . . • H5 62
Mouila . . . . • G5 94
Moulins . . . . • J7 52
Moulmein . . . . • B3 76
Moundou . . . . • C6 90
Mount Adams . . . . ▲ B1 112
Mountain Nile = Bahr
    el Jebel. . . . . ✦ E2 96
Mount Anglem . . . . ▲ A8 104
Mount Apo . . . . ▲ H5 76
Mount Ararat . . . . ▲ L4 84
Mount Arrowsmith . . . . . ▲ C6 104
Mount Aspiring . . . . ▲ B7 104
Mount Assiniboine . . . . . ▲ H6 108
Mount Augustus . . . . . . ▲ C4 102
Mount Baco . . . . ▲ G3 76
Mount Baker . . . . ▲ B1 112
Mount Bartle Frere . . . . . ▲ J3 102
Mount Bruce . . . . ▲ C4 102
Mount Cameroun . . . . . . ▲ D5 88
Mount Carmel . . . . ▲ D3 112
Mount Columbia . . . . . . ▲ H6 108
Mount Cook . . . . ▲ C6 104
Mount Cook . . . . ▲ C6 104
Mount Egmont . . . . ▲ E4 104
Mount Elbert . . . . ▲ E3 114
Mount Elgon . . . . ▲ E3 96
Mount Essendon . . . . . . ▲ D2 102
Mount Evelyn . . . . ▲ F2 102
Mount Everest . . . . ▲ J4 80
Mount Fairweather . . . . . ▲ D5 108
Mount Gambier . . . . . . • H7 102
Mount Garnet . . . . • J3 102
Mount Hermón . . . . ▲ C3 86
Mount Hood . . . . ▲ B1 112
Mount Huxley . . . . ▲ B7 104
Mount Isa . . . . • G3 102
Mount Jackson . . . . ▲(2)MM2 128
Mount Karisimbi. . . . . . . ▲ D4 96
Mount Kenya = Kirinyaga. . ▲ F4 96
Mount Kilimanjaro. . . . . . ▲ F4 96
Mount Kirkpatrick . . . . . ▲ (2)AA1 128

Mount Kosciuszko . . . . . ▲ J7 102
Mount Liebig . . . . ▲ F4 102
Mount Logan . . . . ▲ C4 108
Mount Magnet . . . . • C5 102
Mount Maunganui . . . . . • F3 104
Mount McKinley . . . . . . ▲ (1)G3 118
Mount Meharry . . . . ▲ C4 102
Mount Menzies . . . . ▲ (2)L2 128
Mount Minto . . . . ▲ (2)Y2 128
Mount Mulanje . . . . ▲ F3 98
Mount Murchison . . . . . . ▲ C6 104
Mount Nyiru . . . . ▲ F3 96
Mount Olympus . . . . ▲ B1 112
Mount Ord . . . . ▲ E3 102
Mount Ossa. . . . . ▲ J8 102
Mount Owen . . . . ▲ D5 104
Mount Paget . . . . ▲ P9 126
Mount Pleasant, Ia., U.S . . • B2 114
Mount Pleasant, Mich., U.S . • D2 114
Mount Pleasant, S.C., U.S. . • F3 116
Mount Pulog . . . . ▲ G3 76
Mount Rainier . . . . ▲ B1 112
Mount Robson . . . . ◙ H6 108
Mount Roosevelt . . . . . . ▲ F5 108
Mount Roraima . . . . ▲ E2 124
Mount Shasta . . . . ▲ B2 112
Mount Somers . . . . • C6 104
Mount Stanley . . . . ▲ D3 96
Mount Tahat . . . . ▲ D3 88
Mount Travers . . . . ▲ D6 104
Mount Tuun . . . . ▲ D3 74
Mount Vernon, Al., U.S . . • C3 116
Mount Vernon, Ill., U.S . . • C3 114
Mount Vernon, Wash., U.S . • B1 112
Mount Victoria, Myanmar . ▲ A2 76
Mount Victoria, Papua
    New Guinea . . . . . . ▲ E6 100
Mount Waddington . . . . . ▲ E6 108
Mount Washington . . . . . ▲ S8 108
Mount Whitney . . . . ▲ C3 112
Mount Wilson . . . . ▲ E3 112
Mount Woodroffe . . . . . . ▲ F5 102
Moura . . . . • C6 54
Moussoro . . . . • C5 90
Moutamba. . . . . • G5 94
Mouth of the Shannon . . . ► B9 50
Mouths of the Amazon . . . ► D3 122
Mouths of the Danube. . . . ◜ E4 60
Mouths of the Ganges. . . . ► S4 60
Mouths of the Indus. . . . . ► J5 82
Mouths of the Irrawaddy . . ► A3 76
Mouths of the Krishna. . . . ► D5 80
Mouths of the Mekong . . . ► D5 76
Mouths of the Niger . . . . ► F4 94
Moûtiers . . . . • B5 56
Moyale . . . . • F3 96
Moyen Atlas . . . . ▲ D2 92
Moyenvic . . . . • J6 48
Moynitty . . . . • N8 68
Mozambique . . . . ■ E3 98
Mozambique Channel . . . . ▪ F4 98
Mozdok . . . . • L2 84
Mozirje. . . . . • K4 56
Mpanda . . . . • E5 96
Mpika . . . . • E2 98
Mporokoso . . . . • E5 96
Mpumalanga . . . . ▪ D5 98
Mragowo. . . . . • L4 44
Mtsensk . . . . • G4 64
Mtwara . . . . • G6 96
Muang Khammouan . . . . . • C3 76
Muang Khong . . . . • D4 76
Muang Khôngxédôn . . . . • D3 76
Muang Pakxan . . . . • C3 76
Muang Sing. . . . . • C2 76
Muar . . . . • C2 78
Muarabungo . . . . • C3 78

Name	Ref	Page
Mubende	E3	96
Muckadilla	J5	102
Mucur	S5	62
Mudanjiang	E1	74
Muddy Gap	E2	112
Mufulira	D2	98
Muğla	L7	62
Mühldorf	H2	56
Mühlhausen	F5	46
Muhu	M7	42
Mukacheve	M9	44
Mukuku	D2	98
Mulaku Atoll	B8	80
Mulde	H5	46
Muleshoe	F2	118
Mulhacén	G7	54
Mulhouse	C3	56
Muli	G5	50
Mullewa	C5	102
Mullheim	C3	56
Mullingar	E8	50
Mulobezi	D3	98
Multán	K3	82
Mumbai	B5	80
Mumbwa	D2	98
Muna	B4	79
München	G2	56
Mungbere	D3	96
Munich = München	G2	56
Munster, France	C2	56
Münster, Germany	K3	48
Muojärvi	Q4	42
Muonio	M3	42
Muqdisho	H3	96
Mur	L4	56
Murat	K4	84
Murchison	D5	104
Murcia	J7	54
Murdo	F2	112
Mures	J3	60
Muret	G10	52
Murfreesboro	D2	116
Murghob	K2	82
Muriaé	J8	124
Müritz	H3	46
Murmansk	S2	42
Murom	H3	64
Muroran	L2	74
Muros	A2	54
Muroto	H7	74
Murphy	E2	116
Murray	H6	102
Murray Bridge	G7	102
Murray River Basin	H6	102
Murska Sobota	M4	56
Murter	L7	56
Murupara	F4	104
Mururoa	M8	100
Murwara	D4	80
Murzūq	H3	92
Mürzzuschlag	L3	56
Muş	J4	84
Musala	F2	62
Musandam Peninsula	G3	87
Muscat = Masqat	H5	87
Musgrave Ranges	E5	102
Muskegon	C2	114
Muskogee	B2	116
Musoma	E4	96
Mustafakemalpaşa	L4	62
Mut, Egypt	E2	90
Mut, Turkey	R8	62
Mutare	E3	98
Mutoray	U5	68
Mutsu	L3	74
Muyezerskiy	R5	42
Muyinga	E4	96
Muynak	K9	68
Muzaffarpur	E3	80
Mwali	G2	98
Mwanza	E4	96
Mweka	C4	96
Mwene-Ditu	C5	96
Mwenezi	E4	98
Mwenezi	E4	98
Mwinilunga	C2	98
Myanmar	B2	76
Myingyan	B2	76
Myitkyina	B1	76
Myjava	N2	56
Mykolayiv	N8	44
Mykonos	H7	62
Mymensingh	F4	80
Mynbulak	L9	68
Myōjin	K4	72
Myrtle Beach	F3	116
Mys Alevina	S5	70
Mys Enkan	P5	70
Mys Govena	V5	70
Mys Kanin Nos.	H1	64
Mys Kekurskij	S2	42
Mys Lopatka	T6	70
Mys Navarin	X4	70
Mysore	C6	80
Mys Shelagskiy	V2	70
Mys Terpeniya	Q7	70
Mys Yuzhnyy	T5	70
Mys Zhelaniya	M2	68
My Tho	D4	76
Mytilini	J5	62
Myvatn	(1)E2	42
Mzimba	E2	98
Mzuzu	E2	98

N

Name	Ref	Page
Naalehu	(2)F4	118
Naberezhnyye Chelny	K3	64
Nabeul	E12	58
Nabire	E3	79
Nablus	C4	86
Nacala	G2	98
Náchod	F7	44
Nacogdoches	C3	116
Nadiad	B4	80
Nadvirna	M1	60
Nadym	P1	64
Nadym	P2	64
Næstved	G1	46
Nagano	K5	74
Nagaoka	K5	74
Nagaon	F3	80
Nagasaki	E7	74
Nagaur	B3	80
Nagercoil	C7	80
Nagorsk	K3	64
Nagoya	J6	74
Nagpur	C4	80
Nagqu	F2	80
Nagyatád	N4	56
Nagykanizsa	N4	56
Nagykőrös	H5	72
Naha	H5	72
Nahr en Nile = Nile.	F2	90
Naiman Qi.	G2	72
Nain.	U5	108
Nairn	J4	50
Nairobi	F4	96
Naivasha	F4	96
Naizishan	C3	80
Najibabad	C3	80
Najin	F2	74
Najrān	H4	90
Nakamura	G7	74
Nakhl	A7	86
Nakhodka	G2	74
Nakhon Ratchasima	C3	76
Nakhon Sawan	B3	76
Nakhon Si Thammarat	B5	76
Nakina	P6	108
Naknek	(1)F4	118
Nakonde	E5	96
Nakuru	F4	96
Nal'chik	K2	84
Nälüt	H2	92
Namagan	N9	68
Namakzar-e Shadad	G1	87
Namapa	F2	98
Nam Co	F2	80
Namdalen	G4	42
Nam Dinh	C2	112
Namib Desert	A4	98
Namibe	A3	98
Namibia	B4	98
Namibia	B4	98
Nam Ping	B3	76
Namp'o	C4	74
Nampula	F3	98
Namsos	F4	42
Namur	G4	48
Namwala	D3	98
Namwŏn	D6	74
Nan	C3	76
Nanaimo	B1	112
Nanao	J5	74
Nanchang	F5	72
Nanchong	D4	72
Nancy	J4	56
Nanda Devi	C2	80
Nänded	C5	80
Nandurbar	B4	80
Nangapinoh	E3	78
Nangatayap	E3	78
Nang Xian	F3	80
Nanjing	F4	72
Nanning	D2	76
Nanortalik	X4	108
Nanping	F5	72
Nansei-shotō	H5	72
Nantes	D6	52
Nanton	D1	110
Nantong	G4	72
Nanyang	E4	72
Nanpalkovo	N3	68
Napas	C4	70
Napier	F4	104
Naples = Napoli	J8	58
Naples	E4	116
Napo	C4	124
Napoli	J8	58
Nara	J6	74
Narbonne	H10	52
Nardò	N8	58
Nares Strait	J2	106
Narev	N5	44
Narew	L5	44
Narmada	C4	80
Narnaul	C3	80
Narni	J6	102
Narrandera	C6	102
Nart	F2	72
Narva	Q7	42
Narva	P7	42
Narva Bay	P7	42
Narvik	J2	42
Nar'yan Mar	K1	64
Năsăud.	M2	60
Nashua.	F2	114
Nashville.	D2	116

Name	Ref	Page
Našice	F4	60
Nasik	B4	86
Nasir	E2	96
Nassarawa	F3	94
Nassau	F4	116
Nässjö	H8	42
Nasugbu	G4	76
Naswã	G5	87
Nata	D4	98
Natal	K5	124
Natashquan	U6	108
Natchez	C3	116
Natchitoches	C3	116
National Park	E4	104
Nattingou	E2	94
Natuna Besar	D2	78
Naumburg	G5	46
Na'ūr	C5	86
Nauru	G6	100
Nautonwa	D3	80
Navahermosa	F5	54
Navoi	M9	68
Navojoa	E6	110
Navsari	B4	80
Nawabshah	J4	82
Naxçivan	L4	84
Naxos	H7	62
Naxos	H7	62
Nayoro	M1	74
Nazaré	A5	54
Nazareth	C4	86
Nazarovo	S6	68
Nazca	C6	124
Nazca Ridge	E3	126
Naze	H5	72
Nazino	P6	68
Nazran'	L2	84
Nazrēt	F2	96
Nazwã	G5	82
Nazyvayevsk	P3	64
Ndele	C2	96
Ndjamena	B5	90
Ndjolé	G5	94
Ndola	D2	98
Neapoli	F8	62
Nebbi	E3	96
Nebitdag	E7	82
Nebraska	G2	112
Neckar	D4	46
Neckarsulm	E7	46
Necker Island	K3	100
Necochea	K6	126
Nédély	C4	90
Needles	D2	118
Nefedovo	P3	64
Neftcala	N4	84
Neftekamsk	K3	64
Nefteyugansk	P2	64
Negage	B5	96
Negār	G2	87
Negēlē	F2	96
Negele	F2	96
Negotin	E3	60
Negro, Argentina	J7	126
Negro, Brazil.	E4	124
Negros	G5	76
Negru	R6	60
Nehbandān	G3	82
Neijiang	C5	72
Nei Monggol	E2	72
Neiva	B3	124
Neixiang	E4	72
Nek'emtē	F2	96
Nellore	C6	80
Nel'ma	P7	70
Nelson	N5	108
Nelson, Canada	C1	112
Nelson, New Zealand	D5	104
Nelspruit	E5	98
Néma	D5	92
Néman	M2	44
Néman	N10	42
Nemperola	B5	79
Nemunas	P3	44
Nemuro	N2	74
Nene	L7	70
Nenjiang	M7	70
Nepa	H5	70
Nepal	D3	80
Nepalganj	D3	80
Neryungri	L5	70
Netanya	B4	86
Netherlands	H2	48
Netherlands Antilles	L6	120
Nettiling Lake	S3	108
Neubrandenburg	J3	46
Neuchâtel	B3	56
Neuenhagen	J4	46
Neuchâtel, Belgium	H5	48
Neufchâteau, France.	L5	52
Neufchâtel-en-Bray	D5	48
Neumünster	F2	46
Neunkirchen	M3	56
Neuquén	H6	126
Neuquén	H4	46
Neusiedler	F10	44
Neusiedler See	M3	56
Neuss	J3	48
Neustadt, Germany	F2	46
Neustadt, Germany	F7	46
Neustadt, Germany	L5	48
Neustrelitz	J3	46
Neu-Ulm	F8	46
Neuwied	K4	48
Nevada	C3	112
Nevada	B3	114
Nevada Auzangate	C6	124
Nevado de Colima	D5	120
Nevado de Huascaran	B5	124
Nevado de Illampu	D7	124
Nevado Sajama	D7	124
Nevados de Cachi	H4	126
Never	L6	70
Nevers	J7	52
Nevėžis	M9	42
Nevinnomyssk	J1	84
Nevşehir	S6	62
New Amsterdam	F2	124
Newark	F2	114
Newark-on-Trent	B1	48
New Bedford	F2	114
New Bern	F2	116
New Britain	+6	100
New Brunswick	T7	108
Newbury	A3	48
New Bussa	E3	94
Newcastle, Australia	K6	102
Newcastle, U.S	L6	50
Newcastle-upon-Tyne	B2	48
Newcastle Waters	F3	102
New Delhi	C3	80
Newfound and Labrador	V5	108
Newfoundland	V7	108
New Georgia Island	F6	100
New Guinea	S10	66
New Hampshire	F2	114
New Haven	F2	114
New Iberia	C3	116
New Ireland	F6	100
New Jersey	F2	114
New Liskeard	C1	114
Newman	C4	102
Newmarket	C2	48
New Mexico	E2	118
Newnan	E3	116
New Orleans	D4	116
New Plymouth	E4	104
Newport, Eng., U.K	A4	48
Newport, Wales, U.K.	K10	50
Newport, Oreg., U.S.	B2	112
New Providence	F5	116
Newquay	G11	50
New Siberia Islands = Novosibirskiye Ostrova	P1	70
New South Wales	H6	102
Newton, Ia., U.S	B2	114
Newton, Kans., U.S	B2	116
New York	E2	114
New York	F2	114
New Zealand	B5	104
Neya	H3	64
Neyrīz	F2	87
Neyshābūr	G2	82
Ngabang	D2	78
Ngaoundéré	G3	94
Ngara	E4	96
Ngo	H5	94
Ngoura	C5	90
Nguigmi	G2	94
Nha Trang	D4	76
Nhulunbuy	G2	102
Niafounké	E5	92
Niagara Falls	E2	114
Niamey	E2	94
Niangara	D3	96
Nia-Nia	D3	96
Nias	B2	78
Nicaragua	G6	120
Nicastro	L10	58
Nice	C7	56
Nicholls Town	F4	116
Nicobar Islands	A5	76
Nicosia = Lefkosia	R9	62
Niedere Tauern	J3	56
Niefang	G4	94
Nienburg	E4	46
Nieuw Amsterdam	F2	124
Nieuw Nickerie	F2	124
Nieuwpoort	E3	48
Niğde	S7	62
Niger	G5	92
Niger	E2	94
Nigeria	F2	94
Niigata	K5	74
Nihau	(2)A2	118
Nijar	H8	54
Nijmegen	H3	48
Nikolayevsk-na-Amure	Q6	70
Nikol'sk	J3	64
Nikopol'	F5	64
Nikšić	F7	60
Nile	F3	90
Nîmes	K10	52
Nimule	E3	96
Nine Degree Channel	B7	80
Nin'gan	E1	74
Ningbo	G5	72
Ningde	F5	72
Ninghai	G5	72
Ninohoe	L3	74
Niobrara	F2	112
Nioro	D5	92
Nioro du Sahel	C1	94

O

Place	Ref	Page
Oahu	L3	100
Oakland	B3	112
Oakley	A2	116
Oak Ridge	D3	114
Oamaru	C7	104
Oaxaca	E5	120
Ob'	N2	64
Oban	G5	50
O Barco	D2	54
Oberhausen	J3	48
Oberstdorf	J6	48
Obi	C3	79
Óbidos	F4	124
Obigarm	K2	82
Obihiro	M2	74
Obninsk	G3	64
Obo	D2	96
Obskaya Guba	N4	68
Obuasi	D3	94
Ob'yachevo	J2	64
Ocala	E4	116
Ocean Falls	F6	108
Oceania	G7	100
Oceanside	C2	118
Och'amch'ire	J2	84
Odate	L3	74
Odda	D6	42
Odemira	B7	54
Odemiş	L6	62
Odense	F1	46
Oder = Odra	F3	64
Odesa = Odesa, Ukraine	F5	64
Odessa, U.S	F2	118
Odienné	C3	94
Odorheiu Secuiesc	N3	60
Odra	F6	44
Oelsnitz	H6	46
Oeno	N8	100
Oestev	H7	126
Ofaqim	B5	86
Offenbach	D6	46
Offenburg	C2	56
Ogaki	J6	74
Ogasawara-shotō	T7	66
Ogbomosho	E3	94
Ogden	D2	112
Ogle	E5	56
Ogre	N8	42
Ogulin	L5	56
Ohai	A7	104
Ohio	D2	114
Ohio	C3	114
Ohrid	C3	62
Ohura	E4	104
Oiapoque	G3	124
Oil City	E2	114
Oita	F7	74
Ojinaga	F3	118
jos del Salado	H4	126
Oka	G6	70
Okato	D4	104
Okavango Delta	C3	98
Okaya	K5	74
Okayama	F7	74
Okha	Q6	70
Okhansk	L3	64
Okhotsk	Q5	70
Okhtyrka	F4	64
Okinawa	H5	72
Okinawa	H5	72
Oki-shotō	F6	74
Oklahoma	B2	116
Oklahoma City	B2	116
Okranger	E5	42
Oksino	K1	64
Okxinden	H4	62
Oktyabr'sk	L5	64
Oktyabr'skiy	K4	64
Okushiri-tō	K2	74
Olancha	C3	112
Öland	J8	42
Olathe	C2	116
Olavarría	J6	126
Ólbia	D8	58
Old Crow	(1)K2	108
Oldenburg, Germany	D3	46
Oldenburg, Germany	F2	46
Old Head of Kinsale	D10	50
Olean	E2	114
Olekma	L5	70
Olekminsk	L4	70
Olenek	J3	70
Olenëk	L2	70
Olhão	C7	54
Olib	K6	56
Olinda	L5	124
Olonets	F2	64
Olongapo	G4	76
Oloron-Ste-Marie	E10	52
Olot	N2	54
Olovyannaya	K6	70
Olpe	K3	48
Olsztyn	K4	44
Olt	M4	60
Oltenița	P5	60
Oltu	K3	84
Olvera	E8	54
Olympia	B1	112
Olympus	E4	62
Olympus	Q10	62
Olyutorskiy	W4	70
Oma	D2	80
Omagh	E7	50
Omaha	G2	112
Omak	C1	112
Omapere	D2	104
Omarama	B7	104
Omaruru	B4	98
Ombrone	F6	58
Omdurman = Umm Durman	F4	90
Omegna	D5	56
Omolon	T3	70
Omo Wenz	F2	96
Omsk	N6	68
Omū	M1	74
Omuta	F7	74
Ondangwa	B3	98
Ondjiva	B3	98
Ondo	E3	94
One and a Half Degree Channel	B8	80
Onega	G2	64
O'Neill	G2	112
Oneonta	F2	114
Oneşti	P3	60
Onezhskoye Ozero	F2	64
Ongin	C5	74
Ongole	D5	80
Onguday	R7	68
Oni	K2	84
Onitsha	F3	94
Onon	J7	70
Onon	J7	70
Ontario	N6	108
Onyx	C1	118
Oodnadatta	G5	102
Oostelijk-Flevoland	H2	48
Oostende	E3	48
Oosterschelde	F3	48
Opala	C4	96
Opava	G8	44
Opelika	D3	116
Upelousas	C3	116
Opheim	E1	112
Opole	G7	44
Opotiki	F4	104
Opunake	D4	104
Opuwo	A3	98
Oradea	J2	60
Oran	K9	54
Orán	J3	126
Orange	C5	98
Orange, Australia	J6	102
Orange, France	K9	52
Orangeburg	E3	116
Oranienburg	J4	46
Orbetello	F6	58
Orco	C5	56
Ordu	G3	84
Örebro	H7	42
Oregon	B2	112
Oregon	A3	114
Orel	G4	64
Orem	D2	112
Orenburg	L4	64
Orestiada	J3	62
Orford Ness	D2	48
Orihuela	K6	54
Orillia	E2	114
Orinoco	D2	124
Orinoco Delta = Delta del Orinoco	E2	124
Oristano	C9	58
Orivesi	Q5	42
Orkney Islands	K5	50
Orlando	E4	116
Orléans	G6	52
Ormara	H4	82
Ormoc	G4	76
Örnsköldsvik	K5	42
Orofino	C1	112
Orogen Zizhiqi	L6	70
Orosei	D8	58
Orotukan	S4	70
Oroville	B3	112
Orroroo	G6	102
Orsha	F4	64
Orsk	L4	64
Orşova	K5	60
Ørsta	D5	42
Orthez	E10	52
Ortigueira	C1	54
Orties	F4	56
Orümiyeh	L5	84
Oruro	D7	124
Orvieto	G6	58
Ōsaka	H6	74
Osäm	M6	60
Osceola	B2	114
Oschersleben	G4	46
Osh	N9	68
Oshamambe	L2	74
Oshawa	E2	114
Oshkosh, Nebr., U.S.	F2	112
Oshkosh, Wis., U.S.	C2	114
Oshogbo	E3	94
Osijek	F4	60
Oskaloosa	B2	114
Oslo	F7	42
Oslofjorden	F7	42
Osmancık	F3	84
Osmaniye	G5	84
Osnabrück	L2	48
Osorno	G7	126
Ossora	U5	70
Ostashkov	F3	64
Østerdalen	F6	42
Östersund	H5	42
Ostfriesische Inseln	C3	46

Name		Grid	Page
Ostiglia	•	G5	56
Ostrava	•	H8	44
Ostrołęka	•	L4	44
Ostrov, *Czech Republic*	•	H6	46
Ostrov, *Russia*	•	E3	64
Ostrova Medvezh'i		T2	70
Ostrova Vrangelya		V4	106
Ostrov Ayon		N3	68
Ostrov Belyy		N3	68
Ostrov Beringa		V6	70
Ostrov Bol'shevik		V2	68
Ostrov Bol'shoy Begichev		J2	70
Ostrov Bol'shoy Lyakhovskiy		Q2	70
Ostrov Bol'shoy Shantar		P6	70
Ostrov Chechen'		M2	84
Ostrov Iturup		P1	74
Ostrov Kolguyev		H4	68
Ostrov Komsomolets		T1	68
Ostrov Kotel'nyy		P1	70
Ostrov Kunashir		P1	74
Ostrov Novaya Sibir'		S2	70
Ostrov Oktyabr'skoy		S2	70
Ostrov Onekotan		S7	70
Ostrov Paramushir		T6	70
Ostrov Shiashkotan		S7	70
Ostrov Simushir		S7	70
Ostrov Urup		S7	70
Ostrov Ushakova		Q1	68
Ostrov Vaygach		K3	68
Ostrov Vise		P2	68
Ostrov Vosrozhdeniya		K9	68
Ostrov Vrangelya		W2	70
Ostrowiec Świętokrzyski	•	L7	44
Ostrów Mazowiecka	•	L5	44
Ostrów Wielkopolski	•	G6	44
Ostuni	•	M8	58
Ōsumi-shotō		F8	74
Osuna	•	E7	54
Oswego	•	E2	114
Oświęcim	•	J7	44
Otago Peninsula		C7	104
Otaki	•	E5	104
Otaru	•	L2	74
Oti		E3	94
Otjiwarongo	•	B4	98
Otočac	•	L6	56
Otog Qi	•	D3	72
Otoineppu	•	M1	74
Otorohanga	•	E4	104
Ōtsu	•	H6	74
Ottawa		E1	114
Ottawa, *Canada*		E1	114
Ottawa, *U.S*	•	B2	116
Ottumwa	•	B2	114
Ouachita Mountains		C3	116
Ouadâne	•	C4	92
Ouadda	•	C2	96
Ouagadougou	•	D2	94
Oualâta	•	D5	92
Ouargla	•	G2	92
Ouarzazate	•	D2	92
Oudenaarde	•	F4	48
Oudenbosch	•	G3	48
Oudtshoorn	•	C6	98
Oued Medjerda		D12	58
Oued Meliane		D12	58
Ouésso	•	H4	94
Ouezzane	•	D2	92
Oujda	•	E2	92
Oulu	•	N4	42
Oulujärvi		P4	42
Oulujoki		P4	42
Oulx	•	B5	56
Oum-Chalouba	•	D4	90
Ounarjoki		N3	42
Our		J4	48
Ouray	•	E3	112
Ourense	•	C2	54
Ourthe		H4	48
Outer Hebrides		D4	50
Outjo	•	B4	98
Out Skerries		M1	50
Ouyen	•	H7	102
Ovalle	•	G5	126
Overflakkee		G3	48
Overton	•	D3	112
Övertorneå		M3	42
Oviedo	•	E1	54
Owaka	•	B8	104
Owando	•	H5	94
Owensboro	•	C3	114
Owen Sound	•	D2	114
Owo	•	F3	94
Owyhee		C2	112
Oxford, *New Zealand*		D6	104
Oxford, *U.K.*	•	A3	48
Oxnard	•	C2	118
Oyama		K5	74
Oyapock		G3	124
Oyem	•	G4	94
Oyonnax	•	A4	56
Ózd	•	K9	44
Ozero Alakol'		Q8	68
Ozero Balkhash		N8	68
Ozero Baykal		H6	70
Ozero Beloye		G2	64
Ozero Chany		P7	68
Ozero Il'men'		F3	64
Ozero Inder		J8	68
Ozero Karaginskiy		S3	42
Ozero Khanka		G1	74
Ozero Kovdozero		R5	42
Ozero Leksozero		R4	42
Ozero Njuk		R4	42
Ozero Pirenga		R3	42
Ozero Pyaozero		R3	42
Ozero Sredneye Kuyto		R4	42
Ozero Taymyr		U3	68
Ozero Tengiz		N4	64
Ozero Topozero		R4	42
Ozero Umbozero		T3	42
Ozero Vygozero		G2	64
Ozero Yalpug		R4	60
Ozero Zaysan		Q8	68
Ozhogino		R3	70
Ozieri		C8	58

P

Name		Grid	Page
Paamiut	•	X4	108
Paarl	•	B6	98
Pabianice	•	J6	44
Pachino	•	K12	58
Pachuca	•	E4	120
Pacific Ocean		M3	100
Packwood	•	B1	112
Padang	•	C3	78
Padangsidempuan	•	B2	78
Paderborn	•	D5	46
Pádova	•	G5	56
Padre Island	•	B4	116
Paducah, *Ky., U.S*	•	C3	114
Paducah, *Tex., U.S.*	•	F2	118
Paekdu San.	•	D3	74
Paeroa	•	E3	104
Pafos	•	Q10	62
Pag	•	L6	56
Pag		K6	56
Pagadian	•	G5	76
Pagai Selatan		B3	78
Pagai Utara		B3	78
Pagalu = Annobón		F5	94
Pagan		E4	100
Pagatan		F3	78
Page	•	D1	112
Pagri	•	E3	72
Pahatua		E5	104
Paide	•	N7	42
Päijänne		N6	42
Paisley	•	H6	50
Paita	•	A5	124
Pakaraima Mountains		E2	124
Pakistan	▲	J4	80
Pakokku	•	A2	78
Pakotai		D2	104
Pakrac	•	N5	56
Paks	•	F3	44
Pakxé	•	D3	78
Palagónia	•	J11	58
Palagruža		L6	56
Palamós	•	P3	54
Palana	•	U5	70
Palangkaraya	•	E3	78
Palanpur	•	B4	80
Palatka	•	E4	116
Palau	▲	D5	100
Palau	•	D7	58
Palau	•	D5	100
Palawan		F5	76
Palazzolo Arcéide.	•	J11	58
Palembang	•	C3	78
Palencia	•	F2	54
Paleokastrítsa	•	B5	60
Palermo	•	H10	58
Palestine	•	B3	116
Paletwa	•	A2	78
Pali	•	B3	80
Palikir		F5	100
Palk Strait.		C7	81
Palma	•	N5	54
Palma del Rio	•	E7	54
Palmas.	•	L4	124
Palmas.	•	H6	94
Palmdale	•	C2	118
Palmerston		C7	104
Palmerston Island.		K7	100
Palmerston North.		E5	104
Palm Harbor	•	E4	116
Palmi	•	K10	58
Palmyra Island.		K5	100
Palojärvi		M2	42
Palopo	•	B3	76
Palu	•	A3	76
Poluostrov Taymyr		R3	68
Pamiers		G10	52
Pamlico Sound.		F2	116
Pampa	•	F1	118
Pampas		J6	126
Pamplona, *Colombia.*	•	K7	124
Pamplona, *Spain*	•	J2	54
Panaji	•	C3	80
Panagyurishte	•	M7	60
Panaji	•	B5	80
Panama	▲	H7	122
Panamá	•	B2	122
Panama Canal = Canal de Panamá		J7	122
Panama City	•	D3	116
Panarik.	•	D2	78
Panay.	•	G4	76
Pančevo.		H5	58
Panevėžys	•	P2	42
Pangkalpinang	•	D3	78
Pangnirtung.		G5	108
Pangutaran Group		G5	76
Panjgur		F7	80
Pantanal.		H1	124
Pantelleria		H1	58

Name	Ref	Page
...ola	L9	58
...pa	E2	60
...pakura	E3	104
...paroa	E3	104
...pa Stour	L1	50
...penburg	C3	46
...pey	(1)F2	42
...pua	E3	79
...pua New Guinea	E6	100
...pun	B3	76
...ara	G5	124
...ara	H4	124
...ara	H7	124
...aracatu	E3	126
...aracel Islands	H4	100
...aracín	J6	60
...araguá	C5	62
...araguay	J3	126
...araguay	C5	122
...araíba	K5	124
...araiba	E3	94
...aramäo	F2	124
...arana	L3	126
...araná	H6	124
...araná	J5	126
...araná	H6	124
...araná	K4	126
...aray-le Monial	K7	52
...archim	G3	46
...ardo	J7	124
...arduboce	E7	44
...arepare	A3	79
...arga	C5	62
...arigi	B3	79
...arika	F2	124
...arintins	F4	124
...aris, France	H5	52
...aris, U.S.	B3	116
...arkersburg	D3	114
...arla	F6	56
...arma	F6	56
...arma, Italy	F6	56
...arma	D2	114
...arnassus	D6	104
...ärnu	N7	42
...ärnu	N7	42
...aros	H7	62
...aros	H7	62
...arry Islands	L1	108
...arry Sound	D2	114
...arthenay	E7	52
...artinico	H10	58
...artizansk	G2	74
...aru	G4	124
...aryang	D2	80
...asadena, Calif., U.S	C2	118
...asadena, Tex., U.S.	B4	116
...ascani	P2	60
...asinler	J3	84
...ašman	L7	56
...asni	H4	82
...aso de Indios	H7	126
...aso Robles	B1	118
...assau	J8	46
...asso Fundo	L4	126
...assos	H8	124
...astavy	P9	42
...asto	B3	124
...atagonia	G8	126
...atan, India	B4	80
...atan, Nepal	E3	80
...ate Island	G4	96
...aterna	K5	54
...aterno	J11	58
...aterson	F2	114
...athankot	C2	80
...athein	A3	76
...atiala	C2	80
Patmos	J7	62
Patna	E3	80
Patnos	K4	84
Patos de Minas	H7	124
Patra	D6	62
Patraikós Kólpos	D6	62
Patti	J10	58
Paturau River	D5	104
Pau	K1	54
Paulo Afonso	K5	124
Pāveh	M6	84
Pavia	E5	56
Pāvilosta	L8	42
Pavlodar	P7	68
Pavullo nel Frignano	F6	56
Paxoí	C5	62
Payette	C2	112
Payne's Find	C5	102
Paysandú	K5	126
Payson	D2	118
Pazar	J3	84
Pazardzhik	M7	60
Peace	H5	108
Peace River	H5	108
Peach Springs	D1	118
Pebane	F3	98
Pec	C5	124
Pecan Island	C4	116
Pechora	L1	64
Pechora	J4	68
Pechorskoye More	J4	68
Pecos	F2	118
Pecos	F2	118
Pécs	F3	60
Pedra Azul	J7	124
Pedra Lume	(1)B1	94
Pedro Afonso	H5	124
Pedro Juan Caballero	K3	126
Peene	J3	46
Pegasus Bay	D6	104
Pegnitz	G7	46
Pegu	B3	76
Pegunungan Barisan	B2	78
Pegunungan Iban	F2	78
Pegunungan Maoke	E3	79
Pegunungan Meratus	F3	78
Pegunungan Schwaner	E3	78
Pegunungan Van Rees	E3	79
Pehuajó	J6	126
Peine	F4	46
Peißenberg	G3	56
Pekalongan	D4	78
Pekanbaru	C2	78
Peking = Beijing	F3	72
Peleng	B3	79
Pelješac	E8	44
Pello	N3	42
Pellworm	D2	46
Pelly Bay	P3	108
Peloponnisos	D7	62
Pelotas	L5	126
Pelym	M2	64
Pemba	G2	98
Pemba Island	F5	96
Pembina	G1	112
Pembroke, Canada	E1	114
Pembroke, U.S.	H10	50
Pembroke, U.S	E3	116
Peñafiel	F3	54
Peñaranda de Bracamonte	E4	54
Peñarroya-Pueblonuevo	E6	54
Pendleton	C1	112
Pend Oreille Lake	C1	112
Peniche	A5	54
Península de Guajira	K6	120
Península Valdés	J7	126
Péninsule de Gaspé	T7	108
Péninsule d'Ungava	R4	108
Pennines	K7	50
Pennsylvania	E2	114
Penrith	K7	50
Pensacola	G2	120
Penticton	C1	112
Penza	G11	50
Penzance	G11	50
Penzhinskaya Guba	U4	70
Penzhinskiy Khrebet	V4	70
Peoria	C2	114
Peregrebnoye	N2	64
Pereira	B3	124
Pergamino	J5	126
Périgueux	F8	52
Perito Moreno	G8	126
Perleberg	G3	46
Perm'	L3	64
Përmet	C4	62
Pernambuco	K5	124
Pernik	L7	60
Perpignan	H11	52
Perry	E3	116
Persepolis	E2	87
Persian Gulf	C2	87
Perth, Australia	C6	102
Perth, U.K.	J5	50
Pertuis Breton	D7	52
Peru	A C6	124
Peru	C2	114
Peru-Chile Trench	D5	122
Perúgia	G5	58
Pervoural'sk	L3	64
Pésaro	H7	56
Pescara	J6	58
Péscara	H7	56
Peshawar	B2	80
Peshtera	G2	62
Peski Karakumy	G2	82
Peski Kyzylkum	L9	68
Peski Priaral'skiye Karakumy	L8	68
Pessac	E9	52
Petah Tiqwa	B4	86
Petaloú	G7	62
Pétange	H5	48
Petauke	E2	98
Peterborough, Canada	E2	114
Peterborough, U.K	M9	50
Peterhead	L4	50
Peter I Øy	(2)JJ3	128
Petersburg	E3	114
Petersfield	B3	48
Petershagen	D4	46
Petre Bay	(1)B1	104
Petrich	F3	62
Petrila	L4	60
Petrolia	M5	56
Petrolina	J5	124
Petropavlovsk	N4	64
Petropavlovsk-Kamchatskiy	T6	70
Petroşani	L4	60
Petrovsk-Zabaykal'skiy	H6	70
Petrozavodsk	F2	64
Petrún	M1	64
Pevek	W3	70
Pfaffenhofen	G8	46
Pfarrkirchen	H8	46
Pforzheim	D8	46
Pfunds	F4	56
Phalodi	B3	80
Phan Rang	D4	76
Phan Thiet	D4	76
Phatthalung	C5	76
Phet Buri	B4	76
Philadelphia	F2	116

Name		Grid	Page
ortland, Me., U.S	•	F2	114
ortland, Oreg., U.S.	•	B1	112
ort Laoise	•	E8	50
ort Lavaca	•	B4	116
ort Lincoln	•	G6	102
ort Louis	•	(1)B2	98
ort Macquarie	•	K6	102
ort-Menier	•	U7	108
ort Moresby	•	J1	102
ort Nolloth	•	B5	98
orto, Corsica	•	C6	58
orto, Portugal	•	B5	54
orto Alegre	▢	L5	126
orto Amboim		A2	98
ortocheli	•	F7	62
orto Esperidião	•	F7	124
ortoferraio	•	E6	58
ort of Spain		E1	124
orogruaro	•	H5	56
orto Inglês	•	(1)B1	94
orto Nacional	•	H6	124
orto-Novo	•	E3	94
ort Orford	•	B2	112
orto Santana	•	G3	124
orto Seguro	•	K7	124
orto Tolle	•	H6	56
orto Tórres	•	C8	58
orto-Vecchio	•	D7	58
orto Velho	□	E5	124
ortoviejo	•	A4	124
ort Pire	•	G6	102
ortree	•	F4	50
ort Said = Bûr Sa'îd	•	F1	90
ort St. Johns	•	D6	98
ort Shepstone	•	E6	98
ortsmouth, U.K	•	A4	48
ortsmouth, N.H., U.S.	•	F2	114
ortsmouth, Oh., U.S.	•	D3	114
ortsmouth, Va., U.S.	•	D3	114
ort Sudan = Bûr Sudan	•	G4	90
ort Talbot	•	E1	112
ortugal	A	B5	54
ort-Vendres	•	J11	52
ort-Vila		G7	100
ort Warrender	•	E2	102
osadas	•	B3	79
ôßneck	•	G6	46
ostmasburg	•	C5	98
ostojna	•	K5	56
otapovo	•	R4	68
oteau	•	C2	116
otenza	•	K8	58
ot'i	•	J2	84
otiskum	•	G2	94
otosi	•	D4	124
otstam	•	D7	80
ottuval	•	C3	78
oughkeepsie	•	F2	114
ourerere	•	F5	104
ôvoa de Varzim	•	B3	54
ovorino	•	H4	64
owder	✗	E1	112
owell River	•	C7	108
oyang Hu		J5	72
ožarevac	•	J5	60
oznan	•	F5	44
ozoblanco	•	F6	54
abumulih	•	C3	78
achatice	•	H4	46
achuap Khiri Khan	•	B4	76
æsto	•	H1	46
ague = Praha		D7	44
aha		H1	46
aia	•	(1)B2	94
airie du Chien	•	B2	114
aslin Island		(2)B1	98

Name		Grid	Page
Pratas = Dongsha Qundao.	🏝	F2	76
Prato	•	G7	56
Pratt	•	G3	112
Preetz	•	F2	46
Premnitz	•	H4	46
Premuda		K6	56
Prentice	•	B1	114
Prenzlau		C4	44
Preparis Island		A4	76
Přerov		G8	44
Preševo	•	J7	60
Presidencia Roque Sáenz Peña.		J4	126
Presidio	•	F3	118
Presnogorkovka.		N4	64
Prešov		L9	44
Presque Isle	•	G1	114
Preston, U.K.	•	K8	50
Preston, U.S.		B3	114
Pretoria		D5	98
Preveza	•	C6	62
Pribilof Islands.		(1)D4	118
Priboj	•	G6	60
Příbram	•	D8	44
Price	•	D3	112
Prichard	•	D3	116
Priekule	•	L8	42
Prienai		N3	44
Prieska	•	C5	98
Prievidza	•	H9	44
Prijedor	•	D5	60
Prijepolje	•	G6	60
Prikaspiyskaya Nizmennost'		K5	64
Prilep	•	D3	62
Prince Albert.	•	K6	108
Prince Albert Peninsula		H2	108
Prince Charles Island		R3	108
Prince Edward Island	a	U7	108
Prince Edward Island		G10	88
Prince George	•	G6	108
Prince of Wales Island, Canada.		L2	108
Prince of Wales Island, U.S	🏝	E5	108
Prince Patrick Island		Q2	106
Prince Regent Inlet	►	N2	108
Prince Rupert	•	E6	108
Princeton	•	C3	114
Principe	🏝	F4	94
Prineville	•	B2	112
Priozersk		R6	42
Priština	•	J7	60
Privas	•	K9	52
Privolzhskaya Vozvyshennost		H4	64
Prizren	•	H7	60
Probolinggo	•	E4	78
Progreso		G4	120
Prokop'yevsk		R7	68
Proliv Longa	►	X2	70
Proliv Vil'kitskogo.	►	U2	68
Propriano	•	C7	58
Prosna	✗	G6	44
Prosperidad		H5	76
Prostojov		G8	44
Provadiya		Q6	60
Providence		F2	114
Provideniya		Z4	70
Provins	•	J5	52
Provo	•	D2	112
Prudhoe Bay	•	(1)H1	118
Prüm	•	J4	48
Pruszków		K5	44
Prut	✗	R4	60
Prvić	🏝	K6	56
Prypyats'	✗	G2	40
Psara	🏝	H6	62

Name		Grid	Page
Psebay	•	J1	84
Pskov	•	E3	64
Ptuj	•	L4	56
Pucallpa	•	C5	124
Pucheng	•	F5	72
Púchov		H8	44
Pucioasa		N4	60
Puck		H3	44
Pudasjärvi	•	P4	42
Puebla	•	E5	120
Pueblo	•	F3	112
Puente-Genil	•	F7	54
Puerto Acosta	•	D7	124
Puerto Alegre	•	E6	124
Puerto Angel	•	E5	120
Puerto Carreño	•	L7	120
Puerto de Navacerrada	⌂	G4	54
Puerto Leguizamo	•	C4	124
Puerto Libertad	•	D3	118
Puertollano	•	F6	54
Puerto Maldonado	•	D6	124
Puerto Montt	•	G7	126
Puerto Princesa	•	F5	76
Puerto Real	•	D8	54
Puerto Rico	🏝	L5	120
Puerto Rico Trench.	⌂	E1	122
Puerto Santa Cruz	•	H9	126
Puerto Suárez	•	F7	124
Pukatawagan	•	L5	108
Puké	•	G7	60
Pula		J6	56
Puławy	•	M6	44
Pullman	•	C1	112
Puncak Jaya	▲	E3	79
Puncak Mandala.	▲	F3	79
Pune	•	B5	80
Punia	•	D4	96
Puno	•	C7	124
Punta Arena	⊠	B3	112
Punta Arenas	⊠	G9	126
Punta Eugenia		A3	120
Punta Gallinas	⊠	K6	120
Punta La Marmora	▲	D8	58
Punta Mariato		H7	120
Punta Negra	⊠	A5	124
Puntarenas	•	H6	120
Punta San Gabriel		D3	118
Puqi	•	E5	72
Puri	•	E8	80
Purukcahu.	•	E3	78
Purus	✗	E5	124
Pusan	⊠	E6	74
Putao	•	B1	76
Putararu	•	E3	104
Putian	•	F5	72
Putrajaya	⊡	C2	78
Puttalam	•	C7	80
Putten	•	G3	48
Puttgarden	•	G2	46
Putumayo	✗	C4	124
Puuwai	•	(2)A2	118
Puy de Dôme.	▲	I8	52
Puy de Sancy	▲	H8	52
Pweto	•	D5	96
Pyatigorsk	•	K1	84
Pyè	•	B3	76
Pyhäjärvi	✗	M6	42
Pyhäjärvi.	•	D8	62
P'yŏngyang	⊠	C4	74
Pyramid Lake	✗	C2/3	112
Pyrenees	▲	E11	52
Pyrgos	•	D7	62
Pyshchug	•	J3	64
Pytalovo	•	P8	42

175

Q

Qādub	F7	82
Qalamat Naḍqān	D5	87
Qalāt	J3	82
Qal'at Bīshah	D5	82
Qal'eh-ye Now	H3	82
Qamdo	B4	72
Qardho	H2	96
Qartaba	C2	86
Qatanā	D3	86
Qatar	D4	87
Qatar	A	
Qatrāna	D5	86
Qattâra Depression		
Qâyen	G3	82
Qazax	L3	84
Qazimämmäd	N3	84
Qazvīn	E2	82
Qena	F2	90
Qeqertarsuatsiaat	W4	108
Qeqertarsuatsiaq	V2	108
Qeshm	G3	87
Qeshm	G3	87
Qeys	E3	87
Qezel Owzan		
Qezi'ot	B6	86
Qianshanlaoba	Q8	68
Qiaowan	B2	72
Qiemo	R10	68
Qilian	C3	72
Qilian Shan	B3	72
Qingdao	G3	72
Qinghai Hu	B3	72
Qinghai Nanshan	B3	72
Qingjiang	F4	72
Qingyang	D3	72
Qinhuangdao	F3	72
Qinzhou	D2	76
Qionghai	E3	76
Qiqihar	L7	70
Qira	Q10	68
Qiryat Ata	C4	86
Qiryat Shemona	C3	86
Qishn	F6	82
Qolleh-ye Damāvand	F3	82
Qom	F2	82
Qornet es Saouda	D2	86
Qorveh	M6	84
Qotūr	L4	84
Quang Ngai'	D3	76
Quangolodougou	C3	94
Quang Tri	D3	76
Quanzhou	F2	76
Quaqtaq	T4	108
Quarto Sant'Elena	D9	58
Quba	N3	84
Québec	F1	114
Quedlinburg	G5	46
Queen Charlotte Islands	E6	108
Queen Charlotte Sound	E6	108
Queen Elizabeth Islands	M2	106
Queen Maud Gulf	L3	108
Queensland	G4	102
Queenstown, Australia	J8	102
Queenstown, New Zealand	B7	104
Queenstown, South Africa	D6	98
Quelimane	F3	98
Querétaro	D4	120
Quetta	J3	82
Quezon	F5	76
Quezon City	G4	76
Quibala	A2	98
Quibdó	J7	120
Quilpie	H5	102
Quimper	A5	52
Quimperlé	B6	52
Quincy	B3	114
Qui Nhon	D4	76
Quito	B4	124
Qujing	C1	76
Qumaryan	F1	80
Qurlurtuuq	H3	108
Qus	F2	90
Quseir	F2	90
Quzhou	F5	72

R

Raab	L3	56
Raahe	N4	42
Raas Caseyr	J1	96
Rab	K6	56
Rab	K6	56
Raba	A4	79
Rába	E2	60
Rabat	D2	92
Rābigh	C5	82
Rabka	K8	44
Racine	C2	114
Rackeve	F2	60
Rădăuți	N2	60
Radbuza	H7	46
Radeberg	J5	46
Radebeul	J5	46
Radom	L6	44
Radomsko	J6	44
Radstadt	C10	114
Raduznny	P5	108
Radviliškis	N2	44
Rae-Edzo	H4	108
Raethi	E4	104
Rafaela	J4	126
Rafhā	D4	82
Raglan	E3	104
Ragusa	J12	58
Raha	B3	79
Rahad el Berdi	D5	90
Rahimyar Khan	K4	82
Rainy River	B1	114
Raipur	D4	80
Rajahmundry	D5	80
Rajapalaiyam	C7	80
Rajgarh	C3	80
Rajkot	K5	82
Rajnandgaon	D4	80
Rajshahi	E4	80
Rakhiv	M1	60
Rakovník	C7	44
Rakvere	P7	42
Raleigh	F2	116
Ralik Chain	G5	100
Rambouillet	G5	52
Rameswaram	C7	80
Rāmhormoz	F2	82
Ramlat Rabyānah	C3	90
Râmnicu Sărat	Q4	60
Râmnicu Vâlcea	M4	60
Ramree Island	A3	76
Ramsgate	P10	50
Ramtha	D4	86
Ranau	F1	78
Rancagua	G5	126
Ranchi	E4	80
Randazzo	J11	58
Randers	F8	42
Rangoon = Yangon	B3	76
Rankin	F2	118
Ranong	B5	76
Ransiki	D3	79
Rānya	L5	84
Rapa	M8	100
Rapalla	D4	58
Rapallo	E6	58
Raperswil	D3	56
Rapid City	F2	112
Rapid River	C1	114
Rarotonga	K8	100
Rās Abu Shagara	G3	90
Ra's al Hadd	G5	82
Ra's al Hilāl	D1	90
Ra's al Khaymah	F4	87
Ra's al Kūh	D4	87
Ra's al 'Udayd	C3	87
Rās az Zawr		
Rās Banās	G3	90
Ras Bir	H5	96
Ras Dashen Terara	G5	96
Ra's e Barkan	C2	82
Ra's el Nafas	B7	86
Ra's Fartak	F6	82
Rasht	N5	84
Raška	H6	62
Ras Kasar	G4	90
Ra's Madrakah	G6	82
Ras Nouâdhibou	A4	92
Ras Tannūrah	D3	87
Ratak Chain	H4	100
Ratangarh	K4	82
Rat Buri	B4	76
Rathenow	H4	46
Rathlin Island	F6	50
Ratlam	C4	80
Ratnagiri	K6	80
Ratta	C4	77
Ratzeburg	F3	46
Raukumara Range	F4	104
Rauma	L6	42
Rāut	R2	60
Ravalli	D1	112
Ravenna	H6	58
Ravensburg	E3	56
Ravensthorpe	D6	102
Ravnina	H2	84
Rāwah	J6	84
Rawalpindi	K3	82
Rawicz	F6	44
Rawlinna	E6	102
Rawlins	E2	112
Rawson	J7	126
Rayong	C4	76
Razgrad	P6	62
Razlog	L8	62
Reading, U.K.	M10	50
Reading, U.S.	E2	114
Realicó	J6	126
Rechytsa	F4	60
Recife	L5	124
Recklinghausen	K3	46
Recknitz	H1	46
Reconquista	K4	126
Red, Canada/U.S.	G1	112
Red, U.S.	B3	116
Red Cloud	B1	114
Red Deer	J6	108
Redding	B2	112
Redditch	A2	50
Redfield	G2	114
Red Lakes	A1	114
Redon	C6	52
Redondela	B2	54
Red River = Sông Hông	C2	76
Red Sea	D5	82
Red Wing	B2	114
Redwood Falls	A2	114
Reedsport	B2	112
Reefton	C6	104
Regensburg	H7	46
Reggane	F3	92
Réggio di Calabria	K10	58

Name		Grid	Page
Réggio nell'Emilia	•	F6	56
Regina	◻	F1	110
Rehoboth	•	B4	98
Rehovot		B5	86
Reigate	•	M10	50
Reims	•	G5	48
Reindeer Lake	✦	L5	108
Reinosa	•	F1	54
Reisi	•	J11	58
Reliance		K4	108
Rembang	•	E4	78
Rendsburg	•	E2	46
Rengat	•	C3	78
Renmark	•	H6	102
Rennes	•	D5	52
Reno	•	C3	112
Renton	•	B1	112
Reo	•	B4	79
Replot		L5	42
Represa Tucuruí	✦		
Republic of Ireland	▲	D8	50
Repulse Bay	•	J4	102
Requena	•	C5	124
Réservoir Cabonga	✦	E1	114
Réservoir Caniapiscau	✦	T6	108
Réservoir de La Grande 2	✦	R6	108
Réservoir Gouin	✦	F1	114
Réservoir Manicouagan	✦	T6	108
Réservoir Opinaca	✦	R6	108
Réservoir Pipmuacan	✦	G1	114
Reshteh-ye Kūhhā-ye Alborz	▲	F2	82
Resistencia	•	K4	126
Reşiţa	•	J4	60
Resolute	•	N2	108
Resolution Island, Canada	☒	U4	108
Resolution Island, New Zealand	☒	A7	104
Resovo	•	K3	62
Rethel	•	G5	48
Rethymno	•	G9	62
Réunion	☒	(1)B2	98
Reus	•	M3	54
Reutlingen	•	E8	46
Revin	•	G5	48
Revúca	•	K9	44
Rewa	•	D4	80
Reykjanes	☒	(1)B3	42
Reykjavík	☒	(1)C2	42
Reynosa	•	B4	116
Rezé	•	D6	52
Rēzekne	•	P8	42
Rezina	•	R2	60
Rezovo	•	R8	60
Rheda-Wiedenbrück	•	D5	46
Rhein = Rhine	◿	C2	56
Rheine	•	K2	48
Rhin = Rhine	◿	C2	56
Rho	•	C2	56
Rhinelander	•	C1	114
Rho	•	E5	56
Rhode Island	▪	F2	114
Rhodes = Rodos	☒	L8	62
Rhône	◿	K9	52
Ribadeo	•	C1	54
Ribas do Rio Pardo	•	E9	42
Ribeirão Prêto	•	M3	126
Ribeira = Santa Eugenia	•	A2	54
Riberalta	•	D6	124
Ribnica	•	J3	58
Ribniţa	•	S2	60
Riccione	•	H7	56
Richfield	•	D3	112
Richland	•	C1	112
Richmond, Australia	•	H4	102
Richmond, New Zealand	•	D5	104
Richmond, Ky., U.S	•	D3	114
Richmond, Va., U.S	•	E3	114
Ridgecrest	•	C1	118
Ried	•	J2	56
Riesa	•	J5	46
Riga	•	N8	42
Riggins	•	C1	112
Rijeka	•	K5	56
Riley	•	C2	112
Rimavská Sobota	•	K9	44
Rimini	•	H6	56
Ringkøbing	•	E8	42
Ringsted	•	G1	46
Ringvassøya	☒	J1	42
Rio Branco	◻	D5	124
Rio Colorado	•	J6	126
Rio Cuarto	•	J5	126
Rio de Janeiro	◻	N3	126
Rio de Janeiro	•	N3	126
Rio de la Plata	►	K6	126
Rio Gallegos	•	H9	126
Rio Grande, Argentina	•	H9	126
Rio Grande, Mexico	•	F4	118
Rio Grande	◿	L5	126
Rio Grande do Norte	▪	K6	120
Rio Grande do Sul	▪	L4	126
Riohacha	•	K6	120
Riom	•	J8	52
Ripley	•	D3	114
Ripoll	•	N2	54
Rishiri-tō	☒	Q7	70
Rivadavia	•	G4	126
Riva del Garda	•	F5	56
Rivarolo	•	C5	56
Rivera	•	K5	126
Riversdale Beach	•	E5	104
Riverton	•	A8	104
Rivesaltes	•	H11	52
Rivière-du-Loup	•	G1	114
Rivne	•	E4	64
Rivoli	•	C5	56
Riwoqê	•	G2	80
Riyadh = Ar Riyāḍ	■	B4	87
Rize	•	J3	84
Rizhao	•	F3	72
Roanne	•	K7	52
Roanoke	•	D3	114
Roanoke Rapids	•	F2	116
Robe	•	G7	102
Robertval	•	F1	114
Roccastrada	•	F6	58
Rochefort, Belgium	•	H4	48
Rochefort, France	•	E8	52
Rochelle	•	C2	114
Rochester, Minn., U.S	•	B2	114
Rochester, N.Y., U.S	•	C2	114
Rockall	☒	C2	40
Rockford	•	C2	114
Rockhampton	•	K4	102
Rock Hill	•	D4	114
Rock Island	•	B2	114
Rock Rapids	•	A2	114
Rock Springs	•	E2	112
Rocksprings	•	F3	118
Rocky Mount	•	E3	114
Rocky Mountains	▲	G2	46
Radby Havn	•	H9	52
Roding	•	H7	46
Ropdki Planina	▲	M7	60
Rodos	•	L8	62
Rodos	☒	L8	62
Roebourne	•	C4	102
Roermond	•	J3	48
Roeselare	•	F4	48
Roes Welcome Sound	►	P4	108
Rogerson	•	D2	112
Rogliano	•	D6	58
Rohrbach	•	K2	56
Roi Et	•	C3	76
Roja	•	M8	42
Rolla	•	B3	114
Rolleston	•	D6	104
Roma	•	J5	102
Roma, Italy	•	G7	58
Roman	•	P3	60
Romania	◼	L4	60
Romans-sur-Isère	•	L8	52
Rome = Roma	■	G7	58
Rome, Ga., U.S	•	D3	116
Rome, N.Y., U.S	•	E2	114
Romney	•	E3	114
Romny	•	F4	64
Rømø	☒	D1	46
Romorantin-Lanthenay	•	G6	52
Ronce	•	H2	48
Roncesvalles	•	J2	54
Ronda	•	E8	54
Rondônia	▪	E6	124
Rondônia	•	E6	124
Rondonópolis	•	G7	124
Rønne	•	D2	44
Ronne Ice Shelf	▨	(2)MM2	128
Ronse	•	F4	48
Roraima	▪	E3	124
Raros	•	F5	42
Rosário, Argentina	•	J5	126
Rosário, Mexico	•	D6	110
Rosário Oeste	•	F6	124
Rosarito	•	C6	110
Rosarno	•	K10	58
Roscommon	•	D8	50
Roseau	•	M5	120
Roseburg	•	B2	112
Roseires Reservoir	✦	F5	90
Rosenburg	•	G3	118
Rosenheim	•	H3	56
Rosetown	•	K6	108
Rosignano Solvay	•	F7	56
Roşiori de Vede	•	N5	60
Roskilde	•	G9	42
Roslavl'	•	F4	64
Rossano	•	L9	58
Ross Ice Shelf	▨	(2)Z1	128
Roßlau	•	H5	46
Rosso	•	B5	92
Rossosh'	•	G4	64
Ross River	•	E4	108
Ross Sea	▨	(2)AA2	128
Rostock	•	H2	46
Rostov-na-Donu	•	G5	64
Roswell	•	F2	118
Rotarua	•	F4	104
Rotenburg	•	B5	79
Rotenburg	•	E3	46
Roth	•	G7	46
Rothenburg	•	F7	46
Rotterdam	•	K2	52
Rottumeroog	•	J1	48
Rottumerplaat	•	J1	48
Rottweil	•	D2	56
Roubaix	•	F4	48
Rouen	•	D4	52
Round Mountain	•	K6	102
Roundup	•	E1	112
Rousay	☒	J2	50
Rouyn	•	E1	114
Rovaniemi	•	N3	42
Roverto	•	G5	56
Rovigo	•	G5	56
Rovinj	•	J5	56
Rovuma	◿	F6	96
Roxas	•	G4	76

Place	Grid	Page
Roxburgh	B7	104
Royal Tunbridge Wells	C3	48
Royan	D8	52
Roye	E5	48
Rozdil'na	T3	60
Rtishchevo	H4	64
Ruahine Range	E4	104
Ruapehu	E4	104
Ruapuke Island	B8	104
Ruarkela	D4	80
Ruatoria	G3	104
Ruawai	D3	104
Rub' al Khālī	E6	82
Rubtsovsk	Q7	68
Rudbar	H3	82
Rüdersdorf	J4	46
Rudnaya Pristan'	H2	74
Rudnyy	M4	64
Ruffec	F7	52
Rufiji	F5	96
Rugby	A2	48
Rügen	C3	44
Ruhnu	M8	42
Ruhr	L3	48
Rum.	F5	50
Rumāh	B4	87
Rumbek	D2	96
Rumigny	G5	48
Rumoi	L2	74
Ruoqiang	R10	68
Ruo Shui	C2	72
Rupert	D2	112
Ruse	N6	60
Rushville, Ill., U.S.	B2	114
Rushville, Ind., U.S.	C3	114
Russellville	C2	116
Rüsselsheim	D7	46
Russia	A	
Russia	M3	66
Rust'avi	L3	84
Rute	F7	54
Ruteng	B4	79
Rutland	F2	114
Rutog	B2	80
Ruvuma	F6	96
Ruzayevka	H4	64
Ružomberok	J8	44
Rwanda	A D4	96
Ryazan'	G4	64
Ryazhsk	H4	64
Rybinsk	G3	64
Rybinskoye Vodokhranilishche	G3	64
Rybnik	H7	44
Ryl'sk	F4	64
Ryn-Peski	J5	64
Ryōtsu	K4	74
Ryukyu Islands = Nansei-shotō	H5	72
Rzeszów	M7	44
Rzhev	F3	64

S

Place	Grid	Page
Sa'ādatābād	F2	87
Saale	G6	46
Saalfeld	G6	46
Saar	J5	48
Saarbrücken	J5	48
Saaremaa	L7	42
Saarlouis	J5	48
Saatli	N4	84
Saba	M5	120
Sabadell	N3	54
Sabah	F1	78
Sabhā	H3	92
Sabinas	F3	118
Sabinas Hidalgo	F3	118
Sabine Lake	C3	116
Sabkhet el Bardawil	A5	86
Sabôr	C3	54
Sabzevār	G2	82
Sachanga	B2	98
Sachs Harbour	G2	108
Sacramento	B3	112
Sacramento	B3	112
Sad'ah	D6	82
Sadiya	G3	80
Sado	B6	54
Sado-shima	K3	72
Safford	E2	118
Safi, Jordan	D5	86
Safi, Morocco	D2	92
Safonovo, Russia	F3	64
Safonovo, Russia	J1	64
Safranbolu	Q3	62
Saga	C4	80
Sagami-nada	K6	74
Sagar		
Saginaw	D2	114
Sagiz	K5	64
Saguache	E3	112
Sagunt	K5	54
Sahagún	E2	54
Sahara	C3	88
Saharah el Gharbīya	E2	90
Saharanpur	C3	80
Saharsa		
Şahbuz	L4	84
Sahel	C4	88
Sahiwal	K3	82
Sahuaripa	E3	118
Saïda, Algeria	F2	92
Saïda, Lebanon	C3	86
Saïdābād	F2	87
Saidpur	E3	80
Saigon = Hô Chi Minh	B7	76
Saihan Toroi	C2	72
Saïki	D4	80
Saimaa	P6	42
St. Albans	B3	48
St-Amand-Montrond	H7	52
St. André	K4	56
St. Andrews	K5	50
St. Anthony	V6	108
St. Augustin	K4	48
St. Austell	H11	50
St-Avold	J5	48
St. Barthélémy	M5	120
St-Brieuc	C5	52
St. Catharines	L3	110
St-Chamond	K8	52
St-Claude	L7	52
St. Cloud	B1	114
St. David's	G10	50
St-Denis, France	E6	48
St-Denis, Réunion	(1)B2	98
St-Dié	B2	56
St-Dizier	K5	52
Ste-Anne-de-Beaupré	F1	114
Ste-Menehould	G5	48
St-Étienne	K8	52
St-Félicien	F1	114
St. Francis	J5	112
St. Gallen	E3	56
St-Gaudens	F10	52
St. George, Australia	J5	102
St. George, U.S.	D3	112
St. Georges	F1	114
St. George's	M6	120
St. George's Channel	F10	50
St-Germain-en-Laye	E6	48
St-Girons	G11	52
St. Helena	C7	88
St. Helena Bay	B6	98
St. Helens, U.K	K8	50
St. Helens, U.S	B1	112
St. Helier	C4	52
St-Jean-d'Angely	E8	52
St-Jean-sur-Richelieu	F1	114
St. John	T7	108
St. John's	W7	108
St. Joseph	B3	114
St. Kilda	D4	50
St. Kitts-Nevis	A M5	120
St. Laurent	G2	124
St. Lawrence	L2	110
St. Lawrence Island	(1)C3	118
St-Lô	A5	48
St. Louis, Senegal	B5	92
St. Louis, U.S.	B3	114
St. Lucia	A M6	120
St. Maarten	M5	120
St-Malo	D5	52
St. Marys	D2	114
St. Matthew Island	(1)C3	118
St. Moritz	E4	56
St-Nazaire	C6	52
St. Niklaas	G3	48
St-Omer	E4	48
St. Paul	G2	112
St. Paul	B2	114
St. Peter-Port	C4	52
St. Petersburg = Sankt-Peterburg	F3	64
St. Petersburg	E4	116
St-Pierre-et-Miquelon	V7	108
St-Pol-sur-Ternoise	E4	48
St. Pölten	L2	56
St-Quentin	F5	48
St. Stephen	G1	114
St. Thomas	D2	114
St-Tropez	B7	56
St. Truiden	H4	48
St-Valéry-sur-Somme	D4	48
St. Veit an der Glan	B3	60
St. Vincent and the Grenadines	A M6	120
St-Vincent-les-Forts	B6	56
St-Vith	J4	48
Saipan	E4	100
Sakarya	N4	62
Sakarya	N4	62
Sakata	K4	74
Sakchu	C3	74
Sakha	N3	70
Sakhalin	Q6	70
Sakhon Nakhon	C3	76
Saki	M3	84
Sakishima-shotō	H6	72
Sakskøbing	G2	46
Sal	(1)B1	94
Šal'a	G9	44
Salacgrīva	N8	42
Sala Consilina	K8	58
Salado	J4	126
Salāāh	F4	82
Salamanca	E6	54
Salamina	F7	62
Salamīyah	E1	86
Salar de Uyuni	H3	126
Salawati	D3	79
Salayar	B4	79
Saldus	M8	42
Sale	J7	102
Salekhard	M4	68
Salem	B2	112
Salem, India	C6	80

Name	Sym	Grid	Page
Salem, U.S.	•	C3	114
Salerno	•	J8	58
Salgótarján	•	J9	44
Salida	•	E3	112
Salihli	•	L6	62
Salima	•	E2	98
Salina	•	J10	58
Salina, Kans., U.S.	•	G3	112
Salina, Ut., U.S.	•	D3	112
Salinas, Brazil	•	J7	124
Salinas, Ecuador	•	C2	124
Salinas, Mexico	•	F4	118
Salinas, U.S.	•	B1	118
Salisbury, U.K.	•	A3	48
Salisbury, U.S.	•	E3	114
Salkhad	•	D4	86
Salmás	•	L4	84
Salmon	•	D1	112
Salmon River Mountains	▲	C1/D1	112
Salon-de-Provence		L10	52
Salonta	•	J3	60
Sal'sk	•	H5	64
Salsomaggiore Terme.	•	E6	56
Salt	•	C4	86
Salta	•	H3	126
Saltillo	•	F3	118
Salt Lake City	□	D2	112
Salto	•	K5	126
Salton Sea	✦	C2	118
Salûm	•	E1	90
Saluzzo	•	C6	56
Salvador	□	K6	124
Salvadore	•	H5	122
Salween	✦	N4	84
Salyan	•	H2	56
Salzburg	•	J3	56
Salzgitter	•	F4	46
Salzwedel	•	G4	46
Samaipata	•	E7	124
Samar	•	H4	76
Samara	•	K4	64
Samarinda	•	F3	78
Samarkand	•	J2	82
Sambalpur	•	D4	80
Sambas	•	D2	78
Sambava	•	J2	98
Sambre	✦	F4	48
Same	•	F4	96
Sami	•	C6	62
Sämkir	•	M3	84
Samoa	A	J7	100
Sambor	•	L5	56
Samoded	•	H2	64
Samokov	•	L7	60
Samos	•	J7	62
Samos		J7	62
Samothraki	•	H4	62
Samothraki		H4	62
Sam Rayburn Reservoir	✦	C3	116
Samsang	•	D2	80
Samsun		F9	42
Samsun	•	G3	84
Samtredia	•	K2	84
Samut Songkhram	•	B4	76
San	•	D2	94
San	✦	L4	44
San'a	•	H4	90
Sanaga	✦	G4	94
Sanana	•	C3	79
Sanana		C3	79
Sanandaj	•	M6	84
San Angelo	•	F2	118
San Antonia Abad.	•	M6	54
San Antonio	•	E3	120
San Antonio-Oeste	•	H7	126
Sanāw	•	F6	82
San Benedetto del Tronto	•	H6	58
San Bernardino	•	C2	118
San Borja	•	D6	124
San Carlos	•	D3	124
San Cristóbal	•	C1	74
San Clemente Island			
San Cristóbal	•	C2	124
Sandakan	•	F1	78
Sandanski	•	F3	62
Sanday		K2	50
Sandefjord	•	F7	42
Sanders	•	E1	118
Sanderson	•	F2	118
San Diego	•	C2	118
Sandikli	•	N6	62
Sandnes	•	C7	42
Sandnessjøen	•	G4	42
Sandoa	•	C5	96
San Donà di Piave	•	H5	56
Sandoway	•	F5	80
Sandpoint	•	C1	112
Sandviken	•	J6	42
Sandy Cape	⌑	K4	102
Sandy Lake	•	N6	108
San Felipe.	•	B5	116
San Fernando, Mexico.	•	F3	118
San Fernando, Philippines	•	G5	126
San Fernando, Spain.	•	B5	116
San Fernando de Apure	•	G3	76
Sanford	•	D8	54
San Francis.	•	D2	124
San Francisco, Argentina.	•	E4	116
San Francisco, U.S.	•	A2	116
Sangän.	•	J5	126
Sangar	•	B3	112
Sangha	✦	H3	82
San Gimignano	•	M4	70
San Giovanni in Fiore	•	H4	94
San Giovanni Valdarno	•	G7	56
Sangir	•	L9	58
Sangkulirang	•	G7	56
Sangli	•	C2	79
Sangmélima	•	F2	78
Sangsang	•	B5	80
San Joaquin Valley	✦	G4	94
San Jose	•	D2	80
San José	•	B3	112
San José	☐	B3	112
San Jose de Buenavista	•	H7	120
San Jose de Jáchal	•	G4	76
San José del Cabo	•	H5	126
San Jose de Ocune	•	C4	120
San Juan, Argentina.	•	C3	124
San Juan, Costa Rica	✦	H5	126
San Juan, Puerto Rico.	•	C	120
San Juan Mountains	▲	L5	120
San Julián	•	E3	112
Sankt-Peterburg	•	H8	126
Sankuru	✦	F3	64
Sanliurfa	•	C4	96
San Lorenzo	•	H5	84
Sanlúcar de Barrameda.	•	D3	118
San Luis.	•	D8	54
San Luis Obispo	•	H5	126
San Luis Potosí	•	B1	118
San Luis Río Colorado.	•	D4	120
San Marcos.	•	D2	118
San Marino	•	B4	116
San Marino	■	H7	56
Sanmenxia	•	H7	56
San Miguel	✦	E4	72
San Miguel	•	G6	120
San Miguel de Tucumán	•	E7	124
San Nicolas de los Arroyos	•	H4	126
Sânnicolau Mare	•	J5	126
		H3	60
Sanok	•	M8	44
San Pablo	•	G4	76
San-Pédro	•	C4	94
San Pedro, Argentina.	•	J3	126
San Pedro, Bolivia	•	E7	124
San Pedro Sula	•	G5	120
San Pietro	•	C9	58
San Rafael	•	H5	126
San Remo	•	C7	56
San Salvador	•	G5	116
San Salvador	■	G6	120
San Salvador de Jujuy.	•	H3	126
San Sebastián = Donostia.	•	J1	54
Sansepolcro	•	H7	56
San Séveró	•	K7	58
Sanski Most	•	M6	56
Santa Ana, El Salvador	•	G6	120
Santa Ana, U.S.	•	C2	118
Santa Barbara	•	C2	118
Santa Catalina Island	•	C2	118
Santa Catarina		L4	126
Santa Clara	•	K7	110
Santa Clarita	•	C2	118
Santa Comba Dão	•	B4	54
Santa Cruz, Bolivia.	•	E7	124
Santa Cruz, U.S.	•	B1	118
Santa Cruz de Tenerife.	•	B3	92
Santa Cruz Island.	•	B2	118
Santa Cruz Islands	•	G7	100
Santa Eugenia	•	A2	54
Santa Fé.	•	J5	126
Santa Fe.	□	E3	112
Santa Isabel	•	H6	126
Santa Maria, Brazil.	•	L4	126
Santa Maria, U.S	•	B2	118
Santa Pola	•	K6	54
Santarém, Brazil	•	G4	124
Santarém, Spain	•	B5	54
Santa Rosa, Argentina	•	J6	126
Santa Rosa, Calif., U.S	•	B3	112
Santa Rosa, N.Mex., U.S.	•	F2	118
Santa Rosa Island	•	B2	118
Santa Vitória do Palmar.	•	L5	126
Sant Celoni	•	N3	54
San Feliu de Guixols	•	P3	54
Santiago.	■	G5	126
Santiago, Dominican Republic	•	K5	120
Santiago, Philippines	•	G3	76
Santiago, Spain	•	B2	54
Santiago de Cuba.	•	J5	120
Santiago del Estero	•	H4	126
Santo Antão		(1)A1	94
Santo António de Jesus.	•	K6	124
Santo António do Içá	•	D4	124
Santo Domingo	■	L5	120
Santo Domingo de los Colorados.	•	B4	124
Santos.	•	M3	126
San Vincenzo	•	E5	58
Sanya	•	D3	76
San Bernardo del Campo.	•	E4	124
São Carlos	•	M3	126
São Félix, M.G., Brazil.	•	G6	124
São Félix, Pará, Brazil.	•	G5	124
São Filipe	•	(1)B2	94
São Francisco.	✦	J6	124
São Jorge.	•	(1)B2	94
São Luís.	□	J4	124
São Miguel.	•	(1)B2	94
Saône	✦	K7	52
São Nicolau	•	(1)B1	94
São Paulo.	•	M3	126
São Paulo.	□	M3	126
São Paulo de Olivença	•	D4	124
São Raimundo Nonato.	•	J5	124

179

Name		Grid	Page
Silvan	•	J4	84
Silver City	•	E2	118
Silver Lake	•	B2	112
Simanggang	•	E2	78
Simao	•	C6	72
Simav	•	C4	84
Simeulue	⌖	A2	78
Simferopol'	•	F1	84
Şimleu Silvaniei	•	K2	60
Simpson Desert	⊗	G4	102
Sinabang	•	B2	78
Sinai	⊗	F2	90
Sinaia	•	N4	60
Şinak	•	K5	84
Sinalunga	•	F5	58
Sinanju	•	C4	74
Sincelejo	•	B2	124
Sindelfingen	•	E8	46
Sines	•	B7	54
Singa	•	F5	90
Singapore	▲ A	C2	78
Singapore	•	C2	78
Singaraja	•	E4	78
Singen	•	D3	56
Singida	•	E4	96
Singkawang	•	D2	78
Singkep	⌖	C3	78
Sinj	•	D6	60
Sinjär	•	J5	84
Sinop	•	F2	84
Sinton	•	B4	116
Sinüiju	•	C3	74
Siófok	•	F3	60
Sioux City	•	C4	56
Sioux Falls	•	A2	114
Sioux Lookout	•	H2	110
Siping	•	C2	74
Sipura	⌖	B3	78
Siracusa	•	K11	58
Sir Banī 'Yās	⌖	E4	87
Siret	•	P2	60
Siret	⌀	Q4	60
Siri Kit Dam	•	B3	76
Sirk	•	G3	87
Sirohi	•	B4	80
Sirsa	•	C3	80
Sisak	•	D4	60
Sisôphôn	•	C4	76
Sisseton	•	G1	112
Sistema Central	▲	E4	54
Sistema Ibérico	▲	G2	54
Sisteron	•	A6	56
Sitapur	•	D3	80
Siteia	•	J9	62
Sitges	•	M3	54
Sitka	•	D5	108
Sittard	•	H4	48
Sittwe	•	F4	80
Sivand	•	E1	87
Sivas	•	G4	84
Siverek	•	H5	84
Sivrihisar	•	P5	62
Siwa	•	E1	90
Siyäzän	•	N3	84
Sjælland	⌖	F9	42
Sjenica Jezero	⌀	G6	60
Skærbæk	•	D1	46
Skagerrak	⌀	D8	42
Skardu	•	L2	82
Skawina	•	J8	44
Skegness	•	C1	48
Skellefteå	•	L4	42
Skiathos	⌖	F5	62
Skien	•	E7	42
Skikda	•	G1	92
Škofja Loka	•	K4	56
Skopelos	⌖	F5	62
Skopje	■	J7	60
Skövde	•	G7	42
Skowhegan	•	G2	114
Skuodas	•	L8	42
Skye	⌖	F4	50
Skyros	•	G6	62
Skyros	⌖	G6	62
Slagelse	•	G1	46
Slaney	⌀	F9	50
Slantsy	•	Q7	42
Slatina	•	M5	60
Slave Lake	•	J5	108
Slavonska Požega	•	E4	60
Slavonski Brod	•	F4	60
Slavyanka	•	F2	74
Sleaford	•	B1	48
Sligo	•	D7	50
Sliven	•	P7	60
Slobozia	•	Q5	60
Slonim	•	N10	42
Slough	•	B3	48
Slovakia	◆ A	H9	44
Slovenia	◆ A	K4	56
Štubice	•	D5	44
Slupca	•	L5	56
Słupsk	•	G3	44
Slyudyanka	•	G6	70
Smålandsfarvandet	⌀	G1	46
Smargon'	•	P9	42
Smederevo	•	H5	60
Smiths Falls	•	B2	116
Smokey Hills	▲	A2	114
Smoky	⌀	H6	108
Smøla	⌖	D5	42
Smolensk	•	F4	84
Smolyan	•	G3	62
Smooth Rock Falls	•	D1	114
Smyrna	•	E3	116
Snæfell	▲	(1)F2	42
Snake	⌀	C1	112
Snake River Plain	⌖	D2	112
Snåsavatnet	⌀	F4	42
Sneek	•	H1	48
Snežnik	▲	K5	56
Snøhetta	▲	E5	42
Snøtinden	▲	G3	42
Snowdon	▲	A8	48
Snowdrift	•	J4	108
Snowville	•	D2	112
Snyder	•	F2	118
Soalala	•	H3	98
Soamianara-Ivongo	•	H3	98
Soa-Siu	•	C2	79
Sobral	•	J4	124
Sochi	•	H2	84
Socorro	•	J4	118
Socotra = Suquṭrā	⌖	F7	82
Sodankylä	•	P3	42
Söderhamn	•	J6	42
Södertälje	•	J7	42
Sodo	•	G4	48
Soest	•	L3	48
Sofia = Sofiya	■	L7	60
Sofiya	■	L7	60
Sofiysk	•	P6	70
Sŏfu-gan	⌖	L5	72
Sognefjorden	⌀	C6	42
Sog Xian	•	F2	80
Sohåg	•	F2	90
Soignies	•	G4	48
Soissons	•	F5	48
Sokch'o	•	E4	74
Söke	•	K7	62
Sokhumi	•	J2	84
Sokode	•	E3	94
Sokol	•	H3	64
Sokolo	•	C2	94
Sokoto	•	F2	94
Sokoto	⌀	F2	94
Solander Island	⌖	A8	104
Solapur	•	C5	80
Solenzara	•	D7	58
Solikamsk	•	L3	64
Sol-Iletsk	•	L4	64
Solingen	•	K3	48
Sollefteå	•	J5	42
Soller	•	N5	54
Solna	•	J7	42
Solomon Islands	◆ A	F6	100
Solothurn	•	C3	56
Solov'yevsk	•	K6	70
Sólta	⌖	D6	60
Soltau	•	E4	46
Solway Firth	⌀	J7	50
Solwezi	•	D2	98
Soma	•	K5	62
Somalia	◆ A	H4	96
Sombor	•	G4	60
Sombrerete	•	E2	118
Somerset	•	E2	114
Somerset Island	⌖	N2	108
Someş	⌀	K2	60
Somme	⌀	E4	48
Sömmerda	•	G5	46
Sømna	•	F4	42
Sondershausen	•	F5	46
Sóndrio	•	E4	56
Songavatn	⌀	D7	42
Songea	•	F6	96
Song Hồng	⌀	C2	76
Songhua	⌀	H1	72
Songhua Hu	⌀	D2	74
Songhua Jiang	⌀	C1	74
Songkhla	•	C5	76
Songnam	•	D5	74
Songnim	•	C4	74
Songo	•	E3	98
Songpan	•	C4	72
Sonid Yuoqi	•	E2	72
Sonid Zuoqi	•	E2	72
Son La	•	C2	76
Sonneberg	•	G6	46
Sonora	•	D3	118
Sonora	•	D2	118
Sonoyta	•	D1	118
Sonsorol Islands	⌖	D1	79
Sopron	•	M3	56
Soracaba	•	M3	126
Sorel	•	F1	114
Sorgun	•	F4	84
Soria	•	H3	54
Sora	•	G1	46
Soroca	•	R1	60
Sorong	•	D3	79
Soroti	•	E3	96
Sørøya	⌖	L1	42
Sorrento	•	J8	58
Sortavala	•	R6	42
Sørvagen	•	G3	42
Sosnogorsk	•	J5	68
Sosnowiec	•	J7	44
Sos'va	⌀	M3	64
Sos'vinskaya	•	M2	64
Soto la Marina	•	G4	118
Soubré	•	C3	94
Sŏul	■	D5	74
Soulac-sur-Mer	•	D8	52
Soumoulami	•	Q4	42
Sŏur	•	C3	86
Sour el Ghozlane	•	P8	54
Souris	⌀	F2	110
Sousa	•	K5	124

182

Name	Grid	Pg
Sousse	H1	92
South Africa	C6	98
South America	F5	122
Southampton	A4	48
Southampton Island	Q4	108
South Andaman	F6	80
South Atlantic Ocean	P6	126
South Australia	F5	102
South Bend	C2	114
South Carolina	E3	116
South Charleston	E2	116
South China Sea	F2	112
South Dakota	F2	112
South Downs	B4	48
South East Cape	J8	102
Southend-on-Sea	C3	48
Southern Alps	B6	104
Southern Cross	C6	102
Southern Indian Lake	M5	108
South Georgia	P9	126
South Harris	F4	50
South Hill	E3	114
South Island	B6	104
South Korea	D5	74
South Orkney Islands	(2)A3	128
South Pacific Ocean	P6	126
South Platte	F2	112
South Ronaldsay	K3	50
South Sandwich Islands	(2)C4	128
South Sandwich Trench	H9	122
South Saskatchewan	D1	110
South Shetland Islands	(1)(2)MM4	128
South Taranaki Bight	D4	104
South Uist	E4	50
Southwest Cape	A8	104
South West Pacific Basin	L9	100
Southwold	D2	48
Sovetsk, Russia	L9	42
Sovetsk, Russia	J3	64
Soweto	D5	98
Sozopol	Q7	60
Spain	F5	54
Spalding	B2	48
Sparks	C1	118
Spartanburg	E3	116
Sparti	E7	62
Spassk-Dal'niy	G1	74
Spearfish	F2	112
Spencer	A2	114
Spencer Gulf	G6	102
Spey	J4	50
Speyer	L5	48
Spiekeroog	C3	46
Spišská Nová Ves	K9	44
Spitsbergen	(1)P2	128
Spittal	J4	56
Split	D6	60
Spokane	C1	112
Spoleto	G6	58
Sprague	C1	112
Spratly Islands	E4	76
Spremberg	K5	46
Spring	B3	116
Springbok	B5	98
Springe	E4	46
Springerville	E2	118
Springfield, Colo., U.S	F1	118
Springfield, Ill., U.S	C3	114
Springfield, Mass., U.S.	F2	114
Springfield, Mo., U.S	B3	114
Springfield, Oh., U.S	D3	114
Spring Hill	E4	116
Springs	D5	98
Springs Junction	D6	104
Springsure	J4	102
Springville	D3	116
Squamish	B1	112
Srbija	H6	60
Srbobran	G4	60
Srednekolymsk	S3	70
Sredinnyy Khrebet	T6	70
Srednesibirskoye Ploskogor'ye	F3	70
Śrem	G5	44
Sretensk	K6	70
Sri Jayewardenepura Kotte	D7	80
Srikakulam	D5	80
Sri Lanka	D7	80
Srinagar	B2	80
Stadlandet	C5	42
Staines	B3	48
Stalowa Wola	M7	44
Stamford, Conn., U.S	F2	114
Stamford, U.S.	F2	114
Stanke Dimitrov	F2	62
Stanley, Falkland Islands	K9	126
Stanley, U.S.	C6	112
Stanovoye Nagor'ye	L5	70
Stanovoy Khrebet	L6	70
Starachowice	K8	44
Stara L'ubovňa	H5	60
Stara Pazova	H5	60
Stara Planina	F1	62
Staraya Russa	F1	64
Stara Zagora	N7	60
Starbuck Island	L6	100
Stargard Szczeciński	H10	42
Starnberg	G2	56
Starnberger See	G3	56
Start Point	B3	52
Staryy Oskol	G4	64
Statesboro	E3	116
Stavanger	C7	42
Stavropol'	J1	84
Stavropol'skaya Vovyshennost'	H5	64
Steens Mountains	C2	112
Stefansson Island	L2	108
Stein	G7	46
Steinach	G3	56
Stendal	G4	46
Steno Antikythiro	F9	62
Sterlitamak	L4	64
Stevenage	B3	48
Stevens Point	C2	114
Stewart	F5	108
Stewart Island	A8	104
Steyr	K2	56
Štip	B2	116
Stillwater	B2	116
Stockerau	M2	56
Stockholm	R7	42
Stockton, Calif., U.S.	B1	118
Stockton, Kans., U.S	G1	118
Stockton-on-Tees	L7	50
Stŏng Trêng	D4	76
Stoke-on-Trent	K8	50
Stolac	F6	60
Stolberg	J4	48
Stollberg	H6	46
Stonehaven	K5	50
Stony Rapids	K5	108
Stora Lulevatten	K3	42
Stord	C7	42
Store Bælt	F1	46
Store Sotra	B6	42
Storlien	G5	42
Storm Lake	A2	114
Stornoway	F3	50
Storozhevsk	K2	64
Storsjön, Sweden	G5	42
Storsjön, Sweden	J6	42
Storuman	J4	42
Storuman	J4	42
Stour	C2	48
Stowmarket	D2	48
Stradella	E5	56
Strait of Bonifacio	D7	58
Strait of Dover	D4	48
Strait of Georgia	B1	112
Strait of Gibraltar	E9	54
Strait of Hormuz	G3	87
Strait of Juan de Fuca	B1	112
Strait of Malacca	C2	78
Straits of Florida	E5	116
Strakonice	J7	46
Stralsund	G9	42
Stranraer	H7	50
Strasbourg	C2	56
Strășeni	R2	60
Stratford	D2	114
Stratford-upon-Avon	A2	48
Stratoni	F4	62
Straubing	H2	56
Straumnes	(1)B1	42
Strausberg	J4	46
Strehaia	L5	60
Strimónas	F4	62
Strómboli	K10	58
Strömsund	H5	42
Stronsay	K2	50
Struga	C3	62
Strumica	E3	62
Sturgeon Bay	C2	114
Sturt Stony Desert	G5	102
Stuttgart	E2	56
Suakin	G4	90
Subcule	H5	90
Subotica	G3	60
Suceava	P2	60
Sucre	D7	124
Sudan	E5	90
Sudan	D2	94
Suday	H3	64
Sudbury	D1	114
Sudd	E2	96
Sudová Vyshnya	N8	44
Suez = El Suweis	F2	90
Suez Canal	F1	90
Suhār	G4	87
Suhl	F6	46
Suide	E3	72
Sufenhe	F1	74
Suihua	M7	70
Suir	C7	52
Suizhong	G2	72
Suizhou	E4	72
Sukabumi	D4	78
Sukadana	D3	78
Sukhona	H3	64
Sukkertoppen = Maniitsoq	W3	108
Sula	K1	64
Sulawesi	A3	79
Sulgachi	N4	70
Sulingen	L2	48
Sullana	A4	124
Sulmona	H6	58
Sulphur Springs	B3	116
Sulu Archipelago	G5	76
Sulu Sea	C2	76
Sulzberger Bay	(2)CC2	128
Sumatera	C2	78
Sumatra = Sumatera	C2	78
Sumba	A5	79
Sumbawa	A4	79
Sumbawabesar	A4	79
Sumbawanga	E5	96
Sumbe	A2	98
Šumen	B2	84
Sumenep	E4	78

Name	Grid	Page
Tankse	C2	80
Tanout	F2	94
Tanta	F1	90
Tan-Tan	C3	92
Tanzania	E5	96
Tao'an	G1	72
Taomasina	H3	98
Taormina	K11	58
Taos	E1	118
Taoudenni	E5	92
Tapachula	F6	120
Tapajós	F4	124
Tapsuy	M2	64
Tapuaenuku	D6	104
Tara	N6	68
Tarābulus	H2	92
Taracua	D3	124
Tarakan	F6	76
Taranaki = Mount Egmont	E4	104
Tarancón	H5	54
Taranto	M8	58
Tarapoto	B5	124
Tarare	K8	52
Tarawa	H5	100
Tarazona	J3	54
Tarbes	F10	52
Tarbet	F4	50
Tarcoola	F6	102
Taree	K6	102
Targovište	N5	60
Târgu Jiu	L4	60
Târgu Mureş	M3	60
Târgu-Neamţ	P2	60
Târgu Ocna	P3	60
Tarif	E4	87
Tarija	J3	126
Tarim	Q9	68
Tarim Pendi	Q10	68
Taritatu	E3	79
Tarko Sale	P5	68
Tarlac	G3	76
Tarn	H10	52
Târnaby	H4	42
Târnovo	K2	62
Tarnów	K7	44
Taro	E6	56
Taroudannt	D2	92
Tarquinia	F6	58
Tarragona	N3	54
Tarso Emissi	C3	90
Tarsus	F5	84
Tartagal	J3	126
Tartu	P7	42
Tartūs	C2	86
Tarvisio	J4	56
Tasbuget	N6	64
Tashkent	M9	68
Tash-Kömür	R7	68
Tashtagol	Z3	108
Tasikmalaya	D4	78
Tasman Bay	D5	104
Tasmania	H8	102
Tasmania	E10	100
Tasman Mountains	D5	104
Tasman Sea	B3	104
Tassili du Hoggar	F4	92
Tassili-n'Ajjer	G3	92
Tasty	M9	68
Tata	F2	60
Tatabánya	F2	60
Tatarbunary	S4	60
Tatariya	J3	64
Tatarsk	P6	68
Tatarski Proliv	P7	70
Tateyama	K6	74
Tatvan	K4	84
Tauberbischofsheim	E7	46
Tauern	J4	56
Tauramuri	E4	104
Taungdwingyi	B2	76
Taungup	F5	80
Taunton	J10	50
Taunus	L4	48
Taupo	F4	104
Taurage	M2	44
Tauranga	F3	104
Tauroa Point	D2	104
Tavda	N3	64
Tavda	N3	64
Tavoy	B4	76
Tawas City	D2	114
Tawau	F2	78
Tawitawi	F1	78
Taxkorgan	P10	68
Tay	J5	50
Tayga	R6	68
Taym	C4	82
Taymā'	G2	90
Taymyr	L2	70
Tay Ninh	D4	76
Tayshet	F5	70
Taza	E2	92
Tazenakht	D2	92
Tāzirbū	D2	90
Tazovskiy	P4	68
Tazovskiy Poluostrov	N4	68
Tbilisi	B1	76
Tchibanga	G5	94
Tchin Tabaradene	G5	92
Tczew	H3	44
Te Anau	A7	104
Te Araroa	G3	104
Te Awamutu	E4	104
Teberda	J2	84
Tébessa	G1	92
Tebingtinggi	B2	78
Tecuci	Q4	60
Tedzhen	H2	82
Tees	L7	50
Tegucigalpa	G6	120
Teheran = Tehrān	F2	82
Tehrān	F2	82
Teignmouth	J11	50
Tejo = Tagus	B5	54
Tekirdağ	K4	62
Tekirdağ	B3	84
Te Kuiti	E4	104
T'elavi	L3	84
Tel Aviv-Yafo	B3	86
Teles Pires	F5	124
Telford	K9	50
Telšiai	M2	44
Teltow	J4	46
Teluk Berau	D3	79
Teluk Bone	B3	79
Teluk Cenderawasih	E3	79
Teluk Kumai	F3	78
Teluk Tomini	D3	79
Tema	D3	94
Temerloh	C6	76
Témpio Pausária	D8	58
Temple	G2	118
Temryuk	G1	84
Temuco	G6	126
Tendaho	H5	90
Ténéré	F7	90
Ténéré du Tafassasset	G4	92
Tenerife	B3	92
Ténès	F1	92
Tenkodogo	D2	94
Tennant Creek	F3	102
Tennessee	J4	110
Tennessee	K6	106
Tenojoki	P2	42
Teo	B2	54
Teófilo Otoni	J7	124
Tepic	F7	110
Teplice	C7	44
Terceira	(1)B2	92
Terek	L2	84
Teresina	J5	124
Tergnier	F5	48
Termez	J2	82
Términi Imerese	H11	58
Termitau	N7	68
Térmoli	C8	60
Ternate	C2	79
Terneuzen	F3	48
Terni	G6	58
Ternitz	M3	56
Ternopil'	E5	64
Temuka	C7	104
Terracina	H7	58
Terrassa	N3	54
Terre Haute	D2	116
Terry	E1	112
Terschelling	H1	48
Teruel	J4	54
Teseney	G4	90
Teshio	L1	74
Teslin	(1)L3	118
Tessalit	F4	92
Têt	H11	52
Tete	E3	98
Teterow	H3	46
Tétouan	D1	92
Tetovo	H8	60
Teulada	C10	58
Tevere	G6	58
Teverya	C4	86
Te Waewae Bay	A8	104
Texarkana	C3	116
Texas	F5	110
Texel	G1	48
Thabazimbi	D4	98
Thailand	C4	76
Thai Nguyên	D2	76
Thames	L10	50
Thane	B5	80
Thanh Hoa	D3	76
Tharad	B4	80
Thar Desert.	B3	80
Thasos	G4	62
Thasos	G4	62
Thaton	B3	76
The Bahamas	A4	116
The Dalles	B1	112
Thedford	F2	112
The Fens	B2	48
The Gambia.	A2	94
Thelon	L4	108
The Minch.	F3	50
The Naze	D3	48
Thenia	N9	54
The Pas	L6	108
Thermaïkós Kólpos.	E4	62
Thermopolis	E2	112
The Solent.	A4	48
Thessalóniki	E4	62
Thetford Mines	F1	114
The Wash.	N9	50
The Weald.	B3	48
The Whitsundays	J4	102
Thiers	J8	52

Name	Grid	Page
Trangan	D4	79
Transantarctic Mountains	(2)B1	128
Trapani	G11	58
Traun	K2	56
Traunreut	J3	56
Traversay Islands	H9	122
Traverse City	C2	114
Travnik	E5	60
Trbovlje	L4	56
Trebič	E8	44
Trebinje	F7	60
Trebišov	J1	60
Trebon	K1	56
Tregosse Islets	K3	122
Trelleborg	G9	42
Tremp	L2	54
Trenčín	H9	44
Trent	M8	50
Trento	G4	56
Trenton, Canada	E2	114
Trenton, U.S.	F2	114
Tres Arroyos	J6	126
Três Corações	H8	124
Tres Esquinas	B4	124
Tres Lagos	G8	126
Treuchtlingen	E5	56
Treviglio	H5	56
Treviso	H5	56
Trichur	C6	80
Trier	J5	48
Trieste	J5	56
Triglav	J4	56
Trikala	D5	62
Trikomon	A1	86
Trincomalee	D7	80
Trinidad	E1	124
Trinidad, Bolivia	E1	124
Trinidad, U.S.	F1	118
Trinidad and Tobago	E1	124
Trinity Islands	(1)G4	118
Tripoli, Greece	E7	62
Tripoli = Trâblous, Lebanon	C2	86
Tripoli = Tarābulus, Libya	H2	92
Tristan da Cunha	B9	88
Trivandrum = Thiruvananthapuram	C7	80
Trnava	E1	60
Troisdorf	C6	46
Trois Rivières	F1	114
Troitsk	M4	64
Troitsko-Pechorsk	L2	64
Trojan	G2	62
Trollhättan	F7	42
Tromsø	K2	42
Trondheim	F5	42
Trondheimsfjorden	F5	42
Trotus	P3	60
Troy, Al., U.S	D3	116
Troy, N.Y., U.S	F2	114
Troyan	M7	60
Trujillo, Peru	B5	124
Trujillo, Spain	E5	54
Truro	U7	108
Trutnov	E7	44
Tryavna	H2	62
Trzebnica	G6	44
Tsetserleg	G7	70
Tshabong	C5	98
Tshane	C4	98
Tshikapa	C5	96
Tshuapa	C4	96
Tsiafajavona	H3	98
Tsimlyanskoy Vodokhranilishche	H5	64
Tskhinvali	K2	84
Tsugaru-kaikyō	L3	74
Tsumeb	B3	98
Tsumkwe	C3	98
Tsuruga	J6	74
Tsuruoka	K4	74
Tsuyama	H6	74
Tual	D4	79
Tuapse	H1	84
Tubarão	M4	126
Tübingen	E2	56
Tubize	D1	90
Tubuai	M8	100
Tubuai Islands	L8	100
Tucson	D2	118
Tucumcari	F1	118
Tucuruí	H4	124
Tudela	J2	54
Tuguegarao	G3	76
Tugur	P6	70
Tui	B2	54
Tuktoyaktuk	(1)L2	118
Tula	G4	64
Tulare	C3	112
Tulcea	R4	60
Tulsa	G4	110
Tulun	G6	70
Tulung La	F3	80
Tulu Welel	E2	96
Tumaco	B3	124
Tumen	E2	74
Tumkur	C6	80
Tunceli	H4	84
Tunduru	F2	98
Tundzha	P8	60
Tungir	L5	70
Tungku	F1	78
Tungusk	S5	68
Tunis	H1	92
Tunisia	E2	92
Tunja	C2	124
Tupelo	D3	116
Tupper Lake	F2	114
Tura, India	F3	80
Tura, Russia	G4	70
Turan	S7	68
Turangi	E4	104
Turayf	G1	90
Turba	H4	82
Turbo	B2	124
Turek	H5	44
Turgay	L8	68
Turgay	L8	68
Turgayskaya Stolovaya Strana	L7	68
Türgovishte	P6	60
Turgutlu	K6	62
Turhal	G3	84
Turin = Torino	C5	56
Turiy Rog	F1	74
Türkeli Adası	K4	62
Turkestan	M9	68
Turkey	D4	84
Turkmenbashi	F1	82
Turkmenistan	G2	82
Turks and Caicos Islands	K4	120
Turku	K6	42
Turnhout	G3	48
Turnu Măgurele	M6	60
Turpan	R9	68
Turpan Pendi	S9	68
Turquino	D2	122
Turugart Pass	P9	68
Turukhan	C3	70
Turukhansk	R4	68
Tuscaloosa	D3	116
Tuscola	D2	116
Tuticorin	C7	80
Tutonchany	E4	70
Tutuila	K7	100
Tuvalu	H6	100
Tuxpan	G7	110
Tuxtla Gutiérrez	F5	120
Tuy Hoa	D4	76
Tuz Gölü	E4	84
Tuzla	F5	60
Tver'	G3	64
Tweed	K6	50
Twin Falls	D2	112
Tylkhoy	U4	70
Tynda	L5	70
Tyne	K6	50
Tynemouth	L6	50
Tyra	S7	68
Tyrnavos	E5	62
Tyrrhenian Sea	F8	58
Tysa	N9	44
Tyumen'	M6	68
Tyva	F6	70

U

Name	Grid	Page
Uaupés	D3	124
Ubá	J8	124
Ubaitaba	K6	124
Ubangi	B3	96
Ube	F7	74
Úbeda	G6	54
Uberaba	H7	124
Uberlândia	H7	124
Überlingen	E3	56
Ubon Ratchathani	C3	76
Ubrique	E8	54
Ucayali	C5	124
Ucharal	Q8	68
Uckermark	J3	46
Uda	F5	70
Udachnyy	J3	70
Udaipur	B4	80
Uddevalla	F7	42
Udine	J4	56
Udmurtiya	K3	64
Udon Thani	C3	76
Ueda	K5	74
Uele	C3	96
Uelen	AA3	70
Uel'kal	Y3	70
Uelzen	F4	46
Ufa	L3	64
Ufa	L4	64
Uganda	E3	96
Uglegorsk	Q7	70
Uglich	G3	64
Ugol'nyye Kopi	X4	70
Uh	K1	60
Uherské Hradiště	G8	44
Uiju	C3	74
Uíl	K5	64
Uíl	K5	64
Uinta Mountains	D2	112
Uitenhage	D6	98
Ujiji	D4	96
Ujjain	C4	80
Ukhta	J5	68
Ukiah	B3	112
Ukkusissat	W2	108
Ukmergė	P2	44
Ukraine	G3	40
Ulaanbaatar	H7	70
Ulaangom	S8	68
Ulan Bator = Ulaanbaatar	D1	72
Ulan-Ude	H6	70

Name		Grid	Page
Ulchin	●	E5	74
Ulety	●	J6	70
Ulhasnagar	●	B5	80
Uliastay	●	T8	68
Ulindi	∠	D4	96
Ullapool	●	G4	50
Ullŏng do	▨	F5	74
Ulm	●	F2	56
Ulongue	●	E2	98
Ulsan	●	E6	74
Ulu	●	M4	70
Ulubat Gölü	✦	L4	62
Ulugqat	●	K2	82
Ulukışla	●	F5	84
Ulungur Hu	✦	R8	68
Uluru	▲	F5	102
Ul'yanovsk	●	J4	64
Umeå	●	L5	42
Umeälven	∠	L4	42
Umfölozi	∠	E5	98
Ummal Arānib	●	H3	92
Umm al Jamājim	●	A3	87
Umm Durman	●	F4	90
Umm Qasr	●	B1	87
Umm Ruwaba	●	F5	90
Umnak Island	▨	(1)E5	118
Umtata	●	D6	98
Unalakleet	●	(1)E3	118
Unalaska Island	▨	(1)E5	118
Ungava Bay	►	T5	108
Ungheni	●	Q2	60
Unije	▨	K6	56
Unimak Island	▨	(1)D5	118
Union	●	B3	114
United Arab Emirates	A	F5	82
United Kingdom	A	G6	50
United States		M5	106
Unraven	●	E1	118
Unst	▨	M1	50
Unzha	∠	H3	64
Upernavik	●	W2	108
Upernavik Kujalleq	●	V2	108
Upington	●	C5	98
Upolu	▨	J7	100
Upper Hutt	●	E5	104
Upper Klamath Lake	✦	B2	112
Upper Lough Erne	✦	E7	50
Uppsala	●	J7	42
Urakawa	●	M2	74
Ural	∠	K5	64
Ural Mountains = Ural'skiy Khrebet	▲	L1	40
Ural'sk	●	K4	64
Ural'skiy Khrebet	▲	L1	40
Urambo	●	E5	96
Uranium City	●	K5	108
Uray	●	M2	64
Urbana	●	D2	114
Urbino	●	H7	56
Urdzhar	●	Q8	68
Uren'	●	J3	64
Urgench	●	H1	82
Uritskiy	●	N4	64
Urla	●	J6	62
Uroševac	●	J7	60
Uro-teppa	●	J2	82
Urt	●	C2	72
Uruguaiana	●	K5	126
Uruguay	A	K5	126
Uruguay	∠	K5	126
Ürümqi	●	R9	68
Uryupinsk	●	H4	64
Urziceni	●	P5	60
Usa	∠	L4	64
Uşak	●	C4	84
Usedom	►	J3	46
Usingen	●	D6	46
Usk	∠	J10	50
Usol'ye Sibirskoye	●	G6	70
Ussel	●	H8	52
Ussuri	∠	G1	74
Ussuriysk	●	J2	72
Ust'-Alekseyevo	●	J2	64
Ust'-Barguzin	●	H6	70
Ust' Chaun	●	W3	70
Ústica	▨	H10	58
Ust'-Ilimsk	●	G5	70
Ust' nad Labem	●	D7	44
Ust'-Ishim	●	N6	68
Ust'-Kamchatsk	●	U5	70
Ust'-Kamenogorsk	●	Q8	68
Ust'-Khayryuzovo	●	T5	70
Ust'-Kulom	●	K2	64
Ust'-Kut	●	G5	70
Ust'-Kuyga	●	P3	70
Ust'-Labinsk	●	H1	84
Ust'-Maya	●	N4	70
Ust'-Nera	●	Q4	70
Ust'-Omchug	●	R4	70
Ust' Ozernoye	●	D5	70
Ust' Penzhino	●	V4	70
Ust'-Tatta	●	N4	70
Ust'-Tsil'ma	●	J4	68
Ust' Usa	●	L1	64
Ust'-Uyskoye	●	L7	68
Usu	●	Q9	68
Utah		D4	110
Utena	●	N9	42
Uthal	●	J4	82
Utica	●	E2	114
Utiel	●	J5	54
Utrecht	●	H2	48
Utrera	●	E7	54
Utsjoki	●	P2	42
Utsunomiya	●	K5	74
Uttaradit	●	C3	76
Uummannarsuaq	►	Y5	108
Uvat	●	N3	64
Uvinza	●	E5	96
Uvira	●	D4	96
Uvs Nuur	✦	S7	68
Uy	∠	L2	64
Uyar	●	S6	68
Uyuni	●	H3	126
Uzbekistan	A	L9	68
Uzhhorod	●	K1	60
Užice	●	G6	60

V

Name		Grid	Page
Vaal	∠	D5	98
Vaasa	●	L5	42
Vác	●	G2	60
Vadodara	●	B4	80
Vadsø	●	Q1	42
Vaduz	●	E3	56
Vaganski Vhr	▲	L6	56
Vakh	∠	Q2	64
Valbonnais	●	A6	56
Valdagno	●	G5	56
Valdepeñas	●	G6	54
Valdivia	●	G6	126
Val d'Or	●	E1	114
Valdosta	●	K5	110
Valdres	▨	E6	42
Valence	●	K9	52
Valencia, Spain	●	K5	54
Valencia, Venezuela	●	D1	124
Valencia de Alcántara	●	C5	54
Valenciennes	●	F4	48
Vălenii de Munte	●	P4	60
Valenza	●	D5	56
Valjevo	●	G5	60
Valka	●	N8	42
Valkeakoski	●	N6	42
Valladolid	●	F3	54
Valledupar	●	C1	124
Vallejo	●	B3	112
Valletta	●	J13	58
Valley of the Kings	◉	F2	90
Valli di Comacchio	✦	H6	56
Valmiera	●	N8	42
Valparai	●	C6	80
Valparaíso, Chile	●	G5	126
Valparaíso, Mexico	●	F4	120
Val'tevo	●	H2	64
Valverde del Camino	●	D7	54
Van	●	K4	84
Vanadzor	●	L3	84
Vancouver, Canada.	●	B1	106
Vancouver, U.S.	●	B1	112
Vancouver Island	▨	F7	106
Vandalia	●	D2	114
Van Diemen Gulf	►	F2	102
Vänern	✦	G7	42
Van Gölü	✦	K4	84
Van Horn	●	F2	120
Vanimo	●	J6	100
Vankarem	●	Y3	70
Vanna	▨	K1	42
Vannes	●	K5	52
Vannøya	▨	C6	42
Vanrhynsdorp	●	B6	98
Vantaa	●	N6	42
Vanua Levu	▨	H7	100
Vanuatu	A	G7	100
Vanzevat	●	N2	64
Varanasi	●	D3	80
Varangerfjorden	►	D3	42
Varaždin	●	D3	56
Varazze	●	D6	56
Varberg	●	G7	42
Vardar	∠	E3	60
Vardø	●	R1	42
Varel	●	D3	46
Varese	●	D5	56
Vârful Moldoveanu	▲	M4	60
Vârfurile	●	K3	60
Varginha	●	M3	126
Varna	●	B2	76
Várnamo	●	H8	42
Vaslui	●	Q3	60
Västerås	●	J7	42
Västervik	●	J8	42
Vasvár	●	M3	56
Vathia	●	E8	62
Vatican City	A	F7	58
Vatnajökull	▨	(1)E2	42
Vättern	✦	H7	42
Vaughn	●	E2	120
Vawkavysk	●	P4	42
Växjö	●	H8	42
Vavuniya	●	D7	80
Vazhgort	●	J2	64
Vecht	∠	J2	48
Vechta	●	J1	46
Veendam	●	J1	48
Vega	▨	F1	42
Vega	●	F4	120
Vegreville	●	J6	106
Vejer de la Frontera	●	D7	54
Vela Luka	●	D7	56
Velenje	●	E3	56
Vélez-Málaga	●	F7	54
Velikiye Luki	●	E3	64
Velikiy Ustyug	●	J2	64
Veliko Tŭrnovo	●	N6	60
Velita Kladuša	●	L5	56

Name		Grid	Page
Vsetín	●	G8	44
Vukovar	●	G4	60
Vuktyl'	●	L2	64
Vung Tau	●	D4	76
Vuotso	●	P2	42
Vyatka	●	K3	64
Vyborg	●	Q6	42
Vychegda	⟋	K2	64
Vyshniy Volochek	●	F3	64
Vytegra	●	G2	64

W

Name		Grid	Page
Wa	●	D3	94
Waal	⟋	H3	48
Wabē Shebelē Wenz	⟋	G2	96
Waco	■	B3	116
Wad Banda	●	E5	90
Waddān	●	C2	90
Waddeneilanden	⬡	G1	48
Waddenzee	⬡	H1	48
Wādī al Fārigh	⟋	C1	90
Wādī al Hamīm	⟋	C1	90
Wadi Halfa	●	F3	90
Wad Medani	●	F5	90
Wafangdian	●	G3	72
Wagga Wagga	●	J7	102
Wahiawa	●	(2)C2	118
Wahpeton	●	C7	104
Waiau	⟋	D6	104
Waidhofen	●	K3	56
Waigeo	⬡	D3	79
Waiheke Island	⬡	E3	104
Waihi	●	E3	104
Waikabubak	●	A4	79
Waikato	⟋	E4	104
Wailuku	●	(2)E3	118
Waimate	●	C7	104
Waingapu	●	B1	102
Wainwright	●	(1)F1	118
Waiouru	●	E4	104
Waipara	●	D6	104
Waipukurau	●	F5	104
Wairoa	●	F4	104
Waitakaruru	●	E3	104
Waitaki	⟋	C7	104
Waitangi	●	(1)B1	104
Waitara	●	E4	104
Waiuku	●	E3	104
Wajir	●	G3	96
Wakasa-wan	►	H6	74
Wakayama	●	H6	74
Wake Island	⬡	G4	100
Wakkanai	●	L1	74
Wałbrzych	●	F7	44
Walcheren	⬡	F3	48
Walcz	●	F4	44
Wales	⬡	J9	50
Walgett	●	J6	102
Walkerville	●	J7	102
Walla Walla	●	C1	112
Wallis et Futuna	⬡	J7	100
Walpole	●	C6	102
Walsall	●	L9	50
Walsenburg	●	F3	112
Walsrode	●	E4	46
Walvis Bay	●	A4	98
Wamba	●	D3	96
Wanaka	●	B7	104
Wandel Sea	►	A1	106
Wandingzhen	●	B2	76
Wanganui	●	E4	104
Wanganui	⟋	E4	104
Wangerooge	⬡	D3	46
Wan Hsa-la	●	B2	76
Wanxian	●	D4	72

Name		Grid	Page
Wanyuan	●	D4	72
Warangal	●	C5	80
Warburg	●	D5	46
Ward	●	E5	104
Wardha	⟋	C4	80
Waremme	●	H4	48
Waren	●	H3	46
Warka	●	L6	44
Warmandi	●	D3	79
Warm Springs	●	C3	112
Warren	●	D2	114
Warrensburg	●	B3	114
Warrenton	●	C5	98
Warri	●	F3	94
Warrington, U.K.	●	K8	50
Warrington, U.S.	●	D3	116
Warrnambool	●	H7	102
Warsaw = Warszawa	■	K5	44
Warszawa	■	K5	44
Warta	⟋	F5	44
Wasatch Range	⬤	D1	118
Wasco	●	C1	118
Washington	●	B1	112
Washington D.C.	■	J6	106
Watampone	●	B3	79
Waterford	●	E9	50
Waterloo	●	B2	114
Watertown, N.Y., U.S	●	E2	114
Watertown, S.D., U.S	●	G1	112
Waterville	●	G2	114
Watford	●	B3	48
Watford City	●	F1	112
Watrous	●	K6	108
Watsa	●	D3	96
Watseka	●	D1	116
Watson Lake	●	(1)M3	106
Wau	●	D2	96
Waukegan	●	C2	114
Waukesha	●	C2	114
Waverly	●	C3	114
Wavre	●	G4	48
Wāw	●	D1	114
Wāw al Kabīr	●	C2	90
Waxxari	●	R10	68
Waycross	●	B2	116
Weaverville	●	B2	112
Weber	⟋	F5	104
Webi Shaabeelle	⟋	G3	96
Weddell Sea	►	(2)A2	128
Weed	●	B2	112
Weert	●	H3	48
Weiden	●	H7	46
Weifang	●	F3	72
Weihai	●	G3	72
Weilburg	●	D6	46
Weimar	●	G6	46
Weinan	●	D4	72
Weipa	●	H2	102
Weiser	●	C2	112
Wejherowo	●	H3	44
Welkom	●	D5	98
Welland	⟋	B2	48
Wellesley Islands	⬡	G3	102
Wellington	■	E5	104
Wells	●	C2	112
Wellsboro	●	E1	114
Wellsford	●	E3	104
Wels	●	K2	56
Wenatchee	●	B1	112
Wenchang	●	E3	76
Wenga	●	B3	96
Wenman	⬡	(1)A1	124
Wentworth	●	H6	102
Wenzhou	●	G5	72
Werdēr	●	H2	96
Wertheim	●	E7	46

Name		Grid	Page
Wesel	●	J3	4?
Wesel Dorsten	●	B5	4?
Weser	⟋	E4	4?
Wessel Islands	⬡	G2	10?
West Antarctica	⬡	(2)GG2	12?
West Bank	a	C4	8?
Western Australia	a	A4	10?
Western Cape	a	B6	9?
Western Ghats	⬤	B5	8?
Western Sahara	a	C4	9?
Westerschelde	►	F3	4?
Westerstede	●	K1	4?
Westerwald	⬤	K4	4?
West Falkland	⬡	J9	12?
West Glacier	●	D1	11?
West Palm Beach	●	E4	11?
West Plains	●	B3	11?
Westport	●	C5	10?
Westray	⬡	J2	5?
West Siberian Plain = Zapadno-Sibirskaya Ravnina	⬤	L3	6?
West Virginia	a	D3	11?
West Wendover	●	D2	11?
West Yellowstone	●	D2	11?
Wetar	⬡	C4	7?
Wetaskiwin	●	J6	10?
Wetumpka	●	D3	11?
Wetzlar	●	D6	4?
Wexford	●	F9	5?
Weyburn	●	F2	11?
Whakatane	●	F3	10?
Whalsay	⬡	M1	5?
Whangarei	●	E2	10?
Wharfe	⟋	L7	5?
Wheeler Peak	⬤	E1	11?
Wheeling	●	E1	11?
White Bay	►	V6	10?
Whitefish Point	►	C1	11?
Whitehorse	□	(1)L3	11?
White Island	⬡	F3	10?
Whitemark	●	J8	10?
White Mountain Peak	⬤	C3	11?
White Mountains	⬤	S8	10?
White Nile = Bahr el Abyad	⟋	F	4?
White Sea = Beloye More	►	G1	6?
White Sulphur Springs	●	D1	11?
White Volta	⟋	D3	9?
Whitney	●	E1	11?
Whyalla	●	G6	10?
Wichita	●	B2	11?
Wichita Falls	●	B3	11?
Wick	●	J3	5?
Wickenburg	●	D2	11?
Wicklow Mountains	⬤	F8	5?
Wieluń	●	H6	4?
Wien	■	M2	5?
Wiener Neustadt	●	M3	5?
Wieringermeer Polder	⬡	G2	4?
Wiesbaden	●	D6	4?
Wiesloch	●	D7	4?
Wiesmoor	●	E4	4?
Wigan	●	K8	5?
Wilbur	●	C1	11?
Wilcannia	●	H6	10?
Wildeshausen	●	D4	4?
Wilhelmshaven	●	D4	4?
Wilkes Land	⬡	(2)U2	12?
Willemstad	□	D1	12?
Williams, Australia	●	B1	10?
Williams, U.S.	●	B3	11?
Williams Lake	●	G6	10?
Williamson	●	E2	11?
Williamsport	●	E2	11?
Willis Group	⬡	K3	10?
Williston	●	F1	11?
Williston Lake	⬤	G5	10?